PATRICK,

DREAM BIG AND CHASE YOUR
DREAMS. YOUR SUCCESS IS
WITHIN YOU. STAY STRONG
IN YOUR FAITH AND PEACE
WILL ALWAYS BE WITH YOU.

CJ

Vanderbilt Issues in Higher Education is a timely series that focuses on the three core functions of higher education: teaching, research, and service. Interdisciplinary in nature, it concentrates not only on how these core functions are carried out in colleges and universities but also on the contributions they make to larger issues of social and economic development, as well as various organizational, political, psychological, and social forces that influence their fulfillment and evolution.

Series Editor
John M. Braxton
Peabody College, Vanderbilt University

Editorial Advisory Board
Ann Austin (Michigan State University)
Marcia B. Baxter Magolda (Miami University)
Alan E. Bayer (Virginia Polytechnic Institute and State University)
Ellen M. Brier (Vanderbilt University)
Clifton F. Conrad (University of Wisconsin)
Mary Frank Fox (Georgia Institute of Technology)
Roger L. Geiger (Pennsylvania State University)
Hugh Davis Graham (Vanderbilt University)
Lowell Hargens (Ohio State University)
James C. Hearn (University of Minnesota)
George D. Kuh (Indiana University)
Michael T. Nettles (University of Michigan)
John C. Smart ((University of Memphis)
Joan S. Stark (University of Michigan)
William G. Tierney (University of Southern California)
Caroline S. Turner (Arizona State University)

Giants among Us

First-Generation
College Graduates
Who Lead
Activist Lives

Sandria Rodriguez

Vanderbilt University Press
NASHVILLE

This book is printed on acid-free paper.
Manufactured in the United States of America

Library of Congress Cataloging-in-Publication Data

Rodriguez, Sandria, 1944-
    Giants among us : first-generation college graduates
who lead activist lives / Sandria Rodriguez.
    p. cm. — (Vanderbilt issues in higher education)
Includes bibliographical references and index.
    ISBN 0-8265-1391-3 (cloth: alk. paper)
    ISBN 0-8265-1392-1 (pbk.: alk. paper)
    1. Socially handicapped—Education (Higher)—
United States—Case studies. 2. Academic achievement—
Social aspects—United States—Case studies.
3. College graduates—United States—Interviews.
I. Title. II. Series.
LC4069.6 .R63 2002
378.1'6912'0922—dc21
                                        2001004324

To my brother,
Burnett Williams, Jr.
1946-1999

Contents

Preface

In my youth I suspected that if I thought too much about the plight of the poor, uneducated, and powerless, I would become dangerously militant, a young Angela Davis probably facing jail time. I was wary of committing, like Rosa Parks, so stunningly simple an act of civil disobedience in so decisive and irrevocable a manner as to take the nation's breath away, bringing unimaginable retaliation upon my family. Because I was raised in the south where civil disobedience was a sure route to uncivilized punishment, in my pragmatic view the most acceptable means of combatting discrimination and poverty appeared, and still appears, to be education. I dare say that even today, few among the thinking would disagree.

The belief that education is key to American democracy is as old as the nation. It was articulated in Thomas Jefferson's 1786 call to establish and improve the law for educating the common people (Ravitch 1983). But education lies near the bottom of the enfranchisement pyramid, below economic and political power, though each influences access to its apex, the democratic pursuit of a good life. As bulwarks protecting American democracy, the triumvirate of educational, economic, and political power has also served the contradictory purpose of walling out "undesirables." The most intangible of the three powers, education is also the most irreducible and has frequently proved a prerequisite to economic and political parity. Thus, education is a pressure point around which the nation has historically managed privilege. A challenge for many in positions of political power has been balancing the nation's inclusionary rhetoric with the simultaneous practice of exclusion. As one of the excluded, I have struggled to keep the seeds of bitterness from sprouting in my heart.

My struggles against bitterness notwithstanding, I have spent much of my life thinking about issues of economic, social, and political inequality, so beginning a study of first-generation college graduates from low socioeconomic-status (SES) backgrounds was more akin to accessorizing a favorite outfit than to breaking in new shoes. Still, the process was fraught with uncertainty. Would I become enraged as I scrutinized the educational histories of the study's participants? Even more problematic, I knew, would be finding my own place as researcher and first-generation college graduate within the spectrum of themes bridging the participants' lives. Although I was not the first person in my family to go to college (my older sister preceded me), in most other respects I fit the stringent criteria for the study, defined in Chapter 1. I was an insider by origin and by life experience, a factor that could impinge upon the study whether or not I tried to suppress it.

In addition to worrying about taking an appropriately objective approach to the study, I was concerned that my identity as a first-generation college graduate from a poor family might lessen the validity of my research in the eyes of potential publishers and readers. Studies of culture, and ethnography in particular, have often been conducted by people of comparative privilege among those considered different or exotic. From Margaret Mead and before to *Mama Lola* and beyond, anthropologists have entered different cultures and, over a period of years, transformed their own and their readers' understanding of others' lives. Besides being written by a non-established writer and a non-anthropologist, my identity places this book even further outside ethnography's traditional realm.

I decided to position my experience as a first-generation college graduate within the context of the study by using my own life-history data as a corollary to—even a reflection of—the excerpts and examples included from the participants' lives. Each of the book's chapters begins with a segment of thematically corresponding data from my life history, so in an important way the book is about my journey toward self-discovery. I leave points of analysis about my own story to the reader's discretion.

What will you find in this book? In Chapter 1 I explain why I think first-generation college graduates from low SES backgrounds who became social or educational activists are worth studying. Chapter 2 contains a selection of five stories culled from the interviews of five of the study's participants. These narratives offer unique but representative examples of the rich details comprising the participants' lives.

Chapter 3, along with Chapters 4 and 5, is devoted to analysis of the study's data. In Chapter 3 I examine how the participants came to perceive themselves within the contexts of their families, their schools, and their larger communities. What roles did these institutions play in the academic success of the participants? I identify and define a number of factors that are generally missing from the literature on first-generation college graduates but may have figured prominently in the formation of the participants' self-concepts and seem to have served as important motivation toward their earning college degrees. Additionally, I locate and discuss probable sources of these factors and their short- and long-range effects on the participants' lives.

Chapter 4 focuses upon the participants' college-going experiences, addressing questions of how they not only gained access to college, but also managed socially, financially, and academically once there. The chapter examines the navigation between the two worlds of home and college and identifies personal qualities that may have aided in the participants' success.

In Chapter 5 I consider the activist experiences of the participants. First, a few of the participants are profiled through descriptions of their activism in their own words. Against this backdrop, I identify themes that were both common across the interviews and germane to the participants' activism, suggesting the possible influence of pre-college and college experiences on the participants' decisions to become activists and on the forms that their activism has taken.

Finally, Chapter 6 offers some conclusions concerning the academic success of these first-generation college graduates and their decisions to become educational or social activists. The chapter then presents recommendations for policy and practice aimed at positively affecting educational opportunities for children and first-generation college students and concludes with recommendations for further study and research.

My secret ambition in writing this book is to foment discontent with second-class citizenship for any American, to advance the truth that education for all protects all, and to foster a groundswell of militancy against substandard schooling anywhere in the nation. More potent than idealism, our understanding of first-generation college students' educational experiences and outcomes may direct our hearts, minds, and efforts toward making their aspirations more readily achievable.

The names of the participants and private persons in their stories have been changed.

Acknowledgments

The number of people who gave me invaluable help with this book is stagger-ing. Friends, colleagues, family, acquaintances, strangers–their contributions made the development and completion of my work possible. I thank them all.

Included in this number are Professors Jennifer Grant Haworth, Clifton Conrad, and Terry Williams, whose critiques, encouragement, guidance, and genuine interest in my research were indispensable. I thank my friends and colleagues who made their histories available to me, applauded my work, of-fered to proofread, and provided constructive criticism of whatever text or idea I shared with them. I am grateful to all the virtual and complete strangers who were invariably open to discussing my research, offering their own sto-ries, and recommending potential interviewees for my study.

My debt and gratitude to the participants in the study cannot be overstated. They are all outstanding individuals who took me, for a time, into their lives. They are shining examples of resiliency, generosity, and positive intention. Without them this book would not have been written.

As for my family, their love, strength, and encouragement never faltered. They believed that I would finish this book and that it would be published.

1 | Freedom's Genesis

Sometime after midnight on a starlit evening in the autumn of 1931, my mother and her siblings were awakened by loud knocks on the front door of their house, the snorting of horses, and the shouts of white men demanding that my grandfather come out. Holding a lamp before her like Lady Liberty's flame, my grandmother opened the door and told the men, who were not hooded, that my grandfather was not there. "My churren are sleeping," she told them. "Please don't wake them up." Two of the men came in and looked around the three-room house. They carried lanterns, which shone upon my mother and her sisters in one bed and her brothers in the other. They looked under the beds, in the kitchen; there was no place to hide inside the house. And my grandfather, warned by a sympathetic white man an hour earlier of his impending lynching, had flown into the night, mysteriously lifted, as it seemed, above woods, swamp, and river never to contact his wife or children again.

The weather turned cold early that year. There was deep snow. My grandmother had work cooking for teachers at the white people's school. She would wrap burlap sacks—or inner tubes from car tires when she could get them—around her feet as protection against the snowdrifts covering the fields and pathways to and from work. My mother missed almost the whole year of school because she had no shoes. She never got beyond fifth grade, and although she could read children's stories and the Bible, she was functionally illiterate. Yet she had an unquenchable love and respect for education. As a mother she imparted that love of learning to her five children, all of whom went to college.

My sisters, my brother, and I are college-educated members of the middle class basically due to my parents' great desire that we make a better living for ourselves than they had been able to do. They made tremendous personal sacrifices to ensure our future. I remember that my mother wore the same coat for ten winters when I was growing up. She would go north to the city during the four months after Christmas to work as a live-in maid for rich white people in order to help my father pay college tuition. From the perspective of our own comfortable stations in life, my siblings and I see clearly that our mother's sacrifices on our behalf, along with those of our father, were nothing short of phenomenal.

Interestingly enough, within the context of her familial background, my mother's aspiration that her children become college educated was an exhibition of deviant behavior. Her own education had not been encouraged, and none of her siblings had urged their children to aspire to earn a college degree. In fact, some of her nieces and nephews did not complete high school. Even as a child I wondered admiringly how my mother could be so vastly different from other members of her family. As an adult my thoughts more often have turned to what my mother could have become if her opportunities had been different.

My parents were giants upon whose shoulders my siblings and I stand. Our children stand there, too, as will their children. My mother was an agent of total change in her ancestral line. She left the long-worn rails of recent generations and imagined a new way over unfamiliar land. She "switched the track," and her children took off in a different direction. Her grandchildren are now on the course that she set so many years ago. Her eldest grandchild attended Illinois State University and North Central College. One of her granddaughters earned a bachelor's degree with honors in three years from Harvard University and graduated from medical school at Columbia University's School of Physicians and Surgeons where she is doing her residency. Another granddaughter recently graduated from the Johns Hopkins University with a bachelor's degree in biology. Yet another granddaughter is a graduate of Chicago's Columbia College with a bachelor's degree in advertising, and a grandson is in his junior year as a business major at Temple University. The youngest grandchild, a college freshman, attends a community college near his home. My family's bright present and future are the result of unflagging sacrifice and beloved intention. My mother and father lifted their descendants by design into an entirely different social and economic class. None of us shows any indication of deviating downward from what for us has become the familial norm.

Chapter 1
Motivation, Means, and Method:
Studying Educational Attainment

While growing up black, female, poor, southern, without strong family support, and during the Great Depression effectively ensured that my mother would not become college educated, those conditions did not prevent her from enhancing the educational levels and lifestyle of her children. Many others of my generation were not so lucky in that no one in their families switched the track on their behalf. Yet possessing what very well may be the same determination and drive that compelled my mother, and being born much later—in some cases three or four decades later—than she was, the extraordinary individuals whom I interviewed for this book were able to rise above formidable obstacles to complete a college degree, the first in the histories of their families to do so. By switching the track for themselves, they have undoubtedly affected the upward mobility—educationally, socially, and economically—of their descendants for generations to come. In addition, they have influenced others along the way to become agents of positive change in their own lives and in the lives of their progeny by becoming first-generation college graduates. This book, while it does not address structural or physiological attributes of the participants, attempts to show how these remarkable people managed to achieve their great feats.

My childhood desire to understand why education would be as important to my mother (in whose family no one had ever completed elementary school) as to my father (whose eldest sister attended secondary school in the 1920s and became a teacher) was given added poignancy when I expanded my circle of family. Right after my college graduation in June, 1966, I married a first-generation college student and lived with his family for the summer. I was struck by the fact that only two of my husband's seven siblings had completed high school and that his family was vociferous in its denigration of the college diploma as "just a piece of paper." My mother-in-law informed me often, apropos of nothing, and always within my husband's hearing, that he wasn't so smart and had gotten a D in high school German. I added to my list of reasons to admire my young husband his will to pursue a college degree in spite of a familial environment that is downright hostile to higher education. I also began questioning my husband's two younger sisters about why they, unlike their brother, had not aspired to go to college.

In 1996 I began my research with a question that had figured prominently in my ruminations for thirty years: Why do people who have little to no support for doing so break with tradition by becoming the first in their families to attend college and, after graduation, intentional catalysts for similar metamorphoses in others' lives? Why wouldn't they take the easier course of maintaining the educational status quo that is their ancestral inheritance, thereby keeping calumny off their heads at home and abroad and peace in the family? As Huckleberry Finn, that uneducated denizen of American fiction so aptly concluded, when you are sharing close quarters with those more powerful and less tolerant than you, ". . . what you want, above all things . . . is for everybody to be satisfied, and feel right and kind towards the others" (Clemens 1977, 102).

Review of the Literature

I was not able to find a wealth of answers to my question in the literature on first-generation college students. Since first-generation college graduates' short- and long-range effects upon society appear to be dramatically significant, I was surprised that so little data has been collected about them. For instance, no one knows how many students who have attended or are currently enrolled in colleges and universities in the United States are first-generation college students, just as no one knows how many of the nation's college graduates have been the first in their families to earn a college degree. In fact, most of our colleges and universities have not amassed the data necessary to determine the numbers or identities of their students who are first-generation (Padron 1992; London 1996), or they have not used or reported the data. What little is known about first-generation college students includes the fact that they are disproportionately represented in community colleges (Birenbaum 1986; Rendon 1994; Richardson and Skinner 1992; Willett 1989). The stigma that is generally attached to community colleges, to their typically working-class students, and to most research that focuses on community college concerns may account in part for the fact that first-generation college students have been so seldom studied (LaPaglia 1995).

As one of the first studies of first-generation college students in the United States, London's *The Culture of a Community College* (1978) explored the various conflicts that working-class individuals experience as they make the transition from their blue-collar communities to the alien world of higher education. While the subjects in London's study were white and working-class and, hence, did not have to grapple with differences of ethnicity, class, or race upon entry into "an urban, white, working-class community college" (1986, 92), London reported painful transitions for many of these students who found that they had to renegotiate relationships with family and friends. Since the students themselves and others felt that enrollment in a liberal arts program of study bespoke aspirations to white-collar status, alliances with those who were not going on to college were now challenged. Consequently, these first-generation college students found themselves in a double bind. On the one hand, having dared to try to rise above their station in life by going to college, to do poorly academically would be personally devastating and publicly shameful. On the other hand, to be very successful academically would signal an incontrovertible change of identity. The distress of facing such a discontinuity helps to explain, London (1986) suggested, the anti-academic tendencies of some first-generation college students.

London's 1986 study sharpens the focus through which we view first-generation college students who must straddle the chasms of culture, race, class, religion, and/or gender when they enroll in college. In a later study of the irreconcilable incongruities faced by first-generation college students, London (1989) aptly described the "leaving off" of the first-generation college students' home culture and the "taking on" of the new college culture as "breaking away." The terms precisely encapsulate the transitional process of the working-class white students in London's earlier research and demonstrate Weber's (1968) theory that the most important social role of education is to inculcate those being educated into the culture of a social class. Membership in a status group, Weber argued, requires a particular style of life and is designated by badges such as vocabulary, accent, social conventions, tastes in clothing and food, habits of consumerism, and attitudes regarding outsiders. Against the backdrop of London's and Weber's findings, it seems clear that for first-generation college students whose race, class, culture, religion, or gender bars them from Weberian certification within the new social class of the college, breaking away must be followed or accompanied by "breaking in," my own term. Breaking in becomes necessary when the culture of a college or university does not open fully or willingly to first-generation students. This observation is supported by Weber, who indicated that those who aspire to a status group but are not from the group's class, religious, ethnic, and racial background may not be awarded full membership. Ironically, a successful bid for socialization into the status group of the college is often a cause of great consternation for first-generation college students. They worry about what their friends and family will say about their new status, which marks them as both different from and better than those they are leaving behind.

In writing of her transition to the academic life, LaPaglia (1994) confirmed that the need for personal reconciliation over upward mobility through education may not stop with one's graduation from college:

> When I think of the impact of this [ethnic factory] background on my life and work, I picture someone with one foot in the working class and one foot on a ladder going up, unwilling to commit to a single, more stable stance. To do so would mean betrayal and treachery in some nebulous way. My awkward posture is made easier, if not more graceful, by the fact that although I have a proper academic rank (professor), degree (doctorate) and discipline (the humanities), I am on the faculty of a community college, which is not seen as "really" academic by those who are affiliated with four-year schools.
>
> Therefore, I usually don't feel like an outsider with my community college colleagues, though interacting with a few of particularly WASPish bent can still make me uncomfortable. (1994, xii)

If breaking in can continue to elude someone of LaPaglia's accomplishments, full acceptance into the culture of college may seem an impossibility for many first-generation college students. Their problems, as reflected in the literature, are many and appear to spiral outward from the simple fact of their first-generation status. A first-generation college graduate herself, Rendon (1994) identified the following as key issues that influence the participation of minorities and the poor in higher education: self-doubt; fear of failure; fear of being stereotyped as incompetent or lazy; intimidation by the institution; doubts about being college material; unclear academic goals; inadequate academic preparation resulting in poor cognitive, reading, writing, speaking, and test-taking skills; fear of cultural discontinuity; loss of identity; breaking of family codes of solidarity; and an invalidating academic environment coupled with peer and community pressure not to excel. Gandara (1995), in addressing why some low socioeconomic-status (SES) Chicanos avoid the fate of their peers and become academic successes, found among fifty subjects who had attained Ph.D., J.D., and M.D. degrees, these important resources: older siblings who served as advisors and role models; a parenting style described as authoritarian; family stories as part of students' self-perceptions; identification with middle-class values as well as their own cultural groups through matriculation in (1) desegregated or predominately Anglo schools in high SES communities and (2) college preparatory classes; childhood homes where bilingual literacy was valued; physical handicaps which channeled energies into reading; and a European or ethnically ambiguous, as opposed to "classically Mexican," physical appearance.

Levine and Nidiffer (1996) studied twenty-four poor first-generation college students and found that one person's intervention, whether relative or professional advisor, at a crucial point in the life of each student made the difference in changing the students' lives. These mentors gave hope, enhanced confidence, knowledge of what was important, and direction to the students. Similarly, the literature on first-generation college students identifies seven factors as important elements in the success of this group: peer support groups; familial encouragement; involvement with faculty; financial aid; academic preparedness; formalized programs to aid in admissions and persistence; and faculty expectations of students (Astin 1993; Chaffee 1992; Chatman 1994; Gandara 1995; Hewlett 1981; Joyce 1987; Kiang 1992; Lara 1992; Levine and Nidiffer 1996; Padron 1992; Rendon 1994, 1992; Richardson and Skinner 1992; Simelton 1994; Stein 1992; Warner 1992; Werner 1995).

Still, significant gaps remain in the literature on first-generation college students. For example, the literature provides few clues as to how intrinsic motivations, along with life experiences, affect the matriculation and success of low SES, first-generation college students. Much that has been written on various social and ethnic groups has indicated that familial support is a key factor in the educational attainment of first-generation college students (Astin 1993; Lara 1992; Levine and Nidiffer 1996; Rendon 1994; and others). But as Cuadraz (1993) has asked, if school success is attributable to familial culture, does it follow that academically unsuccessful students lacked the proper socialization into those familial mores which breed success? Gandara (1995) found that among the low-income Chicanos whom she studied, older children who were themselves unable to attend college greatly enhanced the chance for their younger siblings to do so. Harrington and Boardman (1997) postulated that students who use their own standards in assessing their experiences may have a success-promoting advantage over those who adopt others' evaluations. But assuming that they are correct, what promotes "inner direction" (Shostrom 1965, 1966, cited in Harrington and Boardman 1997)? Why would one child from a low socioeconomic-status family become a college graduate while none of her or his siblings, either older or younger, attempted to earn a college degree? With this question in mind, I explored those family and life experiences that contribute to the matriculation and subsequent educational success of low SES, first-generation college students.

A second gap in the literature is the dearth of information on those college-specific experiences, both in- and out-of-class, that contribute to the educational success of low SES, first-generation college students (Terenzini et al. 1996). And third, the literature shows little exploration of the relationships between college or pre-college experiences and their effects on first-generation students' affective growth and development. At this time, we have limited knowledge about the transforming effects of college on first-generation college students. How do various college experiences, for instance, affect the ways in which first-generation college graduates from low SES families live their lives and influence others as agents of change? In her study of Mexican Americans who began their doctoral work during the college-protest years of 1967 to 1979, Cuadraz (1993) discussed some individuals who went to graduate school at Berkeley as a means of continuing their involvement in the politics of the day. The study indicated that the participants tended to choose professions—such as education, law, and social services—which enabled them to integrate their political ideals into their professional lives. Accordingly, in this study I examined (1) how, with or without the anti-establishment *Zeitgeist*, a low SES, first-generation undergraduate becomes infused with the seeds of activism; and (2) how such activism affects the life of that individual—as a college graduate—as well as the lives of others. The study, then, represents an effort to understand the characteristics that selected first-generation college graduates took with them to college, the forces that aided their achievement in college, and their subsequent influence—as educational or social activists—on the world at large.

Research Questions

When I began this study of first-generation college graduates, I was curious about whether their experiences would resonate with my own. And in spite of all my care to be objective, I think I expected to be inspired by their stories. These were people, after all, who had overcome enormous obstacles in their educational journeys, often from a very young age. They had gotten to and through a baccalaureate institution without most of the support that most students take for granted. And they had been involved in educational or social activism for at least five years after college graduation. I did not know why or how the participants had achieved their levels of educational, economic, social, and service-related success, but it was an easy guess that their stories of personal hardship would be balanced by personal salvation. Eager to begin collecting data, I refined my research questions:

1. What family and life experiences contribute to the matriculation and subsequent educational success of low socioeconomic-status, first-generation college students?
2. What college-specific experiences—both in- and out-of-class—contribute to the educational success of low socioeconomic-status, first-generation college students?
3. How do the various experiences previously described affect students' growth and development in college? What imprint do these experiences make on students' decisions to become educational or social activists? How do they affect the ways in which these first-generation college graduates live their lives and influence others as agents of change?

I defined the special terms that I would use in the study:

1. *First-generation college student:* Several scholars have put forth, implicitly or directly, definitions of first-generation college students. London (1986) and Zwerling (1976) described first-generation college students as having parents and grandparents who typically did not complete high school, never attended college, and earned their livelihoods through blue-collar occupations. Billson and Brooks-Terry (1982) defined first-generation college students as those whose parents had not attended college, even though their siblings may have attended. They examined gradations of first- and second-generationality by asking such questions as whether one or both parents had attended but not graduated from college. Their answers enabled them not only to distinguish between first- and second-generation college graduates but also to draw conclusions about the absence as well as the presence of parental college experience upon first- and second-generation college students. York-Anderson and Bowman (1991) defined first-generation college students as those whose parents and or siblings had not attended college at all or who had attended for less than one year. Terenzini et al. (1996) defined first-generation college students as those whose parents did not have any college experience. For this study I chose participants who were the first persons within their immediate or primary family units ever to matriculate in college.

   I selected so constrained a definition because the proliferation of studies defining first-generation college students as those whose parent(s) did not graduate from college mistakenly, I think, correlate knowledge about the college-going process too directly with degree achievement. It seems to me that knowledge about the college-going process, while inherent in degree achievement, is more directly aligned with the experience of attending college, even if a degree is not earned, than with graduation. Consequently, individuals selected to participate in this study were the first in their immediate or primary family units to have any college-going experience at all. It should be noted that even though the term *first-generation* college student is not to be confused with *first-generation American*, the two are sometimes one and the same—when a person who is a first-generation American is also the first in her or his immediate family to go to college.

2. *Educational* or *social activist: Webster's Ninth New Collegiate Dictionary* defines an activist as one whose "doctrine or practice emphasizes direct vigorous action . . . in support of or opposition to one side of a controversial issue" (1986). In a self-description, the activist, educator, and writer Ruth Sidel stated, "I identify as a teacher, as a social activist, as somebody who looks at the world and wants to make people feel and understand the inequities in our society" (Budhos 1996, 31). I use the term *educational* or *social activist* in reference to an individual who advocates for the advancement of his or her views on education or other social issues. For instance, if an educational or social activist is against specific policies and practices in an educational institution because they marginalize certain groups of students, the activist might analyze those policies and practices, show how they have been veiled in the deceptive rhetoric of sound and equitable education for all students, and reveal their discriminatory and premeditated results—with the clear objective of bringing about their demise (Weis and Fine 1993). In this study, educational or social activists may focus their energies on any level(s) of formal schooling—preschool, primary, middle, secondary, college, or graduate—or upon any social issue. While an educational or social activist does not have to be an educator—or educated, for that matter—the activists in this study qualify at least on the second account.

3. *Successful college student:* A college student who achieves the "overall student educational objectives such as earning a degree, persisting in school, and learning the 'right' things—the skills and knowledge that will help students to achieve their goals in work and life" is successful (Barr and Tagg 1995, 15). In this study, the minimum requirement for a successful student is having been able to earn a baccalaureate degree. All of this study's participants have held their bachelor's degrees for a minimum of five years, ensuring that they have had time to establish track records as activists in the minds of their respective communities.

I launched my search for subjects by seeking out well-known first-generation college-graduate activists and requesting their participation in the study. I
also contacted family, friends, and acquaintances from various communities
who are involved in the field of education, in public service, or in community
activism. I spread the word among my colleagues at work and across the nation, asking them to nominate individuals who they believed would be suitable
for the study. Once I had compiled a list of potential subjects, I then selected
the seventeen participants whose stories form the basis of this study. A review
of demographic information about these men and women reveals that they
represent the five major racial/ethnic categories recognized by the United
States Census Bureau; different age categories from those as young as twenty-
eight to those as old as seventy-four; and childhood homes from China to
Canada to New York to the Deep South to the Midwest to California. Twelve
of the seventeen hold advanced degrees; all are working professionals; and all
come from families who were poor (See Table 1).

Their lives are both illuminating and exhilarating, the same and different,
predictable and incredible. They support what we think we know about first-
generation college graduates, even as they compel us to reconsider. They answer our questions and pose new ones, shedding light on old mysteries while
simultaneously broadening the divide between what we do and do not understand. Yet in all their obfuscation, I have found the stories of these first-
generation college graduates to be continually and profoundly interesting. I
spent approximately four hours interviewing each of the seventeen participants, tape recording each conversation in its entirety. In keeping with my
research questions, I structured all interviews around three life phases of the
participants: the pre-college years, the college-going experience, and the post-
college years of educational or social activism.

After conducting and transcribing the interviews, I recorded and cross-
referenced important data events, experiences, characteristics, and circumstances of each participant. Then I began building upon the emerging themes
by deriving (1) profiles of first-generation college graduates from low SES
families; (2) family, life, and college experiences that promote the academic
and social success of first-generation college students prior to, during, and
after graduation from college; and (3) short- and long-term positive effects of
earning a degree, particularly in the area of social or educational activism on
self and on others.

I recorded these emergent themes in analytic memoranda, categorizing the
continuously emerging data. Coding categories for the study, already suggested
as sampling criteria, were augmented by analytic schemes that were suggested

Table 1. Participant Demographics

Participant	Race/Ethnicity	Sex	Age	Origin	Degrees	Profession
Fred	B	M	60	Ohio	BFA, MA, Ph.D	Baptist Minister
Annie	B	F	49	Alabama	BA, MA	Elementary Teacher
Lorraine	B	F	74	S. Carolina	BA	Docent
Sadie	B	F	41	Mississippi	BA, MA, Ph.D	Communications Professor
Grant	B	M	47	Michigan	BA, LLD	Attorney
Dorothy	B	F	39	Chicago	BA, MA	English Professor
Chang	A	M	45	China	BA, MA	English Professor
Arlene	NA	F	60	Canada	BA	Storyteller
Barbara	W	F	63	Chicago	BA, MA, Ph.D	Humanities Professor
Steve	W	M	44	Chicago	BFA, MFA	Artist
John	W	M	74	Chicago	BA	Business Executive
Ken	W	M	58	New York	BA, MA	Philosophy Professor
Clara	W	F	29	Illinois	BA, MA	Spanish Professor
Jerry	W	M	52	California	BA	Artist
Alex	H	M	52	New York	BA, MA. MA, Ed.D	Elementary Principal
Jorge	H	M	28	Chicago	BA, MA	Business Executive
Maria	H	F	29	Chicago	BA	Business Administrator

B=black; A=Asian; NA=Native American; W=white; H=Hispanic

by the data. Becker, Geer, and Strauss (1961), who studied medical students, used "incidents" and "perspectives" as categories for data analysis. Ely et al. (1991) advanced "thinking units" as a category for data analysis. From my own experience as a first-generation college graduate, corroborated by Gandara (1995) and Levine and Nidiffer (1996), I correctly suspected that parental attitudes toward learning might emerge from the data as a category for analysis. Also, from what I have seen of other first-generation college graduates from low SES backgrounds, I suspected, again correctly, that "ascending cross-class identification" and college learning environments might be other categories for analysis. My intention was not to force preliminary, restrictive, or presumptive structures upon the data analysis procedures but, instead, to allow coding categories to suggest themselves.

For each research question, I isolated common themes and supporting excerpts from as many interviews as I could. Thus, I created a file for each research question based on the common themes and the relevant interview data. Only then did I attempt an outline of what the interviews seemed to reveal. Finally, I set out to descriptively and parsimoniously construct an analysis of the participants' family, life, collegiate, and activist experiences.

2 | The Economics of Oppression

The role of godly power in the lives of the oppressed, I believe, is absolutely necessary. Under the Jim Crow laws of the south during my childhood, religion certainly was the most important connective element in our community. Religion, centered around the church, empowered us against evil and sustained us over the days and weeks until the next church service. "The Lord is my rock and my salvation! Whom shall I fear?" we sang earnestly. In reality, there was much to fear—even prosperity—for out of fortune grew jealousies that sometimes carried heavy penalties for the blessed.

My parents were clearly blessed: my mother by being beautiful and by marrying my father; my father by marrying a good woman, being smart, and coming from a large extended family that had owned their own land since 1865. Just days after slavery was over, my great-great-grandfather had bought the original Williams tract on a farm called Peterson. Subsequently he and his brothers and sisters bought over a thousand acres of woods and fields, and by 1965 no white person had owned a foot of Peterson land in almost a hundred years.

My father grew up in Peterson, in a large, two-story white house with both a parlor and a sitting room; five bedrooms; a large formal dining room; a wide hallway furnished with a table, a leather covered daybed, and two huge ferns on tall stands; and expansive front and back porches. During his youth, my father and his older brother and male cousins rode horseback, hunted, or swam in the Albermarle Sound when they were not busy with farmwork. Boys who were intent on becoming farmers rather than completing elementary school during the 1920s and 1930s may have disappointed their parents, but they proved financially beneficial all the same. And the labor of sons aided my grandfather in buying a new car and paying cash for it during the Great Depression.

After my father married my mother, they sharecropped for a few years, saving practically every penny they made. There were no curtains at their windows because it was cheaper to buy paper shades for ten cents each. My mother had inherited her grandfather's steamer trunk and a small table. My father's parents had given them a bed, a dresser, and a wood-burning stove. My father had hired a handyman to make a kitchen table, benches, and some chairs, including a rocker. My parents kept a large garden and chickens, and my paternal grandparents gave them turkeys, pigs, milk, butter, and a young cow. But people were surprised and envious when they bought Bucklesbury, the farm where my memories begin.

White people were upset that my parents actually had the down payment on the farm and that a white doctor had sold valuable land to black people. Many settled back to wait for foreclosure, but in four years the land was paid for. Then my parents bought a few acres from a black minister and had a house built closer to our school. That was in 1952, the year my father's oldest brother, driving drunk at a speed to outrun the devil, missed the first bend in an S-curve and wrapped his midnight blue 1950 Ford around a black walnut tree. He died immediately, and his first cousin, also drunk, a passenger, and the father of twelve children, died a few hours later.

In three years, my uncle's thick-headed son had entangled himself in debt to a white man who coveted my uncle's land and had found a way to get it. This was the land that had been bought by my great-great-grandparents, the first land that my ancestors had ever owned in America. The bank loaned my parents the money to pay my cousin's debts, and my parents acquired the deed to the land bought in 1865 by Richard and Hannah Williams.

On the morning the deed was to be transferred, the wife of my cousin's debtor, Junior Jordan, came to our house and offered to drive my father to Windsor where their business would be carried out.

"You just as well come on and ride with me, Burnett," she said. "Junior had to go on a little earlier, but he said if you rode along with me, it would save you the gas."

We children stood around our living room, barefoot and silent, curious about this white woman who didn't want our father to drive his own car to town. My father thanked her profusely but declined her repeated offer and would not change his mind. She appealed to my mother for support, but my mother demurred, adding that my dad needed to purchase a few things in town after their business was completed. Suppose my father were alone with a white woman who decided to accuse him of rape or attempted rape. He would lose his life, let alone his property. From that day on, my mother hated Junior Jordan, and over the next few months her low opinion of him proved doubly deserved.

Every day that summer my siblings and I would go with our parents from our new house to work on one of our farms. One day when we were working in Bucklesbury, we were surprised to see a seemingly endless caravan of cars snake its way into the clearing of our land. There were fifteen cars in all, each carrying five plainclothes policemen who spilled out of their vehicles with white-faced purpose, converged upon us to show their warrant and make their explanations, and spread out in all directions to search our dense woods for liquor stills that white people had claimed my father was operating. It had been reported that one of my father's cousins was hauling the liquor, strapped in jugs and fruit jars under the hood of his car, to bootleggers in another county. When the revenuers finally emerged from our woods with their shiny compasses, they had nothing to show for their trouble but muddy boots and bites from mosquitoes, gnats, and yellow flies. Afterward my father began taking a rifle to work. I recently asked him to recall how he felt that day when seventy-five white men descended upon us. "It didn't make me feel too good," he said with characteristic understatement, "because I didn't have what I needed to protect you all. But now it doesn't bother me because it's all in the past."

At the time the white people sicced the revenuers on us, black people set out to conjure us, and they were almost more successful than the whites had been. My father developed a searing pain and stiffness in his right shoulder and arm that made doing most farmwork almost impossible for him. The doctor could not help him, but his mother made my grandfather take her to visit a root doctor in South Norfolk, a hundred miles away. Returning with newly found knowledge, my grandmother told my father that there were two animal shapes hanging from a tree branch or a fence post on his property, and if he found and destroyed the shapes, his pain would disappear. My father laughed at his mother's wasteful expenditure of time and money on procuring a conjurer's advice, but one day when he and my brother were walking down the path toward our old farmhouse, he noticed two wire figures of turtles hanging from a branch of a small tree beside a fence post to our cow pasture. The shell of each turtle had been fashioned from mesh wiring, the head, legs, and tail from carefully folded, thick, single wire strands. The turtles had begun rusting, as if left for ages to the elements. My father pulled the shapes apart and became immediately free of pain.

My parents believed that every positive intervention in our lives was the result of God's grace. My grandmother concurred, but she had not been reluctant to help God along with a little intervention from a high-powered voodoo priest. I remember when she stood up in church after the sermon one Sunday a short time later, began pacing back and forth in front of God and congregation, scourged the entire membership as ignorant backwoods liars and hypocrites, and promised never to set foot—in life—in that church again. She proved as good as her word. In fact, she proved better than her word, never entering *any* church again until she was in her casket.

Chapter 2
In Their Words:
Stories of First-Generation
College-Graduate Activists

In the following narratives, I recount the experiences of five of the participants in this study. I have chosen the narrative approach in order to provide a vivid, contextualized account of the complexity of the participants' lives and the many obstacles and issues they negotiated as first-generation college graduates. And while all seventeen of the individuals I interviewed told compelling life stories, I have chosen to highlight the following five narratives for two reasons.

First, these five are perhaps the most representative of all the others in that they portray a breadth of diversity—in terms of race and ethnicity, geographical location of childhood home, and profession—while also magnifying important commonalities. For instance, three of the five stories presented here are of participants—Annie, John, and Alex—who were born within three years of each other in the United States, but whose school experiences were widely divergent. They hail from different parts of the country, and their stories cut across black, white, and Hispanic racial/ethnic categories. Lorraine and Annie, separated in age by twenty-five years, have in common characteristics including race, gender, and birth and rearing in the rural south. Differences and similarities such as these are not focal to the study but lend significant richness and variety to the findings. They also emphasize our responsibility to improve education for the needy by dashing our naive hopes that systemic injustice automatically erodes with time.

Second, the details of these five stories impart different points of emphasis. Annie's story illustrates, against the harsh background of her early environment, the influence of the school, family, and others on her college success. "I tell my students now that I really grew up as a slave," she said to me. As I heard her story, I understood the reality of her statement, even though she was born in 1946, eighty-one years after slavery was abolished. Alex's story stresses the positive role of the community in a New York City ghetto—and others outside the ghetto who reached in—in his academic success. Arlene, the only Native American in the study, tells a story that emphasizes the impact of the college and informal curriculum on her life, while John's story portrays novel approaches to the activist role and its impact on other's lives. In many respects John is an anomaly among the participants. He recounts assistance from almost no one when he was growing up and seems to have found solace in nature rather than in people. A major reason for including his story is that it *is* so different from the rest and may be detected by others as significant beyond those points of analysis that I make in Chapter 3. Lorraine's story, set on an island off the coast of South Carolina where *Gullah* is still spoken, shows the impact of the community, and especially its history, on her academic and life experiences.

Their stories—told in first person—follow. Each was related in response to the three research questions listed in Chapter 1. While I edited the interview transcriptions to reconstruct them into more holistic, flowing narratives, I was careful to honor as completely as I could the interviewees' exact meanings, words, and nuances. These stories are offered especially for those interested in "whole" narratives that may inspire and enlighten by detailing the education and activist-related experiences of five of the study's participants. Readers who are not interested in the stories can skip to Chapter 3, the beginning of the analysis section.

Annie Jones—of Service

Annie, 49, teaches fourth grade in a public school in Illinois.

I was born in a little town called Luverne, Alabama, on October 6, 1946. My mother was Cora Jones, born Armstrong. My father was Willie Jones. My dad finished third grade; my mother finished fifth grade. My dad really couldn't read or write, but my mother could do both. They had fifteen children, eleven of whom are living. Two died before I was born, and my mother miscarried two. I'm the seventh birth, and I'm the fifth living. I have always heard that there is something special about the seventh child. I don't know what it is, but I happen to be that seventh child.

I am the first in the history of my family to go to college. None of my brothers finished regular high school. My oldest sister finished high school, and my sister next to me finished. I have another sister who never finished, but she did get a GED. I have one brother who finished high school in the special education area. I have three brothers who are older than I am and three who are younger, and one sister who is older than I am and three who are younger. With eleven children in the family, we could have had our own football team if we'd had time to play football.

We grew up in the country, on a farm. I tell my students that I grew up as a slave because my dad was a sharecropper, and sharecropping was really a sophisticated name for slavery. My dad farmed eighteen to twenty acres of cotton, twenty acres of peanuts, and forty to fifty acres of corn. My brothers had to stay home from school to farm the land; the plantation owner who was our landlord required that they stay home and work. The white people were in control, and at the end of the year they would decide whether or not you had a profit. So at the end of each year, you barely broke even or you were in debt, and you had to stay on.

I really liked school when I was growing up, but I never went to school on the first day. When I was small I had to stay home because my older siblings, who would have taken me to school, had to stay home to work in the fields. When I was a bit older, I had to stay home to work in the fields myself. During most of the years that he farmed, my father didn't have tractors or other modern farming equipment. In the later years, I guess five years prior to my dad's leaving plantation life, the white man he worked for did have a tractor. My brother drove the tractor. My dad said he was so used to walking behind a mule that he didn't really want to be bothered with the tractor. But I know that tractor work was easier than walking behind a mule pushing a plow, and my father wanted to spare my brother.

I didn't plow, but I used to put soda or fertilizer around the corn. I hoed peanuts and cotton, and I chopped cotton. There is a difference between hoeing and chopping. We would chop first, and later we would hoe. You chop when the cotton is about six or seven inches high. What you really do is you thin it, leaving two or three stalks per hill. Later, you hoe the cotton and the peanuts, which means you get the grass out. Sometimes we would have to pull the grass out of the peanuts to keep our hoes from disturbing the nuts forming under the ground. Once the cotton was mature, we were in the fields from sunup to sundown picking. In late fall when the weather had cooled, the remaining buds of cotton, or scrap cotton, would be ready for picking. Scrap cotton is very difficult to take from the bolls, so we would pull it, taking the cotton and the boll as well.

After the cotton was in, we would dig the peanuts. First, we would plow them up. Then we would erect poles in the fields about every ten to fifteen feet and wrap the peanut vines around the poles so they would dry. Weeks later, after the peanuts were dry, the men would bring the pea picker into the field to separate the peanuts from the vines. Then the vines would be baled into hay. My job was to help roll the hay away from the machine and put it into stacks. We would store the hay in the barn for feeding the animals over the winter. We would harvest the dried ears of corn and store them in the barn to feed the animals as well as ourselves. All our meal for dumplings and cornbread was made from our corn, ground at the gristmill, and kept in a can in the kitchen. The corn also served as seed for planting the next year's crops.

Digging peanuts was very dirty work. It put layers of dirt in our hair, our eyes, and up our noses. Our bodies hurt from constantly bending over to get the peanut plants, shaking the dirt off the roots, and placing the plants on the stack. But no farm work was easy. The cotton bolls were so sharp! They would prick and cut our hands and arms, but my dad would say that we had to get the cotton harvested before the gale set in. The gale is a consistent rain that mildews cotton and lowers its price. The gale comes around the first of November, and I recall one time we had to pull some cotton during gale season.

Normally little children would pick one row of cotton at a time. When we were older, we had to pick two rows at a time. But there were times when there was so much to do that my sister, brother, and I would pick three rows at a time. It was a lot of work and it had to be done fast. Sometimes my dad would say, "You have to pick a hundred pounds of cotton today." And you knew that you really had to work as a child to pick a hundred pounds of cotton. I started picking cotton when I was eight years old. Picking cotton, like all other work, was a family effort. We knew the problems it would cause my dad, and consequently the rest of us, if we didn't get the work done.

About as soon as we were walking well, we were given responsibilities around the house. My dad would not let us stay in bed after sunup. Even on Saturdays we had to get out of bed; he would find something for us to do. We were in the fields after school Monday through Friday—when we got to go to school—and we would work until dark. On Saturdays we sometimes had to work in the fields from six in the morning until noon. At twelve o'clock we would leave the fields and do the chores around the house. We'd have to sweep the yard, an area around the house that didn't have any grass in it, and we'd go into the woods and get dogwood branches to use as rakes. We had to chop wood for the fire because we had a wood stove for cooking and heating. Washing, ironing, scrubbing the floors, and cleaning the house also kept us busy on Saturday afternoons. I remember my dad putting twelve holes in a wooden block, and we would fill those holes with dried corn shucks. Then we would dip the shucks in hot water and use that to scrub the floors. We had to make the soap that we used to clean the floors. We made all our own soap. You mix lye, water, lard, and tallow. You boil it and let it sit for a day to solidify. Then you cut it into pieces. All this work was just part of the family and community work ethic.

When I was a child, I loved to go to school because I loved the challenge of learning new things and I loved reading. I always felt I was escaping my surroundings when I read and put my mind on other things. I had something more than my siblings had, too, because I had an aunt who really loved me. I would go home with her periodically, and she would take me places. She worked for a white family, and sometimes she would take me to work with her. I remember one day she took me to work and I met the little white girl who lived there, and this girl could read. She had these books and she was reading. I thought, "Oh, I would like to be able to read like that," but I didn't have any books. I used to tell my aunt how I really would like to have some books, and she would say, "Well, maybe one day you will get some." I couldn't understand how this little girl could have so many books and we didn't have any. I would go home and try to read the one book that we had, an old Bible, as best I could. There were so many words that I could not understand, and, of course, my mom and dad couldn't really help me. But I would just try to read the best I could.

Now, I remember that one of my teachers gave me a book. I'll never forget it; it was called *Children Everywhere*. I read that book from front to back forever. There was a story in the book about a woman who worked hard and did her job every day, and her husband was always complaining about the work she was doing. So she told him to stay home and do her work and she would go and do his job. He took her up on this, and she could do his job, but he couldn't do hers. And I thought, "There has to be another job that I can do. I don't want to do this job for the rest of my life." I thought of our lives working on the farm year in and year out, and those people not really paying my dad. They were living in a better house than we were living in, but we were doing the work. I couldn't understand that.

My mom and dad were Christian people, and I used to pray as a child because we believed in prayer. We would pray constantly, and I know that was the backbone of our strength and our endurance. So I said, "Lord, I know there is something else out there for me to do. I can't live like this for the rest of my life." And I thought that through reading, I would find help to change my life. I just wanted to do something different. I recall asking my dad to get me some books to read—to just buy a newspaper—but he said he didn't have the money. I didn't understand why he didn't have twenty-five cents to buy a newspaper. Twenty-five cents was the cost of a Sunday paper, but during the week you could get a paper for fifteen cents. Not truly understanding my father's situation, I used to cry, and I'd say, "Daddy, just at least buy a newspaper. I just want something to read." I remember crying for about a week, begging my daddy to buy me a newspaper. I didn't realize at that time that my dad was trying to save his money; he had to save up fifteen cents to buy the newspaper. But he apparently got another dime because he got me a Sunday paper. He got that newspaper! I used to read that paper over and over. I didn't want to lose it because I didn't know how long it would take me to get another one. I would come home at night, after we got out of the field, and sit by the lamp and read the newspaper. I read it so often that the words began to disappear. I came to realize that newsprint isn't permanent. But I read that paper for a long time. I read it over and over again because that's all I had to read.

I had tried to learn to read by reading the Bible. I know it can trip up a lot of educated people even now, but I would just say the words I thought I could say. A lot of the time I would ask my mom what a word was, and she would try to help me. As time went on, I came to understand that she didn't know many of those words and was just doing the best she could to help me. Often I would put in my own words or ideas, guessed from the context, to help me pick up whatever meaning I could.

Even in school we did not read phonetically. I remember we would have a picture, like an apple, and we would have to say, "A is for apple, B is for bat, C is for cat, D is for dog," and so on. When I would see other words, I would just kind of put those sounds together. I know that for *bed* I'd have to remember that *b* is like *buh* and *e* is like *eh* for *elephant* and *d* is like *duh* for *dog*. Sometimes when I was putting sounds together, I would actually get the word.

A great influence in my early life as a student was my fourth grade teacher who later became my fifth and seventh grade teacher. He used to read to us. I loved that. I loved hearing the words as he read. In second, third, fourth, and fifth grades, I attended school in a little two-room house where the teachers were a husband and wife team. The wife taught second and third grades, and the husband taught fourth and fifth. There was another lady who taught first grade, but her class met in the church. We didn't have a school like the white children had. We had the old books from the white school. We never got new books. I was a senior in high school before I ever saw a new book. A lot of times we never saw the covers of a book because the white children would have torn the covers off before the books got to us. Our teacher would say, "Maybe we can salvage this one" and would try to find a book for everyone. Actually, there were never enough books for everyone. I remember when three of us had to share the single copy of that little blue-backed speller. I remember sharing math books. Sometimes four or five of us would crowd around a single math book. We never once had enough books for everybody.

I recall being in a class with three grades and about twenty-nine children. Because books were so scarce, we had to take turns taking a book home. And sometimes there were problems. If a child had to walk a long way and it was raining and the child dropped the book and it got wet, the teacher would look skeptically at letting us take the books home. He'd say, "I think you have to leave the books here." When we did take the books home, all of us children had to compromise. If you took the math book today, then I would take the spelling book. My teacher would give us time to do homework in class. If he were working with the fourth graders, the fifth graders would be doing work in the corner. The children who had taken a particular book home would help the others with that subject. There is all this talk about collaborative learning today; we were doing it back then.

All the black children who lived in my area were in my situation; they couldn't go to school every day. I could not understand why we had to work so hard for the white people, while the white children had books to read, a big pretty red brick building for school, and mowed grass for their yard. We were going to school in an old church with no grass. They had swings on their playground. We had to make our toys and the playground equipment that we used. My teacher, the boys, and even the girls, would go into the woods behind the church and cut down logs and bring them back. My teacher would bring his saw and a hole digger to school. I remember that we made what we'd call today a teeter-totter. We called it a seesaw. We made a flying jenny. We would make our own balls and bats. Everybody would bring old socks to school, and we would stuff some of them with cotton. We would then take another sock and unravel it. The socks in those days were made of cotton, and they would be comprised of one continuous string. You'd take that string and wrap it around the sock with the cotton in it until it was as hard as you wanted it to be. How well you wrapped the sock determined whether it was a hardball or a softball. My teacher would cut a limb from the woods, and he would use a brace—a shear, they call them—and he would shave the wood down and make a bat. For the girls, we just had a flat board for softball, and my teacher would curve the end so our hands could fit around it. We would throw ropes in the trees and attach a piece of leather, salvaged from peanut pickers, for the seats. These were our swings. Our teacher would also bring in old tires and attach them by rope to the trees. Some children could swing in the tires while others would use the leather swing. We also played horseshoes. I think my teacher's grandfather owned those horseshoes and would let us use them from time to time.

I knew that I could do something different with my life when I was twelve years old. That's when I received Christ, and it was at that moment that things just opened up for me. I met my first-grade teacher's brother, who was in college at the time. I had never heard of college. I knew my teachers had to have gotten training somewhere, but this was the first time I had direct knowledge of college. And he made it sound like a terrific place to be. He was going to be a teacher. I remember telling my mother I would like to be a teacher. She said that it would be good for me to become a teacher, that there will always be children who need teachers. At the time, we couldn't think about being anything beyond a teacher or a nurse, so I started thinking that I wanted to become a teacher.

Another important thing that happened to me was that in seventh grade, my teacher let me keep attendance. He put me in charge of the register because he thought I had good penmanship. In fact, my penmanship was better than his. I would record the children's names, days present, days absent, what have you. That was fascinating to me. I would do all this recording and take it to the principal's office, and he would send it to, I think, the superintendent. So I felt certain that I wanted to be a teacher. But I thought I wanted to be a physical education teacher because I enjoyed athletics.

I went on to break records when I ran track in high school. I also played basketball and did a little high jumping. In eleventh grade I decided I wanted to be a home economics teacher because my home economics instructor made sewing so much fun. I had seen my mother sew a lot since she made all our clothes and sewed for people in the community. Usually in home economics class, students were required to make one dress for a course project, but I was able to finish my project and make a second dress. I liked sewing, and my teacher was impressed by what I did; yet by the time I got to Tuskegee, I had decided I wanted to work with children and wound up majoring in elementary education. But I first knew that I wanted to teach when I was twelve years old and my teacher gave me the opportunity to help him. That's one of the things that makes me want to strive to help others today—it's my memory of how he gave me that opportunity. Somebody may look at what my teacher did as a small thing, but to me it was gargantuan. He valued what I could do and gave me responsibility and experience in management.

Another thing that helped me greatly was my teacher's praying. I loved to hear him pray. I remember that our devotion did not stop at the usual time one morning. We must have had prayer and singing for about an hour and a half that day. My sister could sing very well, and my teacher could sing very well. After he prayed, someone sang a song. Then he sang a song. Then someone read Scripture, and then my sister sang a song. Everyone was so filled with the Spirit. I accepted Jesus as my Savior that day in the classroom. And I said to the Lord that day, "Lord, just let me treat others like I want to be treated." And it was a philosophy that stuck in my head.

Even though my teacher would go beyond the normal to show that he cared for all his students, he would whip anybody that got out of line. When he did whip students, they knew that they deserved it. And afterward he would let us know that he loved us anyway. He was just a great motivator—through praise and through letting us stay in at lunchtime to work on something we wanted to learn. I loved learning the multiplication tables. We would sing them jazzed up: "Two times one equal two, two times two equal four . . ." He would give us long multiplication problems like 5,292 x 12. We'd do the work on the board, and he would time us to see how fast we were. It was so much fun!

When we'd go out to play at recess, sometimes he'd come out and play with us. When we were making equipment, he might say we needed an eight-foot pole, and we would have to do the measuring. I didn't know it at the time, but we were learning math and we were having to think critically because he'd give us instructions as to what to do. He was a great teacher. He gave us the opportunity to have ownership in what we were learning. He showed us that you don't have to lose your sense of play to be a grown-up. He'd get on the other end of that teeter-totter and we'd go way up in the air because he was a grown-up and much bigger than we were.

In terms of getting the money to go to college, I think I was in the right place at the right time and happened to graduate from high school in the right year. When I got ready to go off to college, my dad was very sad because he wanted me to go to college but he knew he didn't have the money to send me. He wanted me to go because he knew that I wanted to better my life, that I wanted to get an education. So I told him to just let me go and let me try.

Tuskegee had a work-study program at that time. It was a government program that allowed students to begin work in the summer so they could make the money they needed to start paying their tuition and board for the fall semester. Students could work all year to defray college costs. It so happened that my class graduated from high school during the last year of the program. But prior to my going to Tuskegee, I had to have a physical exam, and I had to send in a fifteen-dollar application fee. My dad did not have the money. He could not go to the plantation owner to ask for it because the plantation owner had already told my dad that he would not be getting any more money. The owner had no idea I was going to college at the time.

My family had two cows. One was my mother's, and that was our milk cow. In order to help me, my mother told my dad to sell her cow. My dad had a man come over and put the cow on a truck to take it to sell. Those white people gave my dad sixty-five dollars for that cow! My dad had to give the man some money for driving the cow to be sold. He used some of the money to take me to the dentist and doctor. When I think of how my dad and mom—the whole family—sacrificed for me! My mother was sickly, and my dad gave her five or ten dollars to get some medicine and have her glasses fixed. When he finished taking care of these things, he gave me the rest of the money, fifteen dollars, and that's what I had to go to college.

I remember my mother had sold some candy and bought fabric to make me two dresses and a skirt. I had a couple of blouses, and my high school teacher had given me a blouse and a pair of pants. I had two pairs of shoes. My aunt had given me two sheets. And my mother had given me a couple of mismatched towels that were all we had. Everything I had was in a little foot-locker. Early on I had told my high school teacher that I didn't want to go to college because college students have pretty clothes and I didn't have a lot of things. My teacher said the people at college wouldn't even look at what I was wearing. So I didn't think about that much anymore because I felt good about the clothes my mother had made me.

So I went off to Tuskegee. One of my high school teachers drove us. He and his wife both were high school teachers, and he was the brother of the man who had been my teacher in fourth, fifth, and seventh grades. I thank them every day. My dad didn't have a car and had no concept of where Tuskegee was. When my teacher and his wife came to pick me up, they also picked up two boys and another girl from my high school class. Four of us went to Tuskegee that year, and there were only eighteen in our class.

My teacher and his wife took us to our dormitories. Then we went to his friend's house who lived in Tuskegee and was on the faculty at the college. That family had dinner waiting for us. My teacher had told them about the other girl in our party, and they had made arrangements for her to stay with them. At least my dad had given me fifteen dollars. Her parents hadn't had that. She went to college with nothing. I gave her five of my fifteen dollars so that she would have some money.

I went on back to campus and started a job through the work-study pro-gram. That summer I worked in the laundry. Everybody else thought it was hard work, but it was not hard to me because the work that I had been doing at home was so far beyond it. I worked in the area where we were washing the community linen: sheets and towels. I was catching hot sheets. That was kind of difficult—not so much on my part—but it took two people to do the job and the girl who worked with me was too slow. You had to move those sheets fast or you'd really get burned. One week I had blisters all over my fingers because I was trying to hold the sheets to give her time to catch her part of them. When I was working with the lady who was training us, it was okay because she was fast. I did that for two months until they decided it was too hard for students and gave us other jobs. Some of us became maids in the hotel, but thanks to God, my high school teacher's friend at Tuskegee helped me get a job working in the dormitory at the desk. I just couldn't believe that they would pay me for sitting at the desk and answering the telephone.

They paid us in vouchers—I never saw any money—but I was able to save up enough money that summer to pay my tuition in September. It was a privilege to work. We were only allowed to take nine hours of classes because we had to work. That's why it took me five years to get out of Tuskegee. I continued to work as a desk clerk in the dormitory, and I would baby-sit for people in the community. I started out baby-sitting for one family, and they told another family about me. After a while I had more baby-sitting jobs than I could hold down, but it was good because it allowed me to buy the personal things that I really needed.

I had to work harder at college than most of the other students because I hadn't had the experiences that they had had. When they spoke about the number of credit hours that they needed, I didn't know what they were talking about. I had never heard of credits. And that little country school that I had gone to didn't have a science lab. I was not prepared academically to compete with a lot of the students, but after being at college for a bit, I found that I could do okay.

When I first got to Tuskegee, I met with a student counselor who was assigned to me. Student counselors told us about the classes we would take. They were assigned according to our majors. Later I met with my academic counselor, who is one reason I just thank God that I went to Tuskegee. If I had gone somewhere else, coming from where I came from, I would have been lost. I probably would have flunked out of school, which I almost did at Tuskegee. If it had not been for people like my counselors, who really cared, I would not have made it. If I had been some place like Northwestern, I would have had to go home because with such a large number of students there, people wouldn't have had a chance to listen to my story or they may not have been that concerned.

College was like being in a foreign country, even at Tuskegee, but that is the college I was supposed to go to. By my teacher introducing me to his friend on the faculty, I had someone to talk to if I had any problems. So I had a mentor in the community as well as in the school. And my house mother was the mother of the couple who later became my godparents. When I got married and my godparents came, a friend of mine said, "I never heard of a grown person getting godparents before." I told her that I never went to a church where a minister said to me, "These are your godparents." But I say that they're my godparents because I know that God put me there in front of them. These people took me into their home. They wanted me to come and live with them, and that was a blessing for me. I didn't have any money, and I went through Tuskegee living at their house without paying one nickel. In return I took care of their four children.

My godparents knew they could depend on me. I gave up a lot of social events because I knew why I was there. I wouldn't allow anyone to come to the house when the parents weren't there. I took the kids to baseball, swimming, wherever they needed to go. I read them stories at night, and I made sure they had their baths. I fixed their breakfast in the mornings. I did everything that I could, and the parents knew that. Occasionally the grandmother would come by to check on me and the children when the parents were away, so I knew I could call on her if I ever needed to. But having grown up with eleven children, I knew what to do. I was happy to have the entire family, and they were happy to have me. The parents gave me the key to their car. That's why I say they are my godparents. They provided for me like they were my parents. So I had that side of my family by the time I graduated.

I grew up with my mother and father, and I grew up poor. I went to Tuskegee and started living with people who were upper-middle-class. You might remember Sargent Shriver who ran for Vice-President. That man was a guest in the house where I lived one night. I moved out of my room so he could sleep in my bed. I got to meet all calibers of people. Except for leaving home and going to Tuskegee, I took my first trip out of the county with these people. I stayed in my first hotel—they took me to the Holiday Inn in Birmingham. My godfather had a meeting there one weekend and he called home that Friday evening, about twelve o'clock that night. My godmother said, "Y'all get up." She woke up the kids. I grabbed a bag, and we jumped in that station wagon and headed to Birmingham. And stayed the weekend. This was the kind of stuff I had read of in the newspaper or heard people talk about. I had never thought I would be able to do those things. I was living in a different world.

When I first went to their home, I hardly knew what to do because I had not been accustomed to going into a bathroom to brush my teeth. I had brushed my teeth standing on the back porch. I grew up going outside to use the toilet. Their whole lifestyle, the living experience, was totally new to me. But the kids had to do chores and stuff, even though their father could give them anything. Like my dad, he made them do things.

I first got to know about other cultures through baby-sitting. The husband in the first family I baby-sat for was from Zimbabwe. I was exposed to African culture at their house. I ate African dishes. Their house was the first place where I had ever eaten out of a silver spoon and at a table set with china. I had worked in some white people's houses near my home, but even the white people's houses didn't look like this one. And when I went into those white people's houses to work and they gave me a sandwich, I had to sit on the back porch to eat it. They would have a set table in their dining room, but they didn't have cut-glass crystal glasses and china and silverware like these people had. And I could sit in the dining room with these people and eat and talk with them.

One day in a graduate class at Northeastern Illinois University, when I was working on my master's degree, the instructor went around the classroom asking the students who was the richest person that they knew about. Some said the DuPonts, some said the Waltons, some said the Kennedys. I don't know who the professor said it actually was, but I think it was the guy from Wal-Mart. The professor asked me last and I was glad because I said, "I'm the richest person I know. I had a mother and a father who loved me and took care of all my basic needs, and my father, God, is the maker of this whole world and everything that's in it. Richness depends on your definition of it. I know from whence I came and I know where I am, and I know it is by the grace of God."

I know the acceptance that I received from my godparents was part of my education. During dinner conversations I learned about Booker T. Washington and how he helped people to live in this world with the things that God has provided. I think that he is one of the most misunderstood men of any time. People call him an Uncle Tom, but that's not true. He was interested in and dedicated to helping his people. I have the videotape of Tony Brown playing the part where Booker T. Washington was teaching the children to make bricks and then build a building. Booker T. asked a kid where he was from. The kid said, "Dozier." Booker T. asked him, "Do you think the people of Dozier need to learn to speak French or to build a house?" The answer was, "To build a house." Being at the table with this family was an avenue of my education that I could not get from a book.

Getting to be around people from other parts of the world taught me that when you're with people of other cultures, you can adapt. And when I go back home with my family and get that fruit jar and that tin plate, I can adapt. I think that's what education is about. It was at the table in Tuskegee that I first heard the word *apartheid* because the husband was part of the struggle. In fact, he was exiled from his country. Here was a man who was a leader from his country, and I was sitting with him. While I would listen to them at dinner, I would ask questions. And the next day the wife would congratulate me on the questions that I had asked. I was learning a lot just by contributing to the conversation.

My formal education has been uneven. When I was in second grade, my teacher wasn't very good; eighth grade wasn't that effective. But my teachers generally motivated me to want to learn. When I went from elementary to high school, the children wanted to play a lot, and I was angry because we'd be in the middle of math class and someone would raise their hand and say, "Can we go out to recess?" I wanted to finish my math. Plus, I had to be in the field when I got home. We'd have four more minutes of class left, and I wanted to get all the work done that I could while I was there. I wanted so much to learn, to read, to write. When I was in third grade, my teacher exposed us to a lot of poetry and I began to write poems. In fact, they selected one of my poems for the school poem.

In the college classroom, some of the professors were exciting, and some were intimidating. I loved literature classes. The teachers were excited about their subjects and I wanted to learn all about children's books, to read every children's lit book I saw, to learn all about the authors. On the other hand, I had a very nice biology teacher from Hungary who had an accent. It was very difficult for me to understand her. I would be so frustrated and I'd go to her after class and try to explain what it was that I didn't understand. She would try to explain, but we could hardly communicate. I was interested in the concepts that I picked up in the class, but I just didn't understand the teaching.

I had trouble in math class. The teacher was very knowledgeable; he had written a math book. But his teaching style and my learning style did not match. He'd tell me answers but wouldn't show me the process. He'd stand there and lecture, but that wasn't what I needed. When the teachers were involved with the material and let us have a lot of practical or hands-on experience, I learned better. I would talk to other students to see if I could learn from them. I got a D from that math class, and I had loved math before. My grade wasn't because I couldn't understand math. I just didn't get the help that I needed from that teacher.

After I graduated from Tuskegee, I took a plane to Racine, Wisconsin, where I stayed with my aunt during June and July. That August I came to Illinois and met with the local school system's Director of Personnel. I got an apartment and started teaching in the public schools.

That was an exciting time in my life. Both of my parents had come to my graduation from college. Once my mother had come to Tuskegee for Parents' Day. It was the happiest day of my life to have my mother on that campus. All the other parents were there, and I had thought that my mother wouldn't be able to come. My mother had been married at that time for thirty-five years, and she had never gone anywhere except once. When they were still living in Alabama, my oldest brother who was living in Florida got sick. My aunt in Florida let my parents know, and my mother got on the bus and went to Florida to be with him. She was there about a week or maybe two weeks. That was the first time she had ever left my dad for anything.

After I got a job teaching in Illinois, I kept after my mother to visit me because I wanted the opportunity to wait on her because she had always been busy. My mother came and stayed with me for a month. This was the third time she had left my dad in forty-two years, and I was just so privileged to have her with me that time. She went back home in August, and she died the first day of October. I signed her death certificate on my birthday, October 6th. It had been a pleasure for me to have her with me, and when my sister called and told me that she was dead, the first thing I said was, "Thank You, Jesus." My roommate did not understand, but I said, "Lord, I did everything I wanted to do with my mom." I took her to her first restaurant, to her first movie, and to Chicago. I wanted to do so many things with her because it had been so hard for her raising all of us and, after they moved to Florida, everybody else in the community.

My family moved to Florida because I went to college. When I went off to college in 1964, the white man who owned the plantation where we lived was so angry. He asked my dad how he could send me to college when his own daughter didn't go. He knew my dad didn't have any money. My dad had not gone to him asking for money. The Ku Klux Klan began harassing my family. There were times when my mom and dad and the children who were still at home would be in bed, and they would hear gunshots and bullets sliding across the tin roof of the house.

On the day the plantation owner told my dad he had to move, my dad went out to another plantation to see if he could move there. They told him they didn't have any space. The plantation owner had gone around to every planta-tion around and told the owners that he was going to make my dad move, and they should not let him move to their farms. My dad had to go and find some other place to live. He went to a black family that had their own place, and they had a barn where they kept their corn and hay. The man told my dad that was all he had, but my family was welcome to it. My dad moved my mother and my two sisters and my two brothers into that barn. They took the corn and stuff out, and that's where they lived until my older sister who was in Florida could get them a place to stay.

My older sister and brother came and moved them to Florida. My folks had had to leave everything in the field and all their other farm produce because it *belonged* to the white man. They had had to leave the farm before it was time to settle with the owner for that year, so they had nothing to show for a year's worth of work. You see, there were eleven of us. None of the others had gone to college. I wasn't supposed to go either, and by going I brought trouble on my family.

I didn't know about a lot of the trouble my family experienced until 1980, over twenty years after some of it happened. My mother died in 1981, my dad in 1985. I graduated from college in 1969. My dad didn't tell me what happened when I went to college until 1980. I am the richest person I know because my parents loved me so much that they didn't want me to experience college with all that trouble on my mind. I wouldn't have had the peace of mind to concentrate on trying to learn if I had known how they were being treated. So they kept it from me. I think now of the power they had to keep those people from stopping my education. At one time my dad had begun to drink heavily. He was a hard worker; he would work from Monday morning until Saturday evening. And on Saturday evening he would start drinking, and he would drink hard. Sometimes he wouldn't stop drinking until Sunday evening. But Monday morning he was going to be sober enough to go to work.

My father's drinking was his escape from a hard life. When I found out some of the things my dad had gone through with those people! There was the time when the white man threatened my dad's life because the cotton was not in on time *one time*. My uncle and his children came to help my family pick cotton. My uncle had his own farm. He was trying to get his cotton in, but he left his and came to help my dad because those people were going to hang my dad. I didn't learn about this until I was out of college and teaching.

I do things for people because I know I'm blessed. I thank God every day because I know what I have. I see a lot of my mother in me. My mother was a giving person. And my dad would do anything to help anybody. When my dad used to kill hogs, he would give away a lot of meat—whole hams to my uncles and lots of meat to the people who helped with the slaughtering. He'd give corn, lots of it, to my uncle to feed his cows. One time when our cow was dry and we needed milk, my dad bought milk from his brother. He gave fifty cents for milk and could hardly find a quarter to buy me a newspaper.

I also recall that when I was in college, only my aunt in Racine would send me something occasionally. None of the others helped me, but one of my uncles encouraged me. His church invited me to be their Youth Day speaker. Then he called my father in Florida and told him how proud he was of me and that I had done a good job. That was in 1967.

I often think about people who have influenced me along the way. The teachers that I had in grade school and high school are my motivators for my work now. I know how I was helped when I was a child, and I just know that children today need our help. I know I would not be where I am today without other people. I do the best that I can do in whatever I do, and I help whomever I can. My parents and my godparents also are models. When my parents were living in Florida, people used to bring their children over and leave them with my mother to keep for free. There was one woman who wouldn't ask my mother to keep her three kids. She'd just bring them over to the yard on Friday and wouldn't come back until Sunday night. My mother would bathe them and feed them. She was sick—low blood pressure and all—but she said children can't help how their parents do. It was nothing for her to have six or seven children going to bed at her house at night.

Like my mother, I love children, and that is one of the reasons I am so glad that I became an elementary school teacher. I recall a second grader who was in my first class. I used to tell her that she was going to go to Tuskegee one day. When she graduated from high school, she went to Tuskegee. From the time she was seven years old, I told her she was going and she went. She loved me. I felt good that I had been able to influence her in a positive way. I had a class of only fifteen children that year. I told an administrator the other day that if most educational leaders really knew the difference that small classes make, they'd make sure we had small classes. I was afraid that whole year that they were going to disband my class of fifteen children because it was small, but every child in that class has done something remarkable with his or her life.

One of my little girls was a sweet angel. I'd tell her she was going to be my nurse or my accountant because she was such a neat child with her work. Would you believe she became the secretary to the superintendent in a large school system? I would look at my children and, based on their strong assets, I would name professions for them. In that way, I could highlight their gifts and give them something to work toward. I told another child that he was going to be my lawyer because I could just see him being very vocal. He is in law school at Northwestern right now, about to graduate.

There are elderly people who I like to help as much as I can. Mrs. Miller is a wonderful lady who took me on as her child. I used to date her nephew, but after we weren't going out anymore, she kind of kept me on. Another person I try to help is Mrs. Sarah Franklin who is 87 years old. I go by to check on her. I try to talk with her every day. She is at the point where she doesn't walk, and I fix meals and take them to her. If she needs something, she thinks nothing of calling me to help her. And I'm glad about that. She just walked into my life. We were having Homecoming at church and she walked up to me and said, "My name is Sarah Franklin and I'm going to be your mother and keep an eye on you." That was in 1980. I had started teaching Sunday school in 1979. When I had my surgery in 1982, she would visit me every day. My mother had died in 1981, and Mrs. Franklin said, "Your mother is dead now, and I'm going to be your mother." I would drive her places, to shopping malls, etc. She looked upon me as her daughter because she never had daughters—only a son. I am happy to help her whenever I can.

My life is enriched by my involvement in church, in teaching, in community service, in the National Association of University Women, and in many other organizations that aim to advance education and to help others. I met my husband through having someone come into the classroom to enhance education for children. Many of the children in my district are very poor, and their parents cannot provide certain educational enrichments for them, so it is important for the schools to do all that they can. We had been studying sand in my class, and I contacted this glass blower and had him come in to demonstrate for the children. I later married the glass blower whom I met in the classroom. I bring in various types of enrichment for students as often as I can. I also do classroom presentations for other teachers on my African travels and other subjects in an effort to help children whenever I can.

The Bible tells us that we all have our gifts and our purposes here on Earth. In an NAUW meeting, my sister-in-law asked one time what we wanted our epitaphs to be. I said I want mine to be "Annie Jones—Of Service." God has given us two dates: our birth date, a dash, and a death date. That dash in between birth and death is our gift to Him. Mine is to help my fellow man in any way that I can. Because that's what Jesus did when He was here. We have to serve each other if we are to serve Him. I never looked at it quite this way until now, but when I look back on my seventh-grade classroom where I accepted my Lord and Savior Jesus Christ, I believe that's what I realized even then. I knew how my teacher was helping us and I, too, wanted to be of service. We got more from my teacher than reading, writing, and arithmetic. He gave us real service. I would like to do the same.

Oona Fa Kno Wha Oona Cum Frum

Lorraine, 74, is a docent on St. Helena Island, South Carolina.

The Confederates were expecting the Union Army to come into Fort Sumter, in the Charleston area, but they bypassed Fort Sumter and came into Port Royal Sound, only a few miles from here. They knew that the only way the South survived financially was by selling sea island cotton, indigo, corn, and rice to England. In return, the South received money and guns from England. To stop the flow of commerce, the Union came in and blockaded Port Royal Sound. It was a Sunday morning, in November of 1861. They began bombarding in Hilton Head early that morning, and by one o'clock that afternoon, the Confederates had conceded defeat. The Union immediately sent down officers to live at a plantation house that is still here. The Secretary of the Interior came down, as did the Secretary of the Treasury, to take over the fields of cotton and other produce that were being grown here on St. Helena and to get them ready for market. The Union officers arrived and found 8,000 enslaved people. There were only a very few who were free, only a few who could read and write. Maybe some who lived in the homes of the slave owners or were servants who took care of the white schoolchildren had learned something from a young charge who would show pictures and words to their mammies. But there were 8,000, maybe 10,000, out here who couldn't read or write, and this was a problem.

Another problem was that the Union soldiers couldn't understand the blacks of this area who spoke a language called *Gullah*. Gullah is a combination of English and *Krio*, which was the official language of Sierra Leone. The slaves that lived here on the island came from Sierra Leone and other coastal West African countries. Those who came from the area between Liberia and the northern part of Sierra Leone were called Golas. And there were also those coming from Angola. As slaves, these two groups converged in this area and in coastal Georgia. To distinguish themselves, one would say, "I'm Gola Tom," and the other one would say, "I'm Angola Mary." They spoke different languages and couldn't understand each other, so they created Gullah, a new language with which they could communicate.

The name Gullah is perhaps a combined form of Gola and Angola. And you can see the difference between the African language of Krio and English in the proverb, "If you don't know where you are going, you should know where you came from." In Gullah we say, "Ef oona na kno wha oona da gwine, oona fa kno wha oona cum frum." Another example of Gullah is that we say, "Ef oona na kno usa oona de go, oona fa kno usa oona commin." In English that is, "If you don't know which side you are on, you should know which side you came from."

The Union's solution to the problems of illiteracy among the blacks and the language barrier between the blacks and the Union officers was Penn School, built on the Oaks Plantation on St. Helena in 1862. Penn was the first school in the South started for blacks. The founder was Laura M. Towne, sent from Philadelphia by the Freedmen's Association. A few months later, Ellen Murray was sent to join Laura Towne. The Freedmen's Association, active in Boston as well as Philadelphia, was a group of humanitarians, mostly Quakers, but others, too, such as Unitarians, who had for years been saying, "It's not fair what you're doing to those human beings. You're dehumanizing them, and they are human. They are not property." But the slave owners had not listened. So when the war came, the white people were afraid and fled the island. There had only been about fifty of them on St. Helena. One reason there were so few is the climate here. It's awfully hot in the summer. Also, whites contracted malaria fever from mosquito bites. The blacks were used to the heat and mosquitoes in Africa. Even though they were third and fourth generation here by the time of the Civil War, they still carried the traits of resistance. Right now, if a mosquito bites me, I will probably rub it, but I do not get any swelling from mosquito bites.

The Yankees started this little school in 1862 to help the newly freed blacks. The first day, nine students attended; the next day, nineteen. At the end of the second week, they had over forty people in one room. Everybody wanted to learn. Parents came to see what these white people were teaching their children, and the parents wanted to learn, too. A powerful incentive for the adults to learn was that they could purchase land if they could sign their names to the deeds. And they wanted to have land. The government sold ten acres, or maybe fifteen, to whoever could afford it. As the blacks could afford more, they were allowed to purchase it. Because of the overcrowding in the school, Laura Towne appealed to the Freedmen's Association, asking that they move the school across the street to the white people's church.

The whites had never had the numbers to fill the first floor of their church, but they had filled the balcony with the so-called black leaders among the slaves. The slave owners knew that the Africans believed in following their leaders, so they brought these blacks in to hear their sermons for purposes of indoctrination and control. The blacks were ordered to go back and tell the others on the plantations that they were to obey the whites, their masters, just as they were to obey God. But now these godforsaken whites had forsaken their church, and Penn School moved in. At this time, a black girl, Charlotte Forten, came from Philadelphia to help with the teaching.

Charlotte Forten's father was a sailmaker, a man of means. Charlotte had been educated at home because her father had not wanted his daughter attending a segregated school. When she finished elementary school, he sent her to friends in Cambridge, Massachusetts, and she went on to college. When she finished college, she applied to teach at Penn. They did not accept her, for even the Yankees were not color blind. A few years later, following the instructions of the poet John Greenleaf Whittier who was her friend, Charlotte reapplied and was accepted. She came to St. Helena, and as the first black instructor at Penn, she taught with Laura Towne and Ellen Murray in the church and in the little study house.

Charlotte Forten was a musician. She played beautiful music and the blacks loved it. We blacks, you know, will sing and sway to the birds' tunes. She invited John Greenleaf Whittier down and asked him to write a song for the people of the island. He wrote the "St. Helena Hymn," and the blacks loved that, too.

Soon the school became overcrowded again, and three additional buildings were acquired. The blacks moved these buildings and joined them together.

The land that was used was purchased from one of the few blacks who was already free. He sold the school ten acres, and when he died, he left additional property to Penn. Not wanting him to be a slave, his master had given him his papers so that he could have the chance to migrate. By contrast, most slave owners in these parts were afraid that their slaves *would* migrate in the middle of the night, following the drinking gourd north. You see, Harriet Tubman was in Beaufort, only about seven miles by boat from St. Helena Island. She had a business there, along with the Underground Railroad. They tried to catch her, but she was too shrewd for them even though she could neither read nor write. "Mother wit" is what they call her gifts.

The gifts of Penn School to the people of St. Helena went far beyond the gift of literacy. In addition to carrying out her teaching duties, Laura Towne started midwifery training at Penn because there were probably 3,000 women here having babies. Of course, the slave owners had been breeding the slaves because every slave was money, and the white men had also made mistresses of black women. Laura Towne taught the blacks good health habits, and they just loved her. I remember that my grandmother spoke of her with reverence and stated proudly that Laura Towne never turned away from the people. She came down here and stayed over forty years. She never returned to her home to live, and when she died, the black women would not let an undertaker or anyone else touch her body. They prepared her for burial themselves.

When Penn School closed in 1948, all the supplies and furnishings belonged to the trustees, who let their friends come in and take whatever they wanted. When Penn museum opened, word circulated that the school was looking for artifacts, and many of the items that had been taken from Penn were given back. I am so happy about the renovation of Penn School. Penn gave me my start, made college an option for me, and made my present comfortable life possible. For every student who ever matriculated at Penn and for posterity, the school deserves to be preserved and its role in the education of islanders deserves to be remembered.

Though we may now be middle class, those who went to college from this area were generally poor people. Some of them in later years were the children of Penn workers, and they earned more income than the average citizen on St. Helena. My mother came from a family of six here on the island. Previous to that, her mother was a Penn student, but instead of going on to graduate, my grandmother got married during her junior year. The custom was that it was good for your daughter to go as far in school as she could, but if an offer of marriage came along, it was better that she get married and let the husband provide. So even though my grandmother wanted to finish school, her mother told her to go ahead and get married. My grandmother was upset. She was a student of both Laura Towne and Ellen Murray, and she had been powerfully influenced by them to complete her education.

My own mother completed the public elementary school here. She left school and went to work because she saw the need. Her father had died when she was three years old, leaving her mother with five children. The baby was six months old. My grandmother later remarried, but she had two more children, and work was hard to find.

My mother's family made their living by farming and raising animals, but to feed a family of nine was difficult. When Mother was twelve years old, she went to Savannah to work. She would stand on a crate to do the washing in the house where she was employed. When she was fifteen, she got a job working for a family who would go to Florida in the summer, and Mother would come back here and dig white potatoes on Cane Island. She was industrious and believed in getting the most and the best that she could. She worked hard all her life, and in her declining years, she moved back to St. Helena.

During the early thirties, Mother came home for a few years, and we all lived with my grandparents. Mother worked in the house that had belonged to Laura Towne. Her employers were people of wealth, and while she worked for them, Mother was able to take us out of the county school and put us in Penn. I had first gone to Penn in the second grade. I had attended during the summer session after the county school, which ran from October to March, was closed for the term so children could work in the fields. But the distance to Penn had been too far for me. If the older children were late for school, they would run and I couldn't keep up with them. Two years later Mother took all five of us out of the county school and sent us to Penn. My grandmother had taught us to read, write, and do multiplication by the time we started school. That's how I got to skip the first year, which would be called kindergarten today.

Education at Penn was quite different from the usual fare at a county school. While at both schools we had Christian studies, in the county schools we also had prayer, music, and scripture before we began classes. The curriculum at Penn was different. We had four days of regular classes and one day of industrial and home arts. The county schools had neither the time nor the money to provide such studies. When I went to county school, there were two rooms with grades three through six in one room and grades primary through second in the other. There was no lunchroom. You had to carry your lunch or go home if you lived close by. We had a stove in each of the classrooms, and the boys had to get the wood and start the fire on cold days. In primary to second grade, we had long benches and a long table that we sat around. There would be forty or more students in a room. The situation was not conducive to learning, but the teachers were good teachers, and the children did learn. If they did not learn, they were not passed to the next grade.

The county did not provide books to the county schools, so the parents had to buy whatever books their children had. Most people didn't have money, so if they had three or four children in school, they couldn't buy the books. Students would have to "look on" with someone else who had a book. In my case, there were two children in the family ahead of me, so I had their books. You had to buy a tablet and your own pencils, and most parents just didn't have the money. If you had a brother or sister in the same room, you would write first and then you'd give them the pencil and let them write. A lot of children didn't have lunch, and food is important when a child is growing and trying to learn. I think about how we struggled! Beaufort County did almost nothing for the education of a black child. We are the products of Penn School and its teachings.

There were only a few white children living on the island when I was a girl. There was not even a busload, but they were given a bus and transported to Beaufort to school. There were no white schools on the island, but there were eight or nine black county schools here. There were no county high schools on the island, and no bus to take black students from the island to the black county school in Beaufort—the Beaufort Training School—called Shanklin School. Most of the black children on the Beaufort side of the bridge went there, but there were two other schools that they could attend, a Baptist church school for girls and Robert Smalls Elementary School.

The county made no provisions for the education of black children on the island after they completed eighth grade. In order to attend a county high school, the children would have had to walk from the island to Beaufort. From where I live here on Frogmore, it is eleven miles one way to Beaufort. From Land's End, it is twenty miles to Beaufort. From Coffin's Point, where the beach is, the students had to walk nine miles just to get to Penn. Black students were expected to walk to school, but the island is eighteen miles long!

Sometimes the parents would try to take the children to school, or the boys would ride a horse, but the parents needed the horse for farming. And a parent transporting children in a buggy or a gig or a cart would have room for only so many. There were only four or five blacks on the island who owned a car, and they were the doctor, storekeepers, and the undertaker. In 1931, two of the Penn trustees each sent a bus to transport the children to school. The trustees were, of course, white people from the North. The black families didn't have money to give to the school. Penn was a white supported institution, and as the Lord touched the hearts of the northern whites, they sent things down here, including clothing by the barrels. If there was a needy family, they would be given clothing. And those who could afford to pay ten cents did so, which let them feel that they had contributed something. At Penn we paid a yearly fee of five dollars, which later went to six. The first graders paid one dollar, just to let the parents feel that they were not on the receiving end without giving something back.

When I lived on the island as a child, blacks did not have a lot of latitude in terms of money, mobility, or interacting with those from the mainland, but we could take the boat that came from Savannah down here to Crow's Bridge on Frogmore. The boat would leave Savannah for Daufuskie Island and Hilton Head and would come here because there were an oyster factory and a shell mill here. We also had a large general store. The Boat would stop at Clear Bridge and go on to the Yard, and then on to Beaufort. They would bring cargo, and they would take cargo. The blacks here on the island would take bushels of potatoes, okra, and greens on the boat to Savannah. They would stay at the foot of the river and sell their produce, often sending some of it to their family members who were living in Savannah. Until 1927, when they built the bridge from Beaufort to the island, people had to row across the water to get to and from St. Helena.

In many ways, Penn School helped to improve life here on the island. People from the community worked in the Penn buildings, on the grounds, and on the Penn farms to help support their families. With its sixty acres of farmland, Penn could grow food for the boarding department and for the day workers and students. We had a few students who were not from the island but from Sheldon, Hilton Head, and maybe Gardens Corners and Garnett. Those few had to stay in the boarding department because distance dictated it. When Penn students reached the eleventh grade, all of them had to go into the boarding department to learn the social graces. Because most of us were taught the facts of life by our grandparents, we didn't know some of the things that we should have been told, things that our parents certainly treated like secrets. So Mr. Lewis, the chemistry and biology teacher, and Mr. Cates, the math teacher, would talk with the boys, while the girls were enlightened by the nurse and the matron of the dormitory.

The girls did all the cleaning at Penn, including the laundry. It was my job to start the fire in the laundry each morning, and I was lucky to get a job. The matron would walk me over to the laundry, make sure there was nobody in the building, lock the door so nobody could come in, and I would start the fire. She would leave, but she could look right across from her station into the building where I was. The boys would be getting ready to go into the fields, and they'd be out there milking before coming in to breakfast. After breakfast, the boys would do the plowing, mostly with mules. Men and women from the community who worked at Penn would come to do their various jobs. Penn brought the community together and boosted the financial condition in many households.

Growing up I remember Mother's telling me that she wanted me to become a trained nurse like Miss Catherine, the daughter of the rich white family that she worked for on the island. I was around five at the time, so I grew up with that. And Miss Catherine would tell me, "You have to finish school, Lorraine, and you have to go to nursing school." I was all for it and I was top of my class all the way up, even in college. But I wasn't the valedictorian at graduation because I had missed a year of college life. What happened is Grandmother's house burned. My little brother had gone to school, and he probably left fire in the house, and the wind. . . . My grandmother was working and there was no fire department. People ran over, but it was too late. My grandmother was crying that she had no place to live, so Mother said, "Lorraine, you just have to stay out of school to help me raise the money to build Mama a house."

No one at Voorhees, the college that I attended in Denmark, South Carolina, wanted to see me leave. Voorhees was excellent in terms of helping me and others to earn the money for college expenses by providing work-study opportunities. But they could not help me to pay my college bills and at the same time earn enough money to replace my grandmother's house. I'll never forget how upset they were that I had to leave. I was the best student in my class, and there was nothing the college could do to prevent the interruption of my education. Leaving college was a bitter pill that I had to take, and I endeavored to swallow it without a gloomy countenance.

My mother was working in New York, and I got a job there doing domestic work. We were lucky enough to buy a house on the [St. Helena] island, and the community moved [the house] to my grandmother's property. After we paid for it, I had to save money for college. That summer I "slept in" out at Long Beach. I saved almost every penny and returned to college the next year. But so much that I needed to know for my senior year was dependent on what I had studied in my junior year. I had forgotten so much while I was working. I hadn't had time to study. I hadn't had books with me. All my books had been destroyed. I had one book. I studied as hard as I could my senior year, but I had lost ground. I'm not sure anyone appreciated how hard I struggled because I was still passing all my classes.

When I finished college, I came back to the island and taught one year in the county schools. When school started in August, we had to go to the county school in Beaufort to get the books for the island students. They were all used books—never a new one. We got what the whites had finished with. There were no supplemental books. When the children finished reading *Dick and Jane* or whatever, there was nothing more for them to read. I had worked for whites in New York, and they threw away books and children's nursery rhymes. I had shipped a trunkful of them here. They would tell me, "Take these books! Take these books! And magazines!"

Nobody here subscribed to magazines except the Penn School people and a few whites. My aunt was working for the mail carrier whose wife was French and not prejudiced at all, even though she couldn't allow me to sit at the table. She would save the newspapers for me. I would get magazines from her like *Good Housekeeping* and *Ladies' Home Journal* to use in making visual aids for the children. I would give the children the magazines to cut things out of. "Find a picture with a horse or some other animal you know," I would tell them. I had grades two and three. I had to keep the third graders busy while I was teaching the second graders, and vice versa. It was hard, but I was vitally interested in the possibilities for the children's future. As much had been done for me. My teachers at Penn had let us pursue learning and had encouraged us to do the things that we were best in while improving in those where we did poorly. I had loved to read, and I'd borrow a book from the Penn library and finish it that day.

When I went to Voorhees, I felt prepared for college in all areas except algebra. We didn't have algebra at Penn after ninth grade, so there was a gap between high school and college algebra. And that has been the weakness of all Penn graduates. Even though they went to Hampton and other colleges, they didn't do well in algebra. But Penn students were far advanced in other disciplines. The President at Voorhees had been Superintendent of Penn, so they knew what to expect of a Penn student. They would say, "You know better. You know the training you had on St. Helena." Penn students did well at college. The transition from high school to college was relatively easy for us. We had positive self images, we knew how to study, and we had a sense of direction. Most college faculty were tough but supportive, just as those at Penn had been. In terms of the adjustment to life away from home, we were already somewhat acclimated to that because Penn had required that we live on campus after the sophomore year.

Penn students were encouraged to go on to college if they could afford it. Scholarships were not available to us. We rented our books at Voorhees, and, lucky for me, the lady who ran the laundry learned that Penn girls knew how to do men's shirts. I got an afternoon job in the laundry. I was also a waitress at Voorhees, just as I had been at Penn. Mother would send my board money to Voorhees, but it was a struggle for us. She went without a lot of things so that I could have. That's why I told my mother she would never want, she would never suffer. "Anything," I told her, "Do what you want to do, as long as it's right. Don't worry about money. I got plenty of money." I didn't always tell my husband, but I'd slip twenty dollars in a letter to my mother, or I would put a fifty-dollar bill in when I was staff and worked overtime. I would always send my mother something. She'd say, "Lorraine, don't send anything." I bought all of her clothes. I just wanted my mother to have the things she missed so that I could get an education.

After teaching a year on the island, I went to New York to work because that's where the opportunities were. I was hired as a receptionist for two doctors at Mt. Sinai Hospital. This job paid three times my teaching salary on St. Helena. And Dr. Lewis encouraged me. He said, "Lorraine, if you want to go to nursing school, since you said that was your ambition, I'll teach you anesthesiology." He'd tell me, "Lorraine, the opportunities for blacks are so hard. They will just do anything to keep a black person down. But don't let it get to you, and don't be bitter because if you hold bitterness, then you are as bad as they are." He would give me extra money. He was a little, short Jewish man— such a good person. His wife was an anesthesiologist, too. I was hoping he would be there years later when I had my operation, but when I went in and inquired about him, the doctor told me that he had died six months before. He said, "You knew Dr. Lewis? He was a sweetheart of a doctor."

My real profession in New York was at Macy's. I began by working with customer accounts, but then the union asked me to be a shop steward. Later I became Section Leader. I supervised forty girls from whom I was able to get very good work. When the union began managing Macy's credit union, they approached me about moving to a position there. I wasn't interested, but when my president told me that they needed me, I took the job. They sent me to Cornell University to take a course in credit union management. I had to learn the labor laws, but it was worth it because it exposed me to the living conditions of other people. The job heightened my caring spirit for other people. I have always wanted to help others because somebody helped me, and I was able to help so many people when I was with the credit union. I could speak with people who were behind in their accounts, and I could make arrangements that would allow them to pay their debts without having to involve an attorney or to garnishee their checks.

I was supervisor of the credit representatives, and you would not believe some of the problems that I encountered. You see, white people do not always understand the problems of black people because many whites have always had. And we haven't. To complicate matters, sometimes black employees would steal or they'd get fired or they'd try to scheme ways to return late from lunch because they were playing cards. And they'd get warnings. With warnings, you don't get raises. If you're not getting raises, you're not going to move up. And Macy's could withhold raises legally. The employees would say, "Lorraine, at least you're fair." I'd say, "Yeah, but we all have to do better, and we can." And I'd try to help them understand how to do better.

During my credit union days, I began volunteering in the schools. I sponsored the Young People's Department as well as the Girls' Club in the community. We didn't have a clubhouse so the teenagers would hold meetings and study sessions in my home, with their parents' permission. After our meetings, I would take the girls home if they lived farther away than the next block. I would call parents and tell them that their children could be expected home in three or five minutes, whatever the case would be, if they were walking by themselves. And I would tell the boys in our group that they didn't fool around with the girls. "You're not a man; you can't support a child," I'd tell them. "You don't need a baby. Wait until you are married." They were afraid of Miss Lorraine, but they loved me, too.

I started baking pies because the boys loved homemade baked goods. We had an ice cream churn, and my mother would make ice cream and bake cakes for the children. I let the children dance in my apartment, and I would take them to museums and other places that their parents didn't take them. We would go rollerskating and ice skating. I would take them to restaurants so the boys would learn to pull the chairs out for the girls and to stand while they were being seated. I have a letter that one of the boys wrote to me about how much I did for him in his youth. How well he remembered me giving him a chance when nobody else would. "Our parents didn't have time. They didn't know a lot of the things that their children needed to learn," he wrote. I am proud that he became a very successful entrepreneur who currently makes about half a million dollars a year.

When the group of children grew too large for social events at my apartment, I spoke with my pastor about letting us use the fellowship hall at the church. "We are going to dance, Reverend, I'll tell you that right now," I said. I reminded the deacons that all of them danced when they were young, and they acquiesced. The children began earning money for special projects by holding dances and selling chicken dinners, which they cooked. We never asked the church for money. Then Pepsi-Cola opened up a club in the area, but by that time there were gangs and fighting encroaching upon our neighborhood.

Throughout the years that I did not live on the island, I always came back four or five times a year. So nine years ago when I was getting ready to move back for good, I had no anxieties about the "slow pace" of life on St. Helena. The retirement farewell held for me on my last day at Macy's was over by noon, the thirtieth of November, and I was on my way to my new home on St. Helena by three o'clock.

The first thing I did when I moved back to the island was to join my church. Then I said I was going to rest and sleep for three months. But I stopped by Penn Center, and they had just hired a new curator. She was from Hampton Institute, just out of college, and didn't know anybody on the island. She didn't know anything about St. Helena, so I volunteered to help her. I didn't know about archives and all that kind of work—but putting the pictures in order, working with the curator if someone came in from the community, introducing her to people, answering the phones, staying at the library while she went to meetings, these things I could do.

I began reading the literature at Penn, and I said, "This is beautiful!" I started digging back into the history of St. Helena. I learned it so I could tell people when they came into the museum. I wanted to be knowledgeable. I already knew the history of Penn, but the history of St. Helena! I didn't know that much. And you never heard Gullah referred to in such a proud and beautiful way. They had just called it the Negro dialect—wouldn't call it Gullah. Other blacks would deride us as "rice eating Geechies" and would be insulted if they were mistaken for one of us. And we were warned away from Gullah. When we got to Penn, we couldn't say "ain't" or "gwine." Some students did because it was all they knew, but they had to change. No more, "I'm gwine" and "Dem people obah dere…Let that tongue hit those teeth!" our Penn teachers would say. When I was teaching on the island, one day a little boy came excitedly to me and said, "Miss Lorraine, cum yonda! Cum yonda!" It took me a minute to realize that he was saying, "Look over there!" I taught those children the same way I was taught at Penn, that there are no such words as *cum yonda*.

I have learned so much about my beautiful language and culture, and I love to share it. The value of remembering "Cum yonda," the value of knowing its origin, the value of appreciating the struggle which fueled its generation— even as we learn standard English—are in direct opposition to the stigma of speaking Gullah or being a Geechie. When Bill Moyers came to film his special on St. Helena Island, I was glad to share my knowledge and experience with him. I have learned so much!

An important event in the preservation and dissemination of the island's culture is Heritage Days, an annual three-day celebration that brings ten to twelve thousand people to St. Helena. Heritage Days has been going on for sixteen years, but just last night people at the old time prayer meeting were saying that we have to keep shouts alive, we have to keep the spirit alive. When

I first moved back to the island, I was at a prayer meeting and noted that there was no shout as part of the service. "No, we don't shout anymore," a deacon told me. "It died out. And what do you know about shouting? They haven't shouted in your time." I started clapping like this, and I started singing, "Abony, Abony, knock a bone fuh me . . ." I started shouting, and he started singing and shouting right there. Well, people gathered around, and the great irony is that I approached some people in my age group and asked them if they would shout, so we shouted on the platform for Heritage Days. From that, we revived the praise house services. This has helped to renew interest in the old ways, and now shouting is a vital part of what gets done here, just as it was in the near and distant past. I am interested in getting more young people involved. Let them be taught how to shout along with singing the old, old songs.

It is culturally and hisorically important that the Penn buildings are being restored, including the site where Dr. King came to plan his march on Washington, and there are plans for further restoration. I initiated the building project for community-based functions of which the Laura M. Towne Park is a part. We also have a Community Development Corporation to help get young people involved in the life of the island. We are going to put an incubator on the corner near the community park where we will help people to launch small businesses. We will have stalls in front of the buildings so people can come and sell their crafts. Homemade quilts, ceramics, picture frames, cabinets, hand-woven baskets, hand-knitted fishing nets, paintings, carvings, all kinds of goods and opportunities will be available to the people. Hair salons, bake shops, and furniture refinishing will also be available. People here can do so many creative things, and we want to expose their work to the public. The incubator will help those who are here and have saleable skills, as well as attract new talent to the area. I am so glad to be a part of all this because it gives me a chance to help.

Yesterday I saw the woman who was my classmate both at Penn and when I was in college. One of her parents was a teacher at Penn. I will never forget the time when I didn't have a dress or shoes to wear to a special event at Voorhees. My friend's mother had sent her two new dresses. One she wore and the other, brand new, she insisted that I wear. Another friend of ours had shoes that she said were too small for her, and she wanted me to wear them and stretch them to her size. So I wore my friends' finery feeling like a princess, not a beggar, because of their genuine desire to help me. As I look back over my life, that day still registers as a special one. I think about those friends. I think about them all the time. I could never forget the things they did for me when we were going to school, and I was poor and they were not.

May I Help You?

Alex, 52, is an elementary school principal.

When I was a kid, I lived with my family on 100th Street in East Harlem in New York City. There were twenty-seven tenements on our street, and they were occupied, according to the *New York Herald Tribune*, by 5,000 men, women, and children. Each tenement had six four-room apartments on each of five levels. The population, even though this was Spanish Harlem, also included blacks, Jews, Italians, Asians, and many other groups. Ours was a cosmopolitan neighborhood with a real sense of community. Every year we held a block party where the summer's luckiest beauty would be crowned Miss 100th Street.

There were lots of kids on our block, and in the summer we would climb the fire escapes and play on the roofs, or we would run in and out of the deluge from open fire hydrants in a futile attempt to stay cool. The street teemed with life and death. People sat on the stoops or leaned out their windows to catch the fresh air. Prostitutes met their johns on the block, and tough-guy gang members claimed the street as their turf. Junkies nodded, and I once saw a man, his stomach split open by a straight razor, holding his guts in place with bloodied hands. After a long day in the factories, tired workers waited for the rum man to begin serving shots. The perennially hopeful waited to check their latest prophecies with the numbers runner. Young lovers waited for the evening shadows to deepen. But for the great majority of the 5,000 who were children, the only action we were looking for was the arrival of the coquito cart.

I was born at home on July 5, 1944, and grew up in an apartment crowded with people. For most of my childhood, my two younger sisters and I were the only children actually living in our home. But every morning, two of our older siblings would bring their children to our house for the day. On school days, they would come before and after school. My younger sisters and I were only a few years older than our nieces and nephews, and we generally felt completely displaced by them. It was as if we were visitors in some noisy, inhospitable place from which we could never return home. Relatives from Puerto Rico and other places would visit us for what seemed like interminable stretches. And on Sundays, my mother's four older children would show up with their entire families in tow.

With all our relatives on hand for meals, we ate in shifts. Because there were so many people to feed, we ate hurriedly and quietly. "Be quiet and eat!" we were told if we talked during the meal. "And clean your plate!" I had no trouble with the latter. But the numbers of people! Sick relatives stayed at our house. Dead relatives were often laid out there. My aunt Emilia passed away when I was a kid, and I remember that she lay in state in our living room for three days. To this day, the smell of carnations, gladiolas, and gardenias reminds me of death.

The 1950s saw the largest migration of all time from Puerto Rico to New York City. Many New Yorkers expected these newcomers to know English already or to learn it very quickly. I started kindergarten around this time and sometimes heard teachers make negative comments about me or other Puerto Rican people because we did not speak English well. I recall hearing people at school say that we were now in America and should forget our Spanish and learn English. These interchanges did not make me feel good. There were no special programs for those of us who did not speak English, and we sank or swam on our own. I did not catch on easily at school, and with the exception of kindergarten, my early years in the classroom were difficult. Groups of us were sent to speech therapy three times a week because we were not fluent in English. But the speech therapist was very nice and recognized full well that we did not have speech problems beyond an inadequate knowledge of the English language.

I went to kindergarten at P.S. 121, a few blocks from my house. My teacher was Mrs. Gilliam, an African American who was bubbly and loved all of us children. I thought she was just wonderful. I had been scared to go to school at first, but after being with Mrs. Gilliam for a couple of days, I was comfortable in my new environment. I learned later that Mrs. Gilliam had grown up in East Harlem. She knew the community and its people. I could tell that she loved me even though she did not speak Spanish. By the end of my kindergarten year, I was speaking English a lot better, and I looked forward to starting first grade at P.S. 109.

Unfortunately, I did not feel welcomed by my first, second, or third grade teachers. It was clear that they did not like me. By second grade, it was also clear that I had some trouble reading. In second and third grades, I was always in the slowest reading group, and my math skills were also quite poor. I did not enjoy school during those years. I felt unsure of myself. But then I got into fourth grade and met Mrs. McShane, and school became a wonderful place again.

Mrs. McShane must have been from Boston. She had an accent, and right away I felt better about my own. When she talked to you, she would put her arm around you. Or she would put her hands on both your shoulders and smile at you. She was dramatic and would assume the voices of different characters as she read aloud. I remember when we were studying the Boston tea party, and Mrs. McShane told us excitedly to play roles. "You're Revolutionaries," she said to a few of us. She huddled with us for several moments like we were co-conspirators before she was off, whispering to the next group who would play the British or the Indians or the French. My love of history began when I was in fourth grade—all because of Mrs. McShane.

Like a bad dream, Mrs. Peters, who had taught me in third grade, recurred as my fifth-grade teacher. Distance from me had not made her heart grow fonder, and one day her great dislike of me and impatience with what she saw as my dullness overpowered her good judgment. She had given an assignment and I had failed to complete it to her specifications. "You stupid little spic!" she hissed. And without thinking about the consequences at all, I slapped her. Hard. I had to go home and tell my mother what I had done, and she had to accompany me to school to meet with the principal and the teacher. I felt horrible. My mother was shy around people whom she did not know, and she was not confident speaking English with them. She knew that we were in big trouble, and she called one of my older sisters to go to school with us in case we needed a translator. By some lucky chance, the principal asked me for my side of the story first. He seemed shocked at my account, which Mrs. Peters admitted was true. I was proud that my mother stood up for me in front of the principal and Mrs. Peters. She told the principal that I was wrong but that the teacher should have known better than to call a little kid names. A few days later, Mrs. Peters was transferred and we got Mrs. Kane as our new fifth-grade teacher. We all loved Mrs. Kane. I realize now that Mrs. Peters could have been in trouble with the principal for calling other Spanish speaking kids "spics" long before my case ever came to his attention. It could be that my incident was just the straw that broke the camel's back. But I went around for quite some time feeling that every kid in fifth grade owed me exclusively for their good fortune.

If I was not setting the world on fire academically by sixth grade, and I wasn't, I was at least consistent in liking the school experience. We would enter the classroom every morning to the calming effect of beautiful classical music that Mrs. Lee, my teacher, would play on the piano. Then we would quietly contemplate the assignments for the morning and for the afternoon that Mrs. Lee had put on the board. She had high expectations of us, but she explained assignments very well and taught us strategies and techniques that we could use to enhance learning. I believe that my experience in elementary school with excellent, caring teachers like Mrs. Lee helped to dissipate the inferiority complex that I had learned in the primary grades. Luckily, I connected with teachers in junior high school who continued to make the world of academia a warm and familiar place.

Some of my best experiences in junior high school were with my counselor and English teacher, Mr. Feldman, a wonderful person from a poor Jewish family who had grown up in New York City. He was not merely concerned about us, he was empathetic. I remember that he helped me to choose a high school, that my choice turned out to be the school where his wife taught, and that he kept up with me via his wife throughout my high school years. Mr. Feldman also made sure that my high school had an academic bent, rather than a vocational one, since he knew that I was interested in going to college. Another excellent influence in junior high was my music teacher, Mr. Fields, a humorous gentleman from Barbados who told me that I had a good voice but didn't know what to do with it. He talked me into playing string bass in the orchestra and singing in the chorus for all three years of junior high. I felt that I learned self-discipline and made academic progress in junior high, even though I still had difficulty with reading and math. My mother could only help me with Spanish, and my dad couldn't help me with schoolwork at all. Yet he had an incredible reverence for education.

My father was a merchant seaman, so he was away on ship for three weeks out of the month and at home the fourth week. Every morning when I was growing up, if my dad was home, he would go to buy fresh bread, milk, and a newspaper. He always bought *The Daily News*, which had pictures, rather than the *New York Times,* which generally did not. Then he would come upstairs and look through the newspaper. On Sundays, he would make an omelette and Spanish coffee for our brunch before he returned to ship. I did not know that my dad could not read until I was older, and I thought it was wonderful that he had modeled reading by buying the paper and looking at it. As I got older, he would sometimes ask me questions about the pictures and what they meant. My father's newspaper is something that just sticks in my mind. He retired the year I went off to college, and he continued to buy bread, milk, and the paper every morning. He was very curious about what was happening in the world, and I was glad when he gained access to cable television and the Spanish television programs.

Both of my parents grew up in Puerto Rico where my mother received an eighth-grade education, while my father only went through third grade. My maternal grandfather had wanted all his children to graduate from eighth grade and resolved to send them on to the Catholic high school if they were inclined to go. Because my mother's two older sisters had gotten married after graduation from high school, my grandfather saw their education as a waste of their time and his money. He refused to let my mother attend high school since he believed she would probably get married after graduation just like her two sisters before her.

My father had a much more difficult life. His own father had been a terrible person who abandoned my grandmother and their young son in San Juan. My grandmother was destitute, so she went home to her brothers on the family farm. She was received as a servant, and my father was not allowed to go to school after he reached third grade. He never talked much about his early childhood, but he did tell me that his uncles worked him almost like an animal. When he was twelve years old, he ran away to his birthplace, San Juan, lied about his age, and got a job as a stevedore on the docks. Years later his mother came to the city, and he supported her and two of his cousins. Much later, when his mother and her second husband were very old and alone in Puerto Rico, my father faithfully sent them money to assist with their upkeep.

My father wanted us to go through high school so that we could do better than he had, but no one in my family ever talked about college. I know that I got the idea that I wanted to earn a college degree from several interventions in my life. One was that I had been a Fresh Air kid and had been sent to camp outside New York City. Sponsored by the *New York Herald Tribune*, the Fresh Air Program matched people from the New York City suburbs and contiguous states with children from the inner city. "Camp" was a two-week period when children such as I could be a part of someone else's family in an entirely different environment. I first went to Fresh Air camp when I was seven years old. When I was eight, I went to Ma and Pa Covey's in Pennsylvania. That experience opened my eyes to a whole new world. Pa Covey commuted by train to his job in Philadelphia where he was a writer for a newspaper. He was up in age, so he worked just two days a week. He and Ma Covey had married later in life, and when I met them Ma Covey was already middle-aged. She had been an English teacher. They had a son, Dan, who was one year younger than I was.

There were lots of books at Ma and Pa Covey's house, and every night Ma Covey would read wonderful stories to Dan and me. And when we sat down for dinner, they always talked about things and asked our opinions. As an eight-year-old, I didn't have lots of opinions, but they would engage both me and Dan. I was shy, but they were expert at finding subjects that I could talk about: how our day had gone, what we had been reading, what we wanted to do the next day. Did we want to go hiking? Swimming? The table was set with dishes that matched, and everyone had a fork, spoon, knife, and napkin. This was new for me since at home we never used both a spoon and a fork. Even as adults, two of my sisters were afraid that they would stab themselves in the jaw or tongue if they were to eat with a fork. They are still more comfortable eating with a spoon.

The Coveys lived at the end of the street on an acre of land. Behind their property was a huge farm, so the land seemed to go on forever. There were apple and other fruit trees, plus trees that were especially good for climbing.

We would pick fruit and Ma Covey would make pies. I had such a nice time with the Coveys that I went back the next year. The Fresh Air Fund generally did not send kids back to the same family two years in a row, but the Coveys asked for me. After my second summer in Pennsylvania, the Fresh Air Fund would no longer pay for me to go to the Coveys, so they began paying for my tickets to and from their home themselves, and I began staying with them for a month. I returned to the Coveys at their expense every year until I was fourteen, when I began working in the summers to save for college. Each visit was a different experience for me. The Coveys were not rich, but they were well off. They were educated and they could do whatever they wanted to do. For example, every year we would go to New Jersey to the seashore. Sometimes we would stay at a little inn for three days. We would collect seashells, and I recall our talking about them and the different places they probably had been. Pa Covey would drive us to New Jersey, and I remember thinking that some day I wanted to be able to do those things for myself and whatever family I happened to have.

Another important intervention in my life occurred when a new group of ministers came to my neighborhood to start a Protestant ministry. Among this group were Max and Amy Korn, a young couple with four kids. I found that being at their house was similar to being at the Coveys. They had loads of books and artwork and were always sharing ideas and engaging everyone around them in discussions. As a means of re-establishing a dissolved church, they had begun Bible study for the young and the old. I started going to Bible study with a couple of my friends. I noticed that Max and Amy would help their children with their homework, so one day I mentioned to Amy that I was having trouble with math. Amy said that she wasn't that great at math, but we could work together to figure it out. She invited me to come over regularly and at a certain time. The Korn children would be doing their homework, and either Max or Amy would help me with my studies, too.

Max already had two degrees and was working on another in education so that he could teach in the public schools. His bachelor's degree was from Dartmouth, and he had earned a master's in divinity from Union Theological Seminary. Amy had been an English teacher and had gotten her bachelor's degree from Mount Holyoke. They were raising their kids to go to college, and they started asking me questions about whether I wanted to go to college. They knew my academic weaknesses, and yet they seemed to see no reason why I should not go to college. They acted as if wanting to go to college were as natural for me as it was for their own children. They had a quality of life that I liked and intended to have. It seemed clear to me that going to college was the best way to achieve my goal.

Just how I would get to go to college was suggested to me one summer when I was at the Covey's. They had a niece who came to visit them. Her parents were divorced, and she was a college student who was working and paying most of her own way through school. Ma and Pa Covey told me about how they had worked their way through school, too. They had come from families who were educated but not wealthy. Ma Covey's father had died when she was very young, so it had been necessary for her to do as much for herself as she could. Pa Covey had begun college, but his studies had been interrupted by WWII. After his return from the war, he had worked while he finished his degree. Here was living proof that you did not have to be rich to go to college. You had to want to go to college, and you had to work to stay there. I realized that you did not have to be Caucasian or from a particular ethnic group to go to college because I had wonderful teachers—black, white, Jewish—all of whom must have gone to college.

Another intervention in my life was a music program offered to students through the New York City public schools. When I was in junior high and high school, free tickets were made available to some performances at the Metropolitan Opera House and at Symphony Hall. We would hear about the free tickets along with the general announcements made over the public address system in the mornings. All one had to do to get the tickets was to go to the dean's office and sign up for them. I was interested in the program at first because I thought that I should be interested. I thought that if you were going to college, you needed to be cultured; and if you were cultured, you needed to enjoy the opera. I had already learned from Mrs. Lee that I enjoyed classical music, so I set out to add some culture to my life.

On days when I had a ticket to a performance, I would take the bus or walk across Central Park to the Met or to Symphony Hall after school. I was fascinated by the staging, the costumes, the music, and the opulent settings. At the Met there were a main floor, a mezzanine, and two balconies. There were huge chandeliers, Corinthian columns, gold walls, and plush seats. I marveled at the audiences of white people who could take off during the day to go to the opera or symphony. For the most part, I saw no minorities in the audience or on the stage, but I did get to see Marian Anderson once, I think at Symphony Hall. My mother's response to my adventures in becoming cultured was, "That's a junk! Why do you go to that stuff?" Yet if I were watching a classical music program on television, she was quite prone to watch it with me. And we had records by Mario Lanza that she enjoyed playing. Actually, we had lots of wonderful records, but most of them were by popular Spanish artists.

My family did not believe that I was serious about wanting to go to college, so they were surprised when I got a summer job the year I turned fourteen and asked my mother to help me open a bank account so I could start saving for college. I worked at Parish Acres, a family camp in Peekskill, New York, run by the Protestant ministry in my neighborhood. During my first summer there, I was one of the general workers who mowed the lawn, painted walls, and did anything else that needed doing. After that first summer, I was promoted to cook's assistant. Every two weeks when I got paid, I would send my money home and my mother would put it in my bank account.

By the time of my graduation from high school, my family was adamant that I should not go off to college. I had not done well on the mathematics section of the New York State Regents Exam, so I was not awarded a Regents diploma. This nixed my application to the New York state colleges and was just another sign to my family that I was not smart enough to go to college. Fueling their case was the fact that I had been told by a high school counselor that I was not college material. My family admonished me to get a good job and help out at home. There was no way that I could have lived at home while attending city college. The mounting pressure to work full-time, the derision I had to endure for being serious about getting a college degree, and the noise and crowds almost always present in my home would have guaranteed my failure. And I could not afford to fail.

Again, help came to me from the East Harlem Protestant Parish. One of the ministers had attended divinity school at Shaw University, a historically black college in Raleigh, North Carolina. He helped me to apply to Shaw because I could afford it, and they would accept me on short notice. I could also have gone to a college in the Midwest except the ticket to get there was too expensive. So Shaw it was, and with two suitcases and a footlocker, I embarked in late August on the long bus ride from New York City to the South.

I arrived at the bus station in Raleigh at four o'clock in the morning. I found a cab driver to take me to the campus, but I did not know exactly where on the campus I should go. The cabbie let me out at a building that turned out to be a women's dorm. Everything was closed, so I sat on my footlocker in the court yard until seven, when people began to stir. The matron at the women's dorm helped me to get my bearings and allowed me to leave my belongings with her while I found my own dorm and room and got myself checked in. I was disappointed to find that I would be sharing a room with four other people.

I was very frightened of not making it in college. The registration process was terrifying. There were long lines, and I was concerned about making the correct choices in courses. I also worried about whether I would have enough money for room and board for the year after paying tuition. I soon found a job cleaning offices to make some extra money. Because my dad had just retired, he could not afford to give me much financial help. I was constantly frightened about my grades. Even though I seemed to be doing well in my classes, I didn't know for sure what my grades would turn out to be. To make matters worse, two of my roommates were not studious and detracted, I felt, from my chances of being successful.

My messages from home seemed promising. My siblings seemed to want me to do well, and my mother was encouraging by asking me how I was doing. But when I went home for the Christmas break, my family constantly said things like, "Now that you're in college, you think you're hot stuff." They denigrated the college-going experience even though they had no direct knowledge of it. They kept reminding me that I had not done so well before. No one praised me for being the second person in my immediate family to earn a high school degree, even though I was one of the youngest children. No one said one word of praise about my being the first in the history of either my mother's or my father's family ever to go to college.

I believe I was the first Hispanic student ever to attend Shaw University, and I was definitely the only one at the institution at the time. But everyone treated me just great. I felt a part of things from the beginning. I remember being at orientation my freshman year and feeling a connection with the student body. Here were all these people from all over the country. Some were struggling academically and financially, just like I was. There were high school valedictorians among us, urbanites, and others who had never before been off the farm. The college made a genuine effort during orientation to make everyone feel at home. Each freshman had been paired with a junior counselor, an upperclassman, who would tell us about all the different processes that we needed to know about and help us to carry out all the new responsibilities that we were facing. They would recommend tutors if we needed them, or they would tutor us themselves for free. I remember that the Dean of Students addressed us at the orientation meeting. She was an older, very fair-skinned black woman who wore her hair in a French roll. She had large lips, and she probably tried to make them appear even larger by applying lots of extremely red lipstick. She looked out at us from the stage of Greenleaf Auditorium and said, "Umm. . . umm. . . umm. . . My people are all the colors of the rainbow!" There were two hundred to three hundred freshmen in the auditorium, and they ranged in color from black to white. Mrs. Adams talked about how beautiful we all were and what potential we had, how confident in us she was and how happy and honored she was to be there to address us. She was obviously proud of her identity, and I believe that all of us who heard her felt proud of ourselves, too.

I had both good teachers at Shaw and others who had the attitude that we would make it on our own with no help from them or we would not make it.

I learned a great deal in history because I liked it, a lot in English, a lot in science, and even a lot in math, in spite of my initial belief that I could not do it. Most teachers were caring, and small classes allowed them to get to know the students.

This was during the sixties and most students had a sense of purpose, both inside and outside the classroom. Everyone I knew was involved to some degree in the Civil Rights Movement. We used to demonstrate in front of segregated establishments such as lunch counters and movie houses. Hundreds of nicely turned-out college students would approach the ticket booth at movie theatres to ask for a ticket. The students were instructed always to line up and approach in pairs. Their requests to purchase a ticket were always refused unless I or a white-looking black was the one asking. We would buy a ticket, go in, stay a little while, and come out and join the line again. The second time we approached the same attendant, we might be refused. We wanted to show that skin color can fool anyone foolish enough to make decisions based upon it. Perhaps more important, we wanted to show that sharing a theater with someone who is black poses no harm, as a result of that person's blackness, to anyone in the theatre. And we wanted to show—and this may be the most important lesson of all—that we weren't tired and we would keep coming back until justice was served.

I left Shaw for economic reasons. At the end of my sophomore year, I knew I did not have the money to return the next fall. That summer I got a job working for a federal program, the Neighborhood Youth Corps, and began paying rent, as my family required, in order to live at home. Since they knew that I had run out of money for college, they fully expected me to continue working full-time and to continue making contributions toward the upkeep of the family. I, on the other hand, was frantically trying to think of an alternative.

The church had started a study club so that kids whose parents could not help them with their schoolwork would have a place to go for tutoring. I asked Amy and a Hispanic woman who worked at the study club if they knew of any scholarships that I might apply for. The Hispanic woman knew about ASPIRA, an organization developed to help Puerto Rican kids get to college. I went down town to talk with the people at ASPIRA. I explained to them that I wanted to become a teacher so that I could work with children much like I had been, in an effort to make their learning experiences less difficult and more meaningful. I explained how I had gotten through my first two years of college, and ASPIRA gave me a scholarship to the University of Wisconsin at LaCrosse. The university gave me a work-study position where I could work for twenty hours a week to pay for my room and board. If I worked thirty hours a week, I could earn money toward my tuition as well. For me this was incredible good luck. LaCrosse was trying to attract more minorities to the campus. There were only two or three Hispanics at LaCrosse the whole time I was there. I didn't mind. I was just grateful for the chance to salvage my dream of earning a college degree.

The bus trip from New York to Wisconsin seemed interminable, but after my experience getting to Shaw, I was prepared for anything. I arrived at LaCrosse, found other students who were going to the campus, and, knowing exactly where I should be dropped off, shared a cab to my dorm. The student body was comprised almost totally of whites with a sprinkling of Native Americans. The college had no systems in place to ease my transition to life on campus or to enhance my chances for success; however, in the elementary education department, there were two teachers to whom their students were everything. One was a rather crusty old woman, but I had encountered a professor much like her at Shaw and knew that her bark was more likely to presage a nip than a real bite. She took a special interest in me, helping me to make informed decisions about which courses I should take and how I should go about becoming successful at the university.

When I was in college, my self-confidence grew with each year that I completed successfully. After my first year at Shaw University, the state of New York awarded me the Regents diploma. I believe that Mr. Feldman, my junior high school counselor and English teacher, had arranged for this because I had succeeded at college in spite of my Regents score in math. It seems silly that receiving the Regents diploma from the state should have meant so much to me. But it did. It said that I was college material and that I was no longer defined by that poor math test score.

I had planned to return to New York City to teach in the public school system when I graduated from college in 1967. I was recruited, however, by the Waukegan, Illinois, public schools. The district was experiencing a steady influx of Spanish-speaking children that the schools were not prepared to serve. I knew that strides in meeting the needs of such children were being made in New York, but here was an area where the pertinent issues were not being addressed. So I moved to Waukegan and began teaching children for whom English was the second language.

I noticed that the students were learning English but without the academic content that they needed, so when the state allocated funds for the establishment of bilingual programs in 1971, I wrote a proposal to acquire funds for a program in Waukegan. I elicited the help of community members in convincing the Board of Education to support the program. I also used their help in screening teachers for the bilingual classes. I found that working with parents helped me to do a better job of helping the kids and the community. For instance, I would notice at school that kids were wearing summer clothing and inadequate outerwear in the dead of winter because their parents were new arrivals or down on their luck and unable to manage. Sometimes parents had problems with landlords or with finding a job, and the welfare of the children would be compromised.

I began intervening by finding out which local agencies could help these people and by getting the people in contact with the agencies. Often I would drive parents to agencies such as the Red Cross and the Salvation Army, and I would translate once I got them there. The Red Cross was very helpful to people who needed a place to stay or clothes to wear after a house fire. I have high praise for the Salvation Army, where people could get recycled clothes, furniture, and household utensils whenever they needed them. Because the schools were concerned about the health of all students, they had to bar children from attending if they had not received the proper immunizations or the required physical examinations by a given date. Sometimes children would not be allowed in school because they had not met the school's health requirements, and the Health Department consistently came to their aid when I would call them. Organizations such as the Puerto Rican Society and the G.I. Forum, an association of Mexican American veterans, were very effective in getting Latino parents involved in helping their communities. Almost everyone that I encountered who received help from social agencies proved time and again that they had more than given back to the community what the community had given to them.

A case in point is a family of ten—eight children and two parents—who came to Waukegan from their home country under the sponsorship of a relative. Once they arrived, the relative moved to Chicago and left them in a practically empty apartment with no employment, little money, no knowledge of English, and no prospects for the future. The father was dejected at not being able to find a job, and, after a short time, left his family and returned to their homeland. I took the mother to food pantries, to the Department of Children and Family Services, to agencies and churches that would give the family clothing. All eight of those children finished high school, and several went on to earn college degrees. The eldest child is a social worker in Waukegan.

I have found that working with and helping people provides countless opportunities to add meaning to my life. I remember discovering that a parent who was volunteering to work at her children's school had been a teacher in her country but was not certified to teach in Illinois. She was working part-time in a laundry or a factory on the days that she was not volunteering. I had helped to draft legislation for a transitional bilingual teaching certificate that had been approved by the state. The purpose of the transitional certificate was to allow teachers who had trained under the normal or two-year system, as well as those whose credentials were earned in another country, to teach for six years in a bilingual program if they passed the English proficiency exam. During the six-year grace period, the teacher would be required to complete the courses necessary to gain the regular Illinois teaching certificate. I suggested that the parent acquire a transitional certificate, and I subsequently hired her as a bilingual teacher. In order to do so, I had to translate her credentials and submit them to the state. She was a wonderful teacher, as were many others whom I was able to help enter the teaching profession in much the same way. While some states remained unable to meet the needs of their growing Spanish-speaking student populations, we were facilitating the certification of bilingual teachers who had earned their college degrees and received their teacher training in their native countries of Puerto Rico, Honduras, Mexico, Cuba, Colombia, Chile, and Venezuela. There were times when the state would not approve the transitional certification, and I would have to appeal the decision, especially regarding teachers from Cuba who had not been able to bring all their credentials with them when they escaped the Castro regime. In the end, our efforts were never unsuccessful, and the children, by gaining excellent, loving instructors, have been the benefactors.

I have had the opportunity during my life to work with all kinds of students. As the principal of a junior high school, I found that some students were spending too much of their time at school unproductively in detention hall. Their infractions included actions such as skipping school, disrupting class, and arriving late to class or to school an excessive number of times. Discussions with students who were in trouble and with instructors seemed to reveal that students who have not completed their assignments feel vulnerable in the classroom and are more likely to exhibit undesirable behavior so that they will be removed from a setting where they are not going to be successful. The faculty and I designed and implemented a plan to enhance student success. First, we put in place a system of encouragement that would build community among students, faculty, and staff even as it rewarded the students for their responsible behavior. Dances, movies, cookouts, and special trips became school-wide activities exclusively for those who had stayed out of trouble.

The second prong of our plan entailed the teachers covering detention hall after school every day. Teachers whose students were in detention would provide the work that needed to be done, and the teacher volunteers would make sure the students received the help that they needed to understand and complete their assignments. This proved to be an excellent program. It was not expensive, since the teachers volunteered their time. The numbers of students in detention were reduced, and we saw fewer repeat offenders. Students felt better about themselves, and many made improvements in their grades. Faculty members felt good about giving and about the greater academic involvement of former class offenders. The parents were very happy with the program. The effort was empowering for practically everyone involved.

I left the junior high school in Waukegan to take a central office position in a K-12 district in Aurora, Illinois. Here was a town with a Hispanic population even larger than Waukegan's. I had gotten my doctorate in Curriculum and Instruction, so when I was offered the position in Aurora as Assistant Superintendent for Personnel, I was not sure I wanted to accept it. I wanted to influence what students were being taught. I envisioned the job in personnel as primarily focusing on contract negotiations, employee discipline, and sessions with lawyers both in and out of the courtroom. I took the job because the Superintendent reminded me that I would be able to influence, perhaps more than any other person, the quality of teachers hired by the district. Immediately I remembered my own teachers from my K-12 days. I had forgotten much of the content that I had learned, but I had not forgotten the teachers who had been kind to their students, who had believed that they could learn, who had demonstrated a conviction that every child in the classroom is a unique manifestation of God's best idea.

No matter how happy I am in my job, I have a tendency to look around to see what else is out there that I may need to do. That's how I happened to come to my present job. Before I left Aurora, I had interviewed for a few school superintendencies and had actually been offered one. For some reason, I had also applied for one principalship. The job was in an elementary school in the poor area of one of the most affluent school districts in northern Illinois. Sixty percent of the students are Hispanic. When I was invited for a second interview, I decided that I would go and have a look at the school. I entered the building just as the first bell was about to ring, and little kids were scurrying to get to their classrooms. Three of them spied me, and, excellent hosts that they were, hurried toward me, their huge smiles welcoming. "May I help you?" they inquired, almost in unison. They must have been about six or seven years old, since two of them had lost their front teeth. I was hooked. Here were first- or second-grade ambassadors carrying out the principles of good customer service with more warmth and skill than is exhibited by trained professionals in some colleges. In my job as Assistant Superintendent for Personnel, I had read stories to classes and otherwise involved myself with the teaching and learning process as often as I could. But here was the potential for more immediate and continual participation. I was offered the job and I took it.

My current work allows me to observe students, detect their needs as whole persons, and do whatever I can to help them grow into the fine citizens that they can all become. We have begun a dual language program that teaches English-dominant and Spanish-dominant kids in both languages, beginning in the earliest grades. We ascribe to the philosophy that when it comes to knowledge and love, more is better. We want children who speak Spanish to know that their knowledge of the language is an asset, not something to be ashamed of, and that learning English well will put them far ahead of the game. We want children who speak English to know that becoming fluent in Spanish is a valuable skill that will expand their opportunities in tomorrow's shrinking world. No matter what a child's first language may be, we want to help them to learn English while retaining a complete and healthy respect for their native tongue. I try to learn greetings, at least, in the many different languages of our students. If we are truly what we speak, then it behooves me, as it does the children, to be *and speak* all that I can.

Look What I Bring to You Good People
Arlene, 60, is a storyteller and social activist in Chicago, Illinois.

I was born on the Six Nations Reserve, which is near Brantford, in southwestern Ontario, Canada. I was born into my tribe and my clan through my mother's lineage. That's how it is with the Iroquois people. I'm a Mohawk, of the Mohawk Nation of the Iroquois Confederacy, and I am of the Bear Clan.

My grandmother raised me, and, as unbelievable as it may seem, I didn't know until I had grown up and been away from the reserve for several years that my grandmother was a clan mother of the Bear Clan. A clan mother is quite powerful. She chooses the chiefs, and if a chief does not perform to particular standards, she can remove him from his position. The clan mother is a leader of the clan, which is like a family, although not all members are brothers and sisters and there are diverse groups within the family or tribe within the nation.

When I lived on the reserve, I was told nothing of my grandmother's clan leadership because of a conflict in her spiritual beliefs and practices. The overt focus of my entire upbringing was the Christian church. My grandmother was a devout Christian, so we went to church every Sunday, sometimes twice; and we often attended prayer meetings at night during the week. Any traditional rituals in which my grandmother was involved were kept from me. Instead of the Indian spiritual ways, we were served a regular diet of the Bethany Bible Mission.

Closer to our home on the reserve was the Medinah Baptist Church where we often attended afternoon services. As if the magic of the church were not potent enough to banish Indian beliefs, somewhere along the line—maybe while sitting in the Medinah Baptist Church—I got the message that there were two kinds of Indians: the good ones who were Christians and the bad ones who practiced the traditional ways. Those of us who had converted to Christianity were assured somehow that those who practiced traditional ways were pagans, and early in my life I learned that I must not associate with the pagans. Not surprisingly, I do not recall having any friends who followed the traditional ways when I was growing up; and, being a good Indian, I knew and was interested in nothing of substance about my culture.

I went to all eight grades of elementary school on the reserve. There were thirteen one-room schools with an Indian teacher at each school. I think this must have been a positive for us. Here was a potential role model who looked like us at the head of each classroom. But my teachers, although they were Indian, taught me nothing about my culture. They did not encourage me to study hard or go to college. Simply put, they did not inspire me to aspire.

When I graduated from eighth grade, I took the bus to a nearby town, Hagersville, for my high school education. In high school, there was no encouragement or inspiration from my teachers for me to become an educated person. In many respects, they were as wooden as the carvings of Indians in headdress that once stood outside small-town general stores. My French teacher, whom I did not like, was diminutive and had thick black hair that was constantly falling into his eyes. I knew he was alive because he was forever brushing his hair away from his face. He sparked no interest in his class at all, but French was a mandatory subject. The only connection my teacher and his class had to my life occurred on those mornings when my grandmother decided that we would have cereal for breakfast. Everything on the cereal box was in French as well as English. Otherwise, French provided nothing that I could use in my daily life. I did like Latin, however, and when I moved from Canada to the United States, the Latin teacher at my new high school was quite impressed by my ability in Latin. To this day, all I can remember in Latin is *Gallia est omnis in partes tres* which means "All Gaul is divided into three parts." Ironically, nobody has ever asked me into how many parts Gaul is divided. In my entire experience in and out of school, with the exception of my high school Latin class, no one has asked what I know in Latin, and no one has cared.

Other courses that I took in school were also impractical. When I was in high school in Ontario, I took a class called agricultural science, a course designed to teach students to become farmers, or farmers' wives, on the reserve.

We learned about corn smut, a disease of corn. In my entire life outside that classroom, I have had no interaction with corn except that I appreciate it as a very, very prominent food for our people. That appreciation is something I learned after I was a grown woman.

During about my junior year in high school, a lot of my friends began leaving school to move to the States. Anything to do with the States was glamorous, especially the American cars that would come over the border sporting their New York license plates. One of my best friends quit school, moved to the States, and began coming home on weekends with new clothes. My mother had remarried and lived in Indiana. On Thanksgiving in 1952, she invited me to move to the States to finish my high school education because only four years are required in the U.S. as opposed to the five forms in Canada. So I moved to the States when I was sixteen years old. I finished high school in 1954. In 1955, I got married.

I married during the June Cleaver era when the husband went to work and the wife stayed at home and raised the children. That's exactly what I did for years and years. The marriage deteriorated, and finally my husband and I were divorced in 1971. I didn't have a clue about how to make a living. When I was married, my husband had allowed (I bristle at that word now) me to work part-time at Sears, Roebuck during the Christmas season. Otherwise I had no experience in the world of work.

At the time of my divorce, I was living in a Chicago suburb. Somehow I managed to get a job with the real estate firm Hogan and Falwell on the twentieth floor of the World Trade Building in downtown Chicago. I commuted to Chicago on the Barrington Northwestern train. On my commute, I would think about the dreams that I had secretly held for myself when I was home raising my children. I would recall seeing two or three people who lived on my block leave their homes early in the morning to commute to Chicago. They had jobs and offices. That had seemed so distant to me, but I dreamed about commuting to Chicago to my office. After I realized that dream, I got the idea that it would be great to be transferred to another city and have an expense account. Eventually that happened for me, too. I changed jobs and trained for a year as a buyer of hats and wigs. When my company transferred me to Omaha, I realized that for the first time in my life I was totally, independently myself. You hear many women talk of no longer being simply the mother of, or wife of, or sister of, or daughter of, as their identity. I came to realize that I existed, I *was*—in and of myself—for the first time in my life. I felt as if I had been reborn, not resurrected, for I was new! I had become the new but original Arlene Drake.

My mother was an influence in helping me to become independent. My grandmother was a very, very strong influence in my life. When you look at me today, in large part you are seeing my grandmother, many of whose values I share. When I consider the role model to go beyond what I was, I can look to my mother. When she was a small child, she was sickly with asthma, so she missed a great deal of school. She left grade school by sixth grade, but what my mother accomplished was to me proof of what a woman can do even though a man abuses and abandons her.

I choke up sometimes when I think of my mom. She told me that the last time she saw my father was when she was expecting me. He abandoned her when she was pregnant with his child. He told her, "You're not going to get anywhere. You're just going to be stuck here on the reserve with a whole bunch of kids. And when you ask your husband or your man for some money, he'll toss you a quarter." I think those words stayed with my mother and spurred her on because she achieved so much that you wouldn't expect of someone who had dropped out of grade school. For example, she became the membership chairman for the Indiana State Board of the PTA. And when she took on that role, she was able to generate more members than anyone in that position had generated before. She would go out and speak at schools and to various community and civic groups. In the early sixties, the subject matter of her talks was called Indian lore. She also hosted a television program here in Chicago on Channel Eleven called *Totem Club*.

I admired my mother tremendously, and I said to myself that one of these days I would like to have a show on Channel Eleven. I was able to accomplish that. In the spring of 1993, I co-hosted *Hot Line 21* for Greenpeace on cable television in Chicago. Claude Rollins, who worked for Greenpeace, had asked me to be his guest on his show, and we had a wonderful time. That next spring he asked me to host the show with him. I just loved it, and the first show that I did was the best. I zeroed in on Native American environmental issues, as well as the First Nations People's environmental issues in Canada. I had Native American guests, one of whom was James Yellowbank, the Hochunk environmentalist and musician.

My television show allowed me to educate others, and even some Native Americans themselves, about the old ways of our people. I could share facts about how the Indians hunted, how they killed only what they could use, how they talked to the animals and thanked them for providing food. Not long ago I saw Pearl Sunrise, a Navajo weaver, and she talked about how the Indian hunter respects other life. When they say, "All my relatives," they mean all the trees, all the birds, every living thing. With the television show, I felt that I was doing what I had set out to do. My mom was like that, too. She accomplished what she set her mind to do.

I never really met my father when I was a child, but my father's mother was very, very loving toward me when she would encounter me at events on the reserve. And she was forever asking me to come and visit with her. I, myself, chose not to get involved with my father's side of the family. I felt a separation from them.

In the middle sixties, I was invited to a reunion on my father's side of the family in New York state. My father comes from a large family. One of his brothers changed his name to Jay Silverheels, and for a number of years he played Tonto on the television show *The Lone Ranger;* his real name was Harry Smith. I went to the reunion with my handsome husband and my two precious children. My father and his latest wife were there; she is three months older than I am. And there were many children as well—three from my father's first wife who was deceased and five from his last wife. A few years later, my paternal grandmother passed away, and my daughter and I went to the funeral. My father literally took me by the elbow and proudly introduced me as his daughter to all these people. My grandmother raised me to be gracious, so I was gracious through the whole thing. But when one of my uncles said to me, "Well, we didn't know about you," I said, "Don't look at me. Look at your brother." At this late date, my father had apparently become quite proud of me. I hadn't even begun to do that which would really single me out; I hadn't even thought about enrolling in college.

Here's how I happened to go to college. After my job in hats and wigs, one of my friends, a Hochunk, suggested that I enroll in NAES College, the Native American Educational Services College in Chicago. NAES had opened its doors in 1975. It is a reservation/urban learning college with campuses in Chicago, Minneapolis-St. Paul, and Fort Peck, Montana, where the Cinnewanen Sioux are. I met with the president of the college and enrolled. NAES granted credits for prior learning, as well as for professional development in a particular field. This was very attractive to me because the program could save me time and money. Even more important, it provided an implicit validation of what I am and what I brought to the college and to the world just by virtue of my experiences.

In addition to studying hard and taking a full load of classes, I worked as a development officer with Wright College, a job that would count toward my degree in community development. I was responsible for contacting people in Chicago as part of a fund-raising campaign. At the time NAES was not accredited, so when I received my degree in April of 1981, it was awarded by Antioch University in Yellowsprings, Ohio. NAES had a bilateral agreement with Antioch, an accredited institution, through which we were granted our degrees.

I wanted to go to college because I realized that I would need credentials in order to grow. At NAES classes were very small, and a lot of individual attention was given to the students. We felt like a family. I joined with all the other students to form an informal support group. We had much in common with each other. Many of us were single heads of households, and some of us were divorced. And we learned so much from each other. For example, I would hear Joan, a Sioux from the Dakotas, as she would come up the stairs near my office to see the college officials. She worked in a factory and was very, very structured and disciplined. Joan's self-motivation had a profound effect on me.

The instructors at NAES were very approachable and accessible—almost like our peers—so there was a comfort in the classroom experience. I felt perfectly comfortable in raising any kinds of questions. My thoughts and concerns were all respectfully received. I did not feel intimidated or that I should suppress any ideas or questions that I might have. This was very different from my education in Canada, in those one-room schools where my teachers had taught me and my mother before me. Prior to my experience at NAES, I do not recall a time that a teacher inspired me or any other Indian student or encouraged us to go on to higher education. And in neither the one-room schools nor in the high school did anyone ever instruct us in the traditional ways of the Native American people.

At NAES, we studied in-depth the history of Native Americans. Often experts in particular areas would come from various parts of the country to provide added insight into what we were studying. I remember a religious leader once came in to teach during a course on contemporary Indian religious issues. Someone came from the southwest to teach about tribal government. Native American languages such as Navajo and Ojibwa (or Chippewa) are also taught at NAES. Mohawk is not, but there are more Ojibwa and Navajo people in Chicago than there are Mohawk. Learning about other Native American people actually compelled me to learn more about the Mohawk and the other Iroquois people. I was proud to learn that the U.S. government itself is based on the government of the Iroquois Confederacy, which goes back hundreds of years. On one occasion the white scholars got together with the Indians to figure out when the Iroquois Confederacy was formed. The Indians said the date was 1390; when the meeting ended, the white scholars said it was 1500. The powers that be ignore history and write their own.

After NAES, some of my classmates went on to get their master's degrees. Joan, whom I mentioned earlier, didn't miss a beat. When she received her bachelor's degree in 1981, she had already made arrangements to go on to the

University of California at Berkeley. In two years, she had earned her M.A. in public health. I decided to take a break from school for a while and accepted a job in Chicago as the Executive Director of the Native American Committee. The whole mission of NAES was to get credentialed leadership onto the reserves and into urban settings, so my job was just following through on what I had studied for. I gave myself a five-year time frame in which to get my M.A. Five years have come and gone, and I haven't done anything to realize that goal.

NAES helped me to become aware of other Indian nations, cultures, and traditions. At NAES, I would hear about the government run boarding schools for Indian children in the States and in Canada. Someone said the children would go into those boarding schools innocent and pure of heart and would leave broken in spirit. I could reach out and touch my best friend, Joan, as an example of this. She went to a boarding school where she was supposed to be deculturalized from her Indian ways when she was four years old. She shared with me how she became very ill—she thinks it was around one Christmastime. The people in charge of the school put her in a room that was dark, and she was still there the next Easter. By then she was all drawn up and could hardly move. A priest came in and bodily picked her up and moved her from that place. These exposures to real-life experiences that people had and that are part of our history became part of my curriculum when I was in college. The knowledge that I received from my fellow students was as great as what I learned in the classroom.

The same was true of my learning about the traditional ways of Native American people. I remember going to a powwow with Joan, who had her two sons and her daughter with her. Her youngest child, her daughter, was decked out in the traditional outfit of Joan's tribe with her hair done in the particular way that her hair should have been done. Even though Joan had been sent to a boarding school at an early age, somehow the schools, government, and churches hadn't been able to take her heritage away from her. And Joan, without the cultural assistance of her Japanese ex-husband, was passing that heritage on to her children.

The transmission of heritage is immensely important, for just as it helps to form the self-identification of a child, it simultaneously helps to preserve the identity of a people. For these reasons, powwows are held quite often at the American Indian Center in Chicago so that Indian people can get together, regardless of their tribe or organization. In the American Indian Center's history, it has been a major struggle just to maintain the heart of the Indian community. It is a struggle—both funding-wise and in terms of the building they're in. I never went to a powwow when I was on the reserve in Canada. We were separate from the people who practiced the traditional ways. When I was in college, I learned about taking part in powwows and eventually thinking, "I'll be darned! That's the grass dance! I know that! Heavenly days! I know this! I know that!" It was quite a springboard for me to begin to realize that, as in the case of my friend Joan, many, many Native Americans were torn from their families but were still able to maintain a strong spiritual link to the traditional ways. I've been trying to learn what I can about the traditional ways, but I'm not always true to myself because I'm not learning every day as much as I possibly could be learning about our people.

In terms of learning, I have no time to lose because during so much of my life, I learned practically nothing about my people. When I was growing up, my grandmother and grandfather spoke Mohawk and Oneida. They were fluent, but they did not teach those languages to us. When Native American children were torn away from their parents and sent to the government-run boarding schools, they were literally beaten when they spoke the language of their people. There is a very haunting film called *Where the Spirit Lives* that tells the stories of these children. I have met many Indians who said that their parents tried to protect them by not teaching them their native language.

In so much of my life, luck has played a strong role in what I have been able to learn and do. For instance, in a recent year my daughter and I went to another of my father's family reunions. The spring before going to that reunion in August, I had read in *The United Tribe*, a newspaper from near Green Bay, Wisconsin, about Jacob Thomas, the chief of the Cayuga tribe. He was going to be at the Unida Tribes conference, and he was going to be presenting the Great Law of Peace of the Iroquois people. It would be a five-day conference, all in English. The reputation of the Great Law of Peace of the Iroquois, which was brought to inspire the peacemaker so we would stop warring with each other, is legendary. But it just was not possible for me to attend the conference. I wanted so much to learn about the Great Law of Peace! When I was at the family reunion in August, I happened to walk down to the river to be by myself for a while. One of my cousins caught up with me and started talking about the Great Law of Peace of the Iroquois! When I was ready to leave the next day, he gave me fourteen tapes of the Great Law of Peace of the Iroquois recited by Chief Jacob Thomas! Very important things have come to me in this serendipitous way. Getting the tapes was so beneficial because it is important to hear the Great Law of Peace recited again and again. Then I'll read a book, for example, *White Roots of Peace,* and I'll see how I can tie together some of what I have been learning. My desire to learn and the way to learn magically find each other.

Here's how I became a storyteller. When I was a small child, my grandmother and I used to take the train to and from Chicago to visit my mother. This led to my becoming a storyteller without realizing that that was what I was doing. After returning from one of our visits, I went to my friend Mary's house and started talking about my trip to Chicago on the train. My story was funny to Mary's family. I was talking about the dress I wore, too long on me, plaid with mostly yellow and blue checks. My grandmother had pinned it up at the waist with straight pins, and I had on jet black stockings and string-up oxfords that my grandmother had bought. I wore a long checked coat, too big on me, that one of my aunts had given my grandmother and she had had cut down for me to grow into. And on top of my head of braids I had a robin's egg blue hat. I told of going down the aisle of the train and of how my stockings started to sag around my skinny legs. These were sexy, jet-black, see-through stockings. Then the pins shortening my dress began coming loose. I was just telling Mary's family my experience, and they thought it was the funniest thing in the world!

Obviously I had other sources and outlets for stories. My grandparents were very involved in community activities, and I attended many events with them. One of the customs at social gatherings was that different people would get up and tell a story, sing a song, or play a game. The events would take the form of a contest, and the person doing the best would get a prize. One night I won the prize, a maroon toss pillow, for telling a story. All I remember about my story is the punch line, "The capital city of Siberia!" I remember that I delivered the line and sat down, and people just cracked up.

I noticed, too, that when my mother and I would drive up to Canada after I moved to the States as a teenager, we would talk about our trip to others, and what we said was always a story. One time when we were driving up to Canada—we were in Michigan somewhere—I had fallen asleep. My mother shook me awake and said excitedly, "Arlene, look what's just up the highway!" Somewhat awake, I looked at all these lights hovering in the darkness ahead of us just above the road, and I said, "Looks like a big ole flying saucer, flying mighty low," and I went right back to sleep. The lights turned out to be on a large truck, but I wasn't awake long enough to discover that fact for myself.

My son was more or less responsible for my beginning to tell stories in schools. He is half Mohawk and half Irish-English. When he was a little boy and his class would talk about Indians at Thanksgiving, the teacher reported that my son would raise his hand and say, "I'm a Mohawk!" And the teacher would say, "Yeah, we know. . . ." Eventually she met me and then she could believe him. I began visiting schools and telling stories of my childhood so that children and their teachers could learn whatever I could offer about Native American people. They could come to understand that some Indians, such as my son, might not look exactly the way some people think Indians should look. Over the years, talks about my childhood have just naturally expanded to some of the other things that I have learned. I began to incorporate the creation story of the Iroquois people. During this past summer, I was at the Field Museum telling stories. While my stories focus more on Iroquois tales, I make use of my varied body of material, telling stories from the Iroquois nation as well as from other tribes.

Storytelling, a major force in my activist work, brings me absolute joy. I do it naturally and people of all ages respond in kind, with joy. I tell my stories; I sing in Mohawk. Afterward people come and talk to me. The little kids want to tell me their stories and what they have read. I try to make my experience and what I have learned real for my audience. I like to invite them into the experience. And I try to keep learning, to keep getting better.

When I was growing up on the reserve, we would sing our hymns in Indian and in English. Since there were six tribes on my reserve, some of the people would get up and speak and sing in their language. I remember one man who would sometimes sing, pray, and speak in *Tuscarora*. I do not speak any of the Iroquois languages, but when I sang *"Jah kah to gee me son gwah way / Ming yon gway day yo sway. . . ."* for my grandmother, I liked to imagine that I was singing *The Twenty-third Psalm*.

Later I learned what the song really means. I was at a conference at the Worthington Cultural Center in Canada, and there were a number of Mohawks there from the Tannedenega Reserve in Ontario. I met a young man named David Skyhawk and asked whether this song I sang was Oneida or Mohawk because the two languages are very, very similar. David Skyhawk began speaking to me in Mohawk when I told him I wanted to learn the language. I reminded him I didn't already speak Mohawk, so he said in English, "Okay. What is your Indian name?" I didn't even have an Indian name, so he gave me one right there on the spot. Then I sang the song to him. He said that it is Mohawk and it means, "Look what I bring to you good people, your good hearts and your good minds." That's what the peacemaker brought to us hundreds and hundreds of years ago. He brought that to all the Iroquois people, all of the various tribes: the Mohawk, the Oneida, the Onondagas, the Cayuga, the Seneca, and later the Tuscarora. He brought this to us in order that we would have good minds and would love one another. That's what *everything* is about. All people need to learn that *now*. And I can see clearly now that David Skyhawk valued immediacy in learning.

When my grandmother passed away in 1963 at the age of seventy-five, my

Auntie Elma became the clan mother of the Bear Clan of the Mohawk tribe because she was the oldest daughter. She focused on the Christian church but maintained her clan mother duties somehow, just as my grandmother had. In October of 1978, she invited me to go with her to a meeting of all the clan mothers and the chiefs of the Mohawk tribe. I went, but it was 1978 and I had a burgundy leather coat and a yellow Camaro. I wasn't really that interested. I didn't get the full impact of what I was experiencing, yet my journey of awakening was underway.

Perhaps my gratitude to my grandparents, my mother, and others who have helped me along the way makes me want to learn and give to others as much as I can. My friend Bea, a Menominee, has been involved in the Chicago Native American community for quite a number of years and credits me with having recruited her to NAES College. At the time, I was a development officer, but I would recruit students. I would call the Executive Directors of Native American organizations and ask them to let me speak to their staffs about NAES. I would promise to take only twenty or thirty minutes of their time, and I would keep my talk simple. I would tell them about myself, about being divorced in 1971 with no clue about what to do, how to write a check, how to use a checkbook, how to go about getting a decent job. I would tell them about how my children had been in their early teens, and how I came to realize that in order to meet my responsibilities and fulfill my dreams, I needed credentials.

I have known the importance of helping others all my life. In Omaha, when I was in the hats and wigs business, I happened to go to an event at the Indian Center there. An Indian woman asked if I would let her little girl spend a day with me at my office. When I was assigned to my job, I had replaced a Caucasian man. He had asked my district manager if I were a Jew. She had said no, that I was a Native American. He had refused to believe that I was American Indian *and* a woman. He reconciled that by saying, "She must be half white," because I was taking his place. I was glad to have that little Indian girl, ten or eleven years old, come and spend the day at work with me. Her mother wanted her to see that I represented a possibility for her. This was "Take Your Daughter to Work Day" before anyone had ever heard of it.

In my life, I try to learn and I try to share with others what I know. I know that peace, love, and understanding start right here, with me. If I feel a sense of joy, of love, and I walk into a school and I smile, people smile back because they're happy. What kind of experience do I want today? What I project is the kind of experience that I can have. Of course, when we look at television or in the newspaper, when we listen to the radio and do whatever we do over the internet, it seems that there is so much to be on guard about. The *Chicago Tribune* columnist Bob Greene wrote a column about a party where people had to be patted down to make sure they were not a danger to the other guests. If people from years ago could see this, they would say, "This is a party?" But we don't have to buy into such craziness and let it control our lives. We go through security checks to get on airplanes, and we understand its purpose. But we ourselves know that we are about peace and love, and we just project that.

Hadioga was a storyteller who would go from village to village a long time ago telling stories at night and during winter between the first and last frost. The grandmothers and grandfathers would be there, and he would find a way of engaging their interest so they wouldn't fall asleep on him. Once he kept them awake by telling them the Iroquois creation story, "Earth on Turtle's Back." I will tell you an abbreviated story about how we came to be.

Listen. . . . Before everything happened, when the Sky Woman came down from the Sky Land, there was nothing but water as far as the eye could see. Animals and birds were swimming on the water. There was just water. Then Sky Woman fell through a hole in the sky and came down. As she was falling downward, the animals saw her and realized that she didn't have webbed feet and couldn't live in the water. So they got together to plan what to do in order to help her. A couple of swans flew up to break her fall, and they were gently bringing her toward the water. Each animal tried to go way down deep in the water because they had heard that way down deep there was earth. And if one of them could go down far enough and bring up some earth, then Sky Woman would have something to stand on, and she could live. So all the animals tried valiantly. The duck tried, then the beaver. The loon tried, but they all failed. And finally, after all the other animals had given up, the tiny little muskrat tried. And she went down and down, and even when it got darker and darker, she kept going down. And when she thought her lungs were going to burst, she kept going. She almost fell unconscious, and she still kept going down and down. And then she reached the bottom, scooped up a little paw of earth, and floated back to the surface. Everyone rejoiced, for she had succeeded in bringing earth up to the surface. But she had to put it somewhere. But where? That's when the great turtle offered that Muskrat put the earth on his back. As soon as Muskrat had done so, Great Turtle's back became larger and larger and larger, as large as Muskrat's endurance and love, as large as his own generous spirit, as large as the compassion of the other animals, until it became the whole world. The swans brought Sky Woman gently to the ground, and she stepped down on earth. When she had fallen through the hole in the sky, Sky

Woman had brought seeds from Sky Land in her hands. The seeds scattered upon the earth, and the grasses and trees began to grow.

Picasso's Principle

John, 52, is an artist and social activist in Waukegan, Illinois.

I was a victim of divorce early in my life—so early I don't even remember it— during World War II. My father married again, again when he was too young, so a problem developed in that marriage as well. I did not get to know my biological mother until I was a teenager. I was at a ball field and two ladies were there. "Johnny, come 'ere! Derrick, come 'ere!" Derrick is my older brother. And I got to meet my mom. What a shock! She had married a Pepsi-Cola bottler in northern California, and I started going to see her in the summer and had a heck of a nice time. They had built a little resort near Mt. Lassen, forty-four miles east of Redding, and it was beautiful. There were a hotel, a gas station, a house overlooking a creek, horses, and all that stuff. I could just romp around and get to know my mom. She was a drinker. She died when she was forty-two and I was twenty-one.

I was born in Fort Wayne, Indiana. When I was a year old and my brother was four and a half, my father married Martha Jane Millhouse, from Hicksville, Ohio. They're still married. I call Martha, Mom. She always tended to the house; she never worked, except during the Christmas season I was nine or ten. Then she worked in gift wrapping to pick up a little something extra for Christmas. My father started off as a factory worker and became a good machinist. He was an only son—a little bit spoiled—and always interested in labor unions. He finally got elected to a union position when I was eight. We moved to California and, after a few moves around the state, settled in San Diego. We bought a house, and that's where I grew up.

My father's union job didn't work out that well for us. The job was very destructive for him and hard on the whole family. I know I grew up angry and sullen over it. It was my father's freewheeling lifestyle—driving around instead of going to work, coming up with a mistress, that type of thing—that was so threatening. I got after him about it, telling him that I wouldn't stand for it. I must have been somewhat effective because he and Martha stayed together.

I grew up by my own devices, pretty much on my own. My mom and dad sort of let me go. Whatever I did was okay. It was as if they forgot about me. Of course, there was discipline and there were rules and stuff. But they never really paid much attention to me, and I was able to roam the hillsides with my bow and arrow when I was a kid. We moved to a new area called Clairemont that overlooked Mission Bay. I loved it because you could see the ocean, which was five miles away.

No one paid much attention to my schooling when I was growing up. I didn't get the message from anyone to go to school beyond twelfth grade. To finish high school, my parents said, was fine. "Get yourself a trade," was the strong message I got at home. At school there was no message at all. I just went through the grades. In the last year of high school, I had a girlfriend, but I went ahead and left home after graduation. I wanted to be an architect, and I went to Berkeley to follow that dream. I had been studying architecture through high school under the guise of taking a trade. I started working for this architect as an apprentice. After a year or so, I looked at the guys in the office and saw that they looked miserable. Their advice was, "John, you don't want to do this. Look at us! We've got ulcers! Go be a plumber or something. Go be happy." So I did a little of both. I stayed with my artwork, and I took up a trade.

I learned how to lay linoleum and carpeting and did that part-time in the evenings and on weekends. I didn't have any financial support from my parents or a scholarship or anything, so I worked for a year and saved. Then I got myself accepted to Berkeley. At that time, Reagan was governor of California, and with the anti–Vietnam War movement, it was a really, really bad scene. The degree of upheaval made it very hard to get an education. In fact, during that time on Friday afternoons, the authorities would have all these paddy wagons roam the streets and round up students as they were walking home from classes. They would bus the kids from Berkeley to a huge concrete slab in Sacramento. All the students would have to spend the weekend on that concrete slab. The accommodations were a few portable toilets. Then early, early Monday morning, around three-thirty or four o'clock, they'd bus the students on back to school. That was Reagan's answer to the anti–Vietnam War demonstrations. He rounded up kids like that for seven or eight months. I got caught a couple of times when I was just walking.

Our classes were disrupted to the point that they were sometimes held out on Haight Ashbury. Classes would meet on the lawn, in the park. That's how I got to meet some of the kids who were really involved in the anti-war movement. I met this guy named Steve Gaskin from San Francisco State; he became the head of the commune, the Farm, where I hooked up with him again years later.

I really didn't want a lot to do with the war protest movement. I was studying cultural anthropology and art and just wanted to focus on my courses. I dropped out of school and went to San Miguel de Allende in Mexico, a hundred miles northeast of Mexico City. I spent a semester there. There were all these people from England, what you'd call beatniks, who were terrific writers. San Miguel was a cool art school, very good for weaving, pottery, sculpture, and painting. It got me going again. I didn't have to be a Vietnam demonstrator just because I was of a particular age. And here were all these people who knew what they were doing with their lives. They were really dedicated artists who had given up everything to be themselves and to move forward with becoming the best artists they could.

I moved forward by going back to San Diego and finishing my degree at San Diego State. I thought I was going to get a master's degree, so I went to New York to the Art League for a semester. I'd heard that the Art League would work you to death and really discipline you, and I wanted that. Schools never really tell you how to be a professional, how to make a living at art; they just tell you that art is something that culture and society need. The Art League did give me some good discipline. I had a hard semester there living in the Village, but I got to meet some interesting people. Then I stayed for a couple of years at Syracuse where I thought I might get a master's degree.

The master's degree course work was too often boring. All you had to do was memorize all the artists in the museums and their histories, and you'd get your master's. I realize now that there is a real value to that. I'm painting every day using knowledge and techniques that artists of long ago learned over the centuries. They may have spent their whole lives and come up with just one thing, but that one thing has lived through the ages. For instance, when I was in college, I started shading my pieces, so that on one side you'll see a little blue streak or hue and on the other side you'll see a little orange or red. Up against an object, this technique gives a real presence of atmosphere. I probably wouldn't have learned that in a lifetime if some professor hadn't come in and said, "John, Rodin did this God knows how many years ago. Go ahead and try it." In that respect, I probably would have been better off studying some of the masters a little more closely, but I didn't. I just pursued my own path, and it's really been pretty hard. I've had a hard life.

My professors did other things that I found life-changing. I remember one time Syracuse had a workshop up in Blue Mountain Lake, above Utica. The whole workshop was on aesthetic ambiguities, and I was totally intrigued. The workshop allowed me to share a mature environment with a number of professors from Syracuse and Montreal who gave me a lot of freedom to experiment. Using glass in my paintings is the result of one of my experiments. I try to do just pure experimentation at least six to eight weeks a year. Much of that practice came from my experience at the Syracuse workshops. Collecting data. Having fun. Trying to reach my limits, to stretch. These habits are legacies, I think, of my art education.

When I went off to college, my parents didn't encourage me at all. They just continued their consistent practice of my youth of leaving me alone. In stark contrast to the way they treated me, they picked on my brother Derrick a lot. Ironically, they had high expectations of him academically and otherwise, and he is the one who was born seven months into the pregnancy and was always a little bit slow. In fact, I had to defend my brother. One of my biggest problems in life has been having to come to his defense and becoming what they call an appeaser or placater. I was always telling lies for him—"I did it! Derrick didn't do this, I did!"—knowing that I wouldn't get a really severe beating for it but he might. Those lies have stayed with me all through my life. It has been somewhat like rescuing somebody over and over again, somebody that shouldn't be rescued. Maybe I shouldn't have lied to help Derrick. Maybe my intervention restricted his ability to have a life of his own. But I was not prepared to tolerate his suffering. Still, the kind of appeasement that I did for Derrick weighs heavily upon me.

Our parents left me alone and sent Derrick to the Navy. When Derrick became a recluse later in life, perhaps no one should have been surprised. He was functioning relatively normally until he was about thirty or thirty-five, and then he became a recluse. I write him twice a year, but I have never gotten a response even though we were good friends. It's he and my dad who never got along. So Derrick just said, "Well, I won't have any contact with any of the family anymore," and went off to work at a winery in northern California. I don't like the idea that he doesn't even send me a Christmas card.

I helped myself to go to college and to do the things that I have done. No one else helped me. No one guided or encouraged me. In my life, I guess you could say that I have been successful at deriving my inspiration and drive from the actual freedom to pursue becoming myself, but every once in a while I get really tired. Trying to live a life of social service sometimes gets me so tired that I have to switch gears. For instance, I taught for just one year at a little private school. There were only twelve students. The school was only two blocks from my home, a little house on a dead-end street. The students would come over to my house instead of going to school. They were fairly gifted, very challenging, and I put so much into teaching them! They seemed always to be with me, and I did wind up fostering one of them, a girl whose mother had a drinking problem. I had my own daughter in high school, so fostering this girl worked out really well. It was hard on me, though, because my house was like a hotel with all of those kids around. They called it Harmon's Hotel. I even heard it referred to that way on the radio once! I tried so hard to connect with and sustain those students! I would promise them that if they really loved art and worked really hard, I would get them into the Art Institute, unrealistic stuff like that, and it was too hard a job for me. So I sold everything I had and went to that famous hippie commune in Tennessee—the Farm.

There were 1,500 people that I had gone to school with in California at the Farm. They specialized in midwifing and published a very good book of some renown, *Spiritual Midwifery*. They also had an eighty-person carpenter crew that went around repairing bridges, tunnels, and other structures. At that time, my only substantial possession was an old Greyhound bus. I built a tepee and kept the twenty-two-foot poles on top of the bus. The tepee was huge, eighteen feet around. I could leave the Farm in my bus, go a distance, pitch my tepee, and just paint. I also taught at the Farm for almost a semester and a half, but my students said, "Get a life, John." They chased me away from teaching, so I left the commune.

While at the Farm, I had met a nurse, one of the midwives, and she went with me all over the country just painting. When we found a place we liked, we'd pitch the tepee. We lived like this for a couple of years. I think I was trying to renew my spirit, which had been depleted by teaching and by the divorce from my first wife. I'll never teach again because it took everything out of me.

My freedom then, now, and always, has been at a heck of a price. My first wife and I were married for sixteen years. When she completed a program to become a social worker, she said, "John, you and I just got married too young, and I never was really attracted to you. Goodbye." And here I was with a daughter in high school! My daughter got through school, moved out, grew up, and was fine. But I paid the price of knowing that my wife had always wanted a little more security, and in the 1970s I could only make around $10,000 a year on artwork. It wasn't enough to raise a family, so I supplemented my income by using the skills I had learned during my college years when I did carpentry and laid linoleum. I looked for newspaper ads that asked for repairs and such on Saturdays, and that would help. We were poor economically, but we had cultural riches. Yet my wife wasn't really willing to accept that kind of life. My hair and my beard were long—I can't blame my wife one bit. That was a traumatic time for me because I had thought I would always be married, but here I was dating. It was so upsetting!

When I went to the Farm, I was finishing a book. The last chapter was about creativity, how women have the ultimate creativity because they can have children. I remarked, "Well, I'm about finished here," and the nurse said, "I can tell that you want another child. I'll give you one." I took a course in midwifery, she became pregnant, and I was given a son, Michael. I delivered him, and it was a real nice experience.

Michael was born while we were traveling in the bus. His mother was a real,

real hippie. She was a nice lady, but I think there has to be something wrong with her because she's always traveling. Raising children and traveling at the same time—in a sense, there's a detachment there. I was raised that way. I knew it couldn't possibly work, so when Michael was a couple of months old, we flipped a coin to see where we would settle down. She wanted to go to Pago Pago in Samoa. We were in the mountains of Colorado, and I said, "I don't care too much for the Colorado mountains because they're not very friendly, so let's go to Vermont and raise our son. We went, and one day I woke up and she was just gone. She said, "I can't stay in one place." That was okay. I had kind of expected it.

Michael and I have been together all of his life. I would stand at my easel, and Michael would be like a little football right under my arm while I painted. I finally did get remarried years later, six years ago, and I'm happily married now. Michael is a freshman in high school. He is in the college prep program. He's very smart, but it seems like everything he does irritates me. He starts homework at ten o'clock and he'll go at it until midnight. I never really harass him, but it bothers me and he knows it bothers me. I offer to help Michael with his schoolwork if he needs any help, and he says, "I'm not a whiner." He's a real Mr. Man.

When I moved to the Chicago area, I became involved in a little business making area rugs with three doctors' wives who wanted their own lives. It worked out really well, and they're still running the store. But I started to feel like I didn't belong. I didn't feel comfortable because the store seemed to be about prestige, and I wanted to do something where I could make a difference in people's lives. That was my job description that I had written way back when I was in college. I needed to be true to my job description, so I looked for a place where I was needed. Waukegan, a working class Illinois city on Lake Michigan, was the worst town I could find with a lake view.

I make a difference in my own life by living as simply as I can. Right now I'm trying to live on $5,500 a year. My costs are down to about $20,000 for my art related expenses, and I try to live on a hundred dollars per week. It's a little bit hard with Michael in high school, with books and things, but there are ways of doing it without Public Aid. And the rest of my income I give away. I'm serious about the job description that I wrote when I was just starting out. I wrote that I wanted to effect social change and that would be my job, so if I have anything extra, and I'm a commercial artist, I'm not really being true to what my job is. When I was at Berkeley, I was particularly affected by something the professors used to say: "Artists are very poor but that's good because then they are living on the edge of a picket fence and they are always telling the truth. You have to tell the truth and money has to be completely out of the picture or very, very secondary." But you get tired. Every once in a while, I'll sell a painting for $10,000 or so and take a little vacation.

I'm into trading. My daughter is getting a divorce because her husband got a girlfriend. So I ran a painting over to her attorney and said, "Here. Now the divorce is paid for." He said, "Are you sure? Do I owe you some money?" He loved it. Everybody's happy. We have, as they say in the business world, a win/win situation. I have three grandchildren. I'm trying to help them and my daughter. I want to make a difference in their lives. My actions and their benefits are clear, uncomplicated, and devoid of politics. Unfortunately, most things are not that simple.

I hate politics, and as an example of politics gone berserk, consider the board for welfare reform that Governor Edgar put me on. I shouldn't call it that. It's properly called the Waukegan Community Federation. We had a board meeting, and all the providers came out the woodwork to try to load up the board. It's a twenty-four-person board with a third of the members from the private sector, a third from public agencies like the schools and police, and a third from provider groups. Well, the providers are so worried about losing their income with all the reform coming that they stacked the board. And there are so many unsavory things that are happening that I should take a tape recorder to the meetings. That's about the only time I feel like carrying one. The whole business of that board kind of eats away at me. We pulled twenty-five women off welfare a while back, and I thought it was going to be real challenging to get their kids good day care and get the women training and a good job in exchange for their welfare checks. I thought I was going to get a lot of heat from their men and their families because they might not want that kind of change, but it seems to be working. The women want their independence. I don't think some of their boyfriends do. We started with twenty-five women, but this is going to go across the board in a couple of years. I'm pushing these reforms because I think they will help to put responsibility, dignity, and hope back into these women's lives, but it's really scary.

I'm the only social deviate on the board. I'm a deviate because I'm truly from the public sector. I've wanted to quit a dozen times but several people have said, "You can't quit. You're the only person holding that thing together." Even though I hate being politically involved, it sometimes seems the only way to make a difference. I hate it. I really hate it, but I have to do it. I unseated some people when they went after the old Andrew Carnegie Library. It is a wonderful, structurally sound building and they were going to tear it down, so I instituted the whole goddamn thing of saving it. When the city officials made their move to tear it down, I organized the wards in town and I hired two people for three months to help me with all the surveying and with getting all the newspaper articles out. I had Ray Bradbury come to town, and he stayed with us a while to make sure it didn't happen. I got the building away from the city. I only paid a dollar for it—that's the beautiful part—and now it's under the auspices of a not-for-profit organization that's dedicated to remodeling it for a children's museum.

When I bought the Globe Department Store in the middle of town, I was going to open a theater and a children's museum in there. But during that same period the politicians threw an uproar because I moved thirty-five artists into the space, and we were having an ongoing display. It was beautiful. The city said they had to buy the building back. My dad had always told me not to fight city hall, so I gave it back to them. They never did pay me for my engineering work. I had had about $12,000 worth of architecture work done, and they promised to pay me for that but they never did carry through. Then I found out they wanted to put city hall there. They had refused to tell me what they wanted to do with it beyond the fact that it was for a very, very important governmental agency.

When they made their presentation to put city hall there, the city council wouldn't even approve it. The mayor only had three votes from the council, so the property sat there for two years. Then the Globe turned into a college, the College of Lake County, which is good in a way, but in a way it isn't. You see, it isn't really a college. It's more like a night school where people get dropped off and picked up. They don't live down here. There are no taxes being paid from all the revenue that is being generated. There are no taxes going to improve society here. But I can't argue against the improvements on the other end. CLC is really helping a lot of first-generation college students who need a boost in getting an education and access to better jobs.

The college isn't directly affecting the education of children in the community, so that's where the art bus comes in. The idea for the bus is from the mid-1980s when the University of Virginia asked me to do a show on a family. I lived for nine months in Hurricane Hollow in Wise, Virginia, way up in the mountains, in coal-mining country. I did a study and a show of about eighteen paintings on the Roscoe family, who were coal miners and bootleggers. In fact, Dep Roscoe, the head male of the family, had been a coal miner for about twelve years when he started his family with Maureena Roscoe. Maureena was more into bootlegging than coal mining, so she got Dep set up out there in the woods with a liquor still. The society was matriarchal, and Maureena wouldn't let Dep back into the house after the children were born. He lived out in the woods for eighteen years with that still, and Maureena sold bottles of whiskey to the sheriff and everybody else. That's how Maureena got all her kids through college. They all became college graduates—an accountant, a lawyer, a doctor, and a writer for a national sports magazine.

Dep began doing drugs at about seventy or seventy-five years of age when a psychiatrist that he went to in Wise got him started. The psychiatrist was a heavy drug peddler. They put Dep in an old-age home, and I got him out. I was willing to take care of him, and I signed the papers and I did take care of him, helped by his son Ralph who wasn't really capable of doing the job. Ralph was emotionally upset all the time. He was gay, and living out in the middle of the woods; when you're gay,being around a lot of coal miners is not good. Ralph needed to go back to New York or somewhere, but he had gotten beat up in the city and had suffered an emotional crisis. He liked me a lot, though, and followed me around, but when he started buying me jewelry, I got worried for a while. He proved to be helpful, though, at getting me from family to family. Without him, I might have gotten shot going on some of those places just trying to say hello.

I did the study of the family and the series of eighteen paintings, and they all went into a mobile that would go from high school to high school as part of a program encouraging kids not to quit school. It was a good program. I used the people and culture of Wise, distilled into the Roscoe family, as the basis for the paintings. For instance, because the people had no transportation, they walked everywhere, and that subject comprises one of my paintings. There was a lot of black lung in that area, and the corner store in Wise, instead of being a 7-11 or a dry cleaners, would be a place to get oxygen. So I brought into the paintings things such as script, walking, oxygen, bootlegging, coal mining, and family life.

It occurred to me that maybe I should start a bus service between three little towns: Wise, Coeburn, and Norton, which are in relatively close proximity to each other. I thought the hospitals should finance the bus because most of those people walking were going to the hospital. Most of the clinics and services were, in one way or another, attached to the hospital, if not actually housed in the hospital buildings. I was able to pull that together and get a little bus going. The traveling art mobile had given me the inspiration. It had a multitude of educational and cultural benefits that were made possible by changes that President Kennedy had instituted. He had built a highway that enhanced access to various towns. He had filled in many of the abandoned mines so they wouldn't fill up with water and pollute the underground water sources. These strides were efforts to make good on his campaign promises. I incorporated that history into my study and added the art bus concept to my ideas for future replication.

When Michael and I came to the Chicago area, I was thinking about starting an art mobile here. Several communities, such as Quincy, Illinois, have asked me to show them how to put the players together financially to start their own art buses. An art bus only costs $15,000 a year, but you do need an administrator, perhaps from the township, to help keep the volunteers organized. And you need an agency like the Park District that does maintenance on its own trucks to volunteer to do the bus maintenance. I would say that if I just stopped painting and did a brochure, I would become instantly rich because there are a thousand communities that could really use these services. Education systems are quick to drop art programs in the schools, and I thought that if I could reach one generation. . . . Waukegan looks as unattractive as it does because we need to bring some art back to it. And the kids who get on that bus, they climb right on. It's good for ages four to twelve. The teenagers need their own place.

I'm thinking about setting up a little store down here where teenagers can sell their artwork, to complete the cycle. They will get on the bus now to help the younger ones to follow directions. If the kids are given an assignment, they listen, they follow it, and they go to work. The only rowdy people generally in the Waukegan area are the parents. They're squabbling outside, and the children are saying, "Shhhhhhhhh!" because art is a kind of quiet thing.

The only really hard case that I have encountered in the bus is Rolling Green. It's a project in North Chicago. The kids are carrying knives and they're really rough and tough, and the parents come outside the bus and say stuff like, "You white honky, what you doing here? What you doing in my neighborhood? How come you threw my kid off the bus?" Well, it's because their kid was trying to stab another kid. I did a lot of finger painting. It's as simple as you can get. Use one little teeny cup of paint on a single still-life subject. I said, "Here's your assignment." Those Rolling Green kids took these big jars of finger paint and dumped them upside down and started throwing them around the bus and I'm by myself. The area really needs help, but these people were out of control. Rolling Green is identical to Cabrini Green where a whole society of people is out of control in a sense, but they're really not because they function very well within their society. There is a lot of rough stuff going on that in our perspective may seem dysfunctional, but they're living and going through life. So, who am I to . . . ? Well, I have a hard time with Rolling Green. My wife really doesn't want me there. She knows I'm going to get killed because I'm throwing kids off the bus.

I turned the whole bus thing over to the township, and I'm working with Christy Wells. Now Christy goes to Rolling Green. She has a photography program, and she has the youth program for the township. Christy lost a volunteer, a graphic artist, because he is taking a night class in typing until mid-November. He couldn't—didn't want to—do Rolling Green. But that's the area that really needs the work. I'm not the person to do it because I'm white, number one, and number two is that I'm not a real teacher; I'm an artist. And I'm too soft-spoken. A man came up and analyzed what I was doing. He lives in the Rolling Green area. He said, "John, you're way too soft-spoken. You have to be much more aggressive. If a kid starts reaching his arm into your supply cabinet, you shut the door on his arm. You don't ask him not to do it." All this interaction would disturb me, and I would go home and be upset for hours and hours. I'm not willing to do that. I'm not so dedicated to that particular niche of our society that I feel a real calling to serve Rolling Green. The calling comes for the Hispanic kids and the black kids and the white kids here in Waukegan who have a certain amount of discipline in their lives and can hear you talk. But I have this lady who serves the white kids on the north side of Waukegan. They're more into crafts. The Hispanic and the black kids are more into the fine arts; they seem more creative. I hate to generalize like that, but it's true.

I'm going to open a store for teenagers because they need a sense of how to run a business. You are never taught in college or high school or anywhere else how to live a life as an artist. Artists have no idea how to do it, and they are always unhappy. They all ultimately fail. There are only maybe a thousand in the country who make a living at art. If the kids had a store, they could show themselves the gestalt of the art experience. I'm hooking up with Hull House to make this happen. Hull House has a 3,000-foot space that they use. There is one area about the size of my shop that they can part with at one o'clock in the afternoons. That would work out perfectly for the kids. They could operate the store from around one-thirty to seven o'clock and go through what a store owner goes through. We could mix things up by bringing in some rough kids as well as some kids from the Honors Program and get them working together on the same objectives. The objectives would include marketing, accounting, and other very simple disciplines that would teach how to survive as an artist. The kids could grapple with real questions: What would I paint to survive? How would I express myself? There is always that fine line between creativity and what people will accept. Are you going to survive if nobody is your patron? They don't really have patrons in this country. They have the Endowment for the Arts, but that's like, "Here's $500 for your show." How far will $500 go?

Other factors complicate the painting life. A case in point is a painting of a little Waukegan house that I made a little prettier and offered to ReMax as a way of helping the homeless. I called it *American Dream Home*. All the realtors of ReMax had to use it for a closing gift. In my opinion, realtors help to create homelessness because for every house that they sell, they jack up the price by at least 6 percent in commission, plus whatever greed is involved. So they create homelessness by putting houses out of reach of so many people. I remember just a few years ago I could buy a very nice house for $17,900, and now that house would cost $179,000. So I feel that realtors play a part in the derailment of the American dream, hence the title of the painting. And that one little print raised $300,000 in two years for the homeless. It all went to the homeless.

We serve the homeless and others through the Cares Foundation. Whenever one of these agencies around here needs $5,000, the Cares Foundation gives them the money. We give money to whomever we can, like a women's shelter called A Safe Place, a food pantry, and various other agencies. During the couple of years that I was selling prints of *American Dream Home*, I went to a mortgage company that wanted ReMax's business, played them against each other, and sold to both of them. Northwest Mortgage Company sold thousands and thousands and thousands of those prints. I had homeless people frame the prints. That fit my job description. The job was nice and simple. We used a frame that was basically done already. All the framers had to do was drop the picture in, put it in a package, and gift wrap the package. If you just go outside the door here, the homeless are walking up and down the street. They are easy to find for a project like this. And as workers, they are not just recipients of goods, not just "the problem"; they are also part of what is supposed to be a solution.

The problem with helping the homeless and others in need is that all the courthouses and all the social workers are trying to protect their own interests. They will create any kind of program to maintain homelessness and other miseries to keep their jobs. They're just lying in wait like tigers and lions right outside the courthouse doors. All their agencies are lined up and down the street in the middle of a town. There should be a little downtown where you can enjoy the courtship of life, but the social agencies are feeding off these problems that the judges let out of the room. And then the problems get paraded up and down the street. No matter what you do to alleviate misery, there are a lot of things maybe you shouldn't do. For instance, at ReMax I stopped the *American Dream Home* venture because they used it for every rag, it seemed, in the country. They publicized, "ReMax is supporting the homeless, *da, da, do,* via this print." And they'd show pictures of it and pictures of me with their owners. They got at least 15 million dollars worth of free publicity out of that print, and I got only $300,000 for the homeless. So maybe I created more homelessness by helping to line the pockets of realtors, by helping to push the price of a house just a little further out of someone's reach. So I decided that I don't want to do this win/win corporate thing. These people don't make me feel good.

I have a painting here of members of the old Negro Baseball League. The League dissolved in the 1950s. One of the guys died just recently, a few weeks ago. Prior to his dying, all of them came to my shop and signed these prints, all 750 of them. I have been working on this project with two Chicago Bears players, Wendell Davis and Thomas Sanders, here in Waukegan. They have a little business, All Stars Sports, in Palatine. They market the prints of the Old Negro League on the Internet, and the proceeds go to retarded children. They paid me $10,000 for the painting, and it cost me about $5,000 because I had to bring the Negro League players to town and keep them over at the Holiday Inn. So that was expensive, but the project is a good one. It is kind of a pure concept of win/win. You just do something and it helps somebody. These Negro League players never got any social security. They are all kind of down and out. Now they're getting 60 percent of the money from the prints. Sixty percent is a good amount. With the United Way, the money to recipients is only about twenty cents on the dollar. The Negro League project is doing a lot better than that and is a good thing for the players and for retarded children.

Another good thing is the youth center that we put together on Belvidere. It is a really nice place and a wonderful service to the community. I put the bus together at the youth center with help from volunteers. We tore the seats out, built cabinets in the bus, installed a sink, and generally completed our transformation. The youth center includes gang outreach in its list of activities, and during the summer, I had one afternoon a week with just the gangs. They were great. They were like angels compared to that Rolling Green bunch. They loved our work, especially the graffiti part. I have these large boxes of chalk, and we'd go out and decorate the sidewalks with chalk. The basis of our relationship was, "What's better than graffiti?" The answer was, "Here it is." I'd like to provide the kids from gang outreach with a store. If I could only stay away from politics and keep my head low. . . but that's just about impossible to do.

There is so much to do that I would love to do. I found this little town, Wayland, Missouri, that's all boarded up. Nobody lives there. It's near the Mississippi River but off the flood plain. Five hundred people live around the town. And still it's all boarded up. It's one of the lowest income towns in the entire United States, and the people there have this attitude that they can't do anything. So I bought the whole goddamn town and credited it to a not-for-profit group. I gave them $50,000 worth of tiger prints with which to raise some start-up funds. So now they have this big committee between here and

Hannibal and St. Louis where they are selling the prints. Columbia University Missouri has a tiger mascot, and the prints are selling like crazy at their football games. Seventeen Amish families live around Wayland. They're standoffish, but they will ride in a car if transportation is arranged for them and they will take a job when their farm duties do not interfere. The committee is paying these Amish people to restore the town, and they are going to need some ongoing financial support. So that's what this next show that I'm doing in St. Louis is about. This whole deal is rife with politics in a way, but so far it's the colorful but fun kind, and the local history is interesting. You see, Mary, who is heading up the construction crew, is working with Everett, the husband of the Mayor Sue Hill, who wants to tear the town down. And Lucretia Craw heads the not-for-profit group. Her great grandfather befriended the Indians of the area and started the community of Wayland during Marquette's time. For many who are involved, the restoration of Wayland will be a labor of love.

Picasso kept saying—and during his last twenty years he probably made so many mistakes he had to say it—that love is the bottom line in the universe. I try to keep sight of that. I know that for everything you do, there's always a shitty part of it. There's always an equal amount of light and dark. Maybe a little bit more dark. Maybe a little bit more negative than positive. But I have to try to keep a positive balance. If I clap my hands, I want the sound that goes out to be a positive rather than a negative sound because I believe that it travels forever through the universe. That's where the love is, then. It's in our actions and in our intentions. And I think that Picasso was right. I think that loving is the most important thing that we can do. Loving fits my job description, it just feels right for me, and I intend to stay with it all of my life.

3 | Building a Rock Foundation

I fell gravely ill when I was a little over a year old. From an energetic toddler, I became listless, refused food, and cried often. The doctor recommended a diet of saltines and Coca-Cola, which proved ineffective, and my parents grew certain that I was dying. Then the doctor decided that I needed an immediate operation and sent me to the hospital. My mother has told me many times how my father argued with Dr. Brand. The doctor became angry, asked my father if he thought he was the doctor and if he wanted to see me die. My father believed that I was suffering from stomach parasites, detectable by movements of my abdominal muscles. The doctor grudgingly agreed to delay operating until six o'clock the next morning, with the stipulation that if there were no greater signs of parasites than what my parents claimed to have seen, he was going to cut me open and look for a way to save my life.

As if fortifying her spirit by denying her body, my mother had not eaten all day. She and my father dozed off and on in hospital chairs that night between bouts of praying for my safety. If God could deliver Daniel, if Christ could command Lazarus to get up and walk, if the Holy Spirit could move upon the face of the waters and bring order out of chaos, surely I could live to hear the story of my deliverance. At six o'clock the next morning, when Dr. Brand strode into my hospital room and began examining me, from my rectum I excreted cluster upon cluster of glistening white worms.

During my youth, I went to the doctor a lot but never to Dr. Brand, whom my parents deeply distrusted. If I complained at all about not feeling well, my parents would cart me off to the doctor. One spring day when I was going on three, I mentioned to my mother that my stomach hurt, whereupon she cleaned me up to send me with my father to the doctor in Windsor, about fifteen miles away. There was a combination dry cleaner, gas station, and general store about two miles from our house where my father stopped to buy gas. I waited in the car while he went inside to pay.

"Daddy, can I have some of that on that sign?" I asked as soon as he was back in the car.

"What sign?"

"That one," I replied, pointing.

"What does that sign say?" he asked.

"Mayola Ice Cream."

"How do you know what it says?" he asked a little incredulously.

"Because I read it," I responded, a little incredulous myself at his obtuseness.

"So what does that say? . . . And that? . . . And that?" He tested me on most of the print visible from our car window.

"Well, I declare!" my father exclaimed over and over. "You can read!" He jumped out of the car and hurried inside the store to buy my ice cream.

I opened my cup and dug in with my little wooden spoon. My father had not started the car. He just sat there, watching me, grinning from ear to ear, and repeating, "I can't believe you can read!

"How do you feel?" he asked finally.

"Fine."

"You want to go to the doctor?"

"Naw," I said.

We sped back home. My father got me out of the car and then left me as he strode to the house, all the while calling to my mother. "Nettie! Nettie! This baby can read!"

I could not tell my parents how I learned to read, but I was absolutely certain of the moment when I knew what reading is. I was in our kitchen perched on a stool between my mother's knees as she sat braiding my hair. It was a lovely day, and our kitchen door was open, so I could see part of the little brick patio outside, the steps leading up to the hallway that split our house in half, some spring flowers that my mother had planted, and a few light blue, yellow, and white butterflies. My mother wanted me to hold my head perfectly still, so I could only look at whatever appeared within my fixed line of sight. In a corner of the kitchen, just before the door to the outside patio was a wooden box that my father used to cart groceries. "Morton Salt." Silently I read the words printed on the side of the box. "When it rains, it pours." I looked for other words and saw that I could read them, too. "Oh, that's what reading is!"

I thought. I knew about reading because my mother was always reading stories to us like "The Frogs Know a Secret," "The Three Billy Goats Gruff," and "The Three Sillies." I did not mention my discovery since I assumed that everyone could read. I knew for a fact that my older sister could. Her teacher would let her bring wonderfully illustrated storybooks home from school for a few days, and while she would go off to school, I would thumb through them. When she was home, she wouldn't let me handle her books. "You might tear them because you're little," she would say. It hurt my feelings that she thought I wouldn't be careful with something I loved as much as I loved her books.

When I was in first grade, I got into an argument at school with my cousin Dorah, one of my father's nieces. "Your ole mama ain't got no education!" Dorah taunted with all the righteousness of a seven-year-old mouth spouting grown-ups' familiar words.

"I'm smart enough for both of us," I shot back immodestly. That silenced Dorah since she believed me, knowing as she did that I had been reading forever and had already read through the first-grade primer. Dorah also knew, as did everyone else, that I was "born for good luck" since I was a girl and looked just like my father. Being smart was part of my good luck package. Unfortunately, I was not smart enough to know that Dorah's statement might hurt my mother, and I related the event in detail when I got home from school that day.

"It's true your mother doesn't have any education," my mother said reasonably, "and that's why all you children have to go to school and study hard so you can be educated."

That we would go to school and study hard was without question. We walked very far to get to school, and because we were the only black family living off our main road, the county turned down my father's request that a school bus pick us up. I can remember standing in the ditch to avoid the rocks that white children would throw at us as their bus roared by in a cloud of dust. When I was in second grade, we moved to a new house within close walking distance of our school. A rule in our home was that we completed our homework before we began our chores; and years later, after we acquired a television, no one was permitted to watch it unless everyone else's schoolwork was done. Our education was clearly our parents' top priority, so it is no wonder that it became ours, too. I recall that when my older sister, who studied very hard but had some difficulty academically, had to repeat college courses during a couple of summer sessions, my mother told her, "You just do your best, and as long as we can work, you can go back."

From first through eighth grades, every day I walked to the same school that my parents had attended before me. It was painted white, and a long porch stretched across its entire width leading to two classrooms at the front of the building and one at the back. When I was in fourth grade, a fourth room and a new teacher were added, making it possible for each classroom to house only two grades at a time. We had an outdoor pump for drinking water and two outdoor toilets—one for boys and one for girls—but often no toilet paper. We had a large, sandy front yard where we held relay races and played other games. In 1954 when I was nine years old, I heard about the Supreme Court decision to end segregation in *Brown v. Board of Education,* and I decided that for fifth grade I would go to the white school. My parents' explanation as to why I could not do so was that Washington, D.C., the federal government, and the United States Supreme Court were a long way from Merry Hill, North Carolina, where I lived.

My decision to enroll at the white school in no way related to wanting to go to school with white students or wanting to be taught by white teachers. My decision had a simple, practical basis: I knew that the physical conditions at the white people's school were better than anything I had ever seen. But I would be in high school, bused almost thirty miles round-trip each day to the county's high school for blacks, before I would experience indoor plumbing or hot lunches at school. In spite of this, my pre-college schooling provided me with many important advantages.

Most adult members of the black community, whether they had children or not, were at least peripherally involved in my education up through eighth grade. Everyone came to our Christmas, Easter, and end-of-the-school-year programs. Church and school comprised the dual center of our community, so children were consistently encouraged on two fronts outside the home. If the county made any concessions to us and our school, they were the result of lobbying by a small group of our fathers. However feeble its flame, this was our brightest example of democracy at work.

Another benefit of my pre-college schooling was that I never felt unwanted at school; my skin color never got in the way. I was always expected to be a high achiever, and I knew that my teachers and principals had my best interests at heart. In high school, my peers and I were earnestly prepared for college to the best of the school's ability; and three of the other ninety-three students who graduated with me also earned verbal or composite SAT scores of about 700, though most of us, despite having studied biology, had never seen an actual microscope.

From high school, some of us going on to college would arrive as first-generation college students—beneficiaries of, among others, high school teachers who had helped us with every aspect of the college application process from choosing where to apply to filling out the financial aid forms. My typing

teacher had not been wildly successful in teaching me to appreciate or perform the act of typing, but he earned an A+ in helping me get into college
with a four-year academic scholarship and a student loan. In college I came
not only to reappraise my view of typing as a necessary skill but also to rue the
poverty which kept me from owning even a secondhand typewriter until after
I had earned my bachelor's degree.

Chapter 3
Family, School, Community:
Vehicles to Realized Potential

Using many of my own family, school, and community experiences as a bridge to understanding the participants in this study, I considered the manner of individual from a low SES background who becomes the first in his or her family to attend college, to earn a college degree, and to choose social or educational activism as an avocation. I began to examine the participants' self-concepts at various crucial points in their lives, with particular attention given to those forces that helped to shape their emerging identities. I searched for clues in their early familial and environmental experiences in an effort to understand the foundations supporting their later academic, social, and economic successes. In a similar vein, I examined their family and life experiences in order to illuminate those processes by which they attained their particular senses of self, their drive to succeed, and their knowledge of how to make success possible. In a very real way, my quest has been to understand a complex question: Who are these people whose stories form the basis of this study?

Instinctively I understood that the question's potential to appear presumptuous and intimidating to the participants could very well equal its complexity and importance to the study. As a good-faith measure, I declared my identity as a first-generation college graduate and shared with the participants relevant parts of my experience at appropriate points in the interview process. This practice seemed to lessen the emotional distance between me and individual participants even as it provided me with an empathetic framework from which to approach the study.

The interviews I conducted are replete with many of the findings already reported in the literature, yet they offer rich insights and understandings that help to build upon what we already know about first-generation college students. For instance, I was surprised to find that almost three-fourths of the participants in the study indicated that they were singled out in some way or made to feel special when they were quite young. Eight years is the oldest age reported by any of these participants at the onset of their "special status," and only one participant reported being as old as eight at the onset. Clearly distinguishable from the family-external "teacher's pet" syndrome, special-status children appear to enjoy an enhanced position within the confines of the family, or in comparison to other family members. Because so many of the participants included some discussion of themselves as special-status children in their life histories, I wondered whether such status plays a role in the likelihood that a child will be able to achieve the remarkable—that is, to become the first in the family to go to college. This question is explored in the first section of this chapter.

In the second section of the chapter, I deal with another surprise finding: the impact on academic success of a phenomenon that I refer to as "positive naming." Two-thirds of the people that I interviewed discussed individuals in their lives who gave them an affirming label or identifier based on a genuine assessment of the interviewee's personal qualities. According to the participants, the effects of positive naming on their lives were pivotal in helping them to improve their self-images, set high goals for themselves, believe in their capability to achieve those goals, and develop and pursue strategies toward their realization. Since the participants' accounts of the roles that others' high expectations played in their academic successes do not differ markedly from past findings, the brief discussion of expectations in this chapter serves primarily as a means of accentuating its distinctiveness from positive naming.

In addition to more discrete factors such as special status, positive naming, and others' expectations, consideration of the spectrum of variables that affected the matriculation and success at college of the first-generation students in this study reveals various findings related to home and school. For instance, only three had parents who completed high school, and many had at least one parent who was functionally illiterate. A related finding showed that only the two youngest participants had believed all their lives that they could go to college.

While this data suggests a considerable amount about the low degree of assurance with which first-generation college students may think about attending college, the interviewees in this study repeatedly emphasized that the degree of parental respect for or interest in education, reading, or knowledge played a far more important role in whether they actually earned a college degree. Sixteen of the interviewees indicated that at least one of their parents (or grandparents) had a strong interest in or respect for knowledge, education, or reading, whether they were literate or not. Not surprisingly, a great majority of the participants revealed that they themselves have been avid readers since childhood. Expanding upon the data in the chapter's third section, I examine the significance of parental attitudes toward education, reading, or knowledge on the academic success of their children.

The fourth section of the chapter addresses the influence of home, school, and community on the academic success of the participants. A key point made repeatedly by the interviewees in this study is that in an ideal world, student success depends on the student *and* on the institutions of home, school, and community. However, the reality of the participants' remembered experiences shows that a positive integration of all these components was rare, almost nonexistent, in their lives. In fact, the participants' stories depict systems of counterproductivity with one or more units recurrently sabotaging the collective goal. Put differently, while the institutions of home, school, and community were committed in theory to working to the advantage of students, at any given point in the school experiences of these first-generation college graduates, one or more of those elements was working, often intentionally, against them.

Finally, in the last section of this chapter I discuss what I refer to as "ascending cross-class identification," a factor of major importance in the success of first-generation college students both prior to and during college. As a strategy employed by the interviewees in adjusting their self-concepts, ascending cross-class identification provides the information needed (1) to recognize aspects of a desired experience or identity and (2) to determine, as well as acquire, the means to their attainment. To perhaps a greater degree than any of the prior sections, the discussion on ascending cross-class identification shows the participants in roles of agency on their own behalf.

In short, in this chapter I examine how the participants came to perceive themselves within the contexts of their families, schools, and larger communities. I identify and define a number of factors that are generally missing from the literature but may have figured prominently in the formation of the participants' self-concepts and served as important vehicles in earning their college degrees. Additionally, I locate probable sources of these vehicles in the participants' experiences and discuss their short- and long-range effects on the participants' lives.

Special Status

> I'm the "genius" in my extended family. When I went to Van Gorder, I
> supposedly went to a "special" school and blah, blah, blah, and yak, yak,
> yak. On my mother's side, I'm the oldest kid and I was the boss; you
> couldn't mess with me. I was the first grandchild *and* male.
>
> *— Jorge*

Throughout this study, interviewees repeatedly identified special status as a
factor of considerable importance in their academic success. Many discussed
forces in their early lives that made them believe they were special through
means independent of their own deliberate actions. Like knighthood, special
status was either bestowed upon or made known to them—with all the rights
and privileges pertaining thereto—by an adult, one possessing the required
rank or stature. While neither knighthood nor special status is owed, unlike
knighthood, special status is not earned. It is akin to love, freely given with no
apparent strings attached. The reasons for its bestowal may vary. The eldest
child or the first male born into a family in some cultures may be awarded
special status. A sickly child may be given special status by parents anxious
about his mortality. A child with unusual natural gifts may receive special status from those who admire her talents. And others, like many of this study's
participants, are simply chosen for reasons that they never knew or questioned.

Special-status children accept the fact that they have been singled out, and
they identify with being special. In Annie's case, this identification was, in part,
the result of fortuitous circumstance, her birth order within her family. Consider, for example, the following quotation from Annie's discussion of her
early family life: "They had fifteen children, eleven of whom are living. Two
died before I was born, and my mother miscarried two. I'm the seventh birth,
and I'm the fifth living. I have always heard that there is something special
about the seventh child. I don't know what it is, but I happen to be that seventh child."

From Annie's earliest years, she was reminded that she was special because
she was the seventh child born to her parents. Just as a baby's entering the
world with the caul on its head is deemed a powerful sign in the lore of many
cultures, being the seventh child born to a woman is considered auspicious
among many African Americans. What effect could such beliefs ,which are, in
fact, superstitions, have upon a person's life?

Caine and Caine (1997) point out that each of us employs deeply entrenched
pictures, beliefs, and assumptions that help us to make sense of the world.
They refer to these views as "mental models" or theories that we actually use

in order to "organize experiences, information, and strategies" and to "shape day-to-day decisions and interactions" (p. 21). If Caine and Caine are correct, and I believe that they are, then Annie's knowledge of her special status as a result of her birth order could very likely have affected her expectations of herself and of the world around her. As a special-status child, and having accepted the definition that marked her as different from the status quo, Annie may have been more attuned and receptive to the possibility of improvement in her life than were the other children in her family, none of whom were the seventh born. Since the conditions of Annie's distinction were duly noted and passed on to her generation in the acculturation process, clearly the adults in her environment held somewhat similar mental models to her own. Recognizing that Annie was special, their interactions with and regarding her may have reflected, even unconsciously, their belief that more, rather than the same, was her due.

This view is supported by examples from the interviews of advantages resulting from the participants' special status. For instance, in explaining why she was the child in her family who happened to visit the home of a little white girl who had lots of books and knew how to read, Annie described an important benefit of the special status afforded her by an aunt. The aunt's treatment of Annie may reflect her deeply ingrained belief that the seventh born is due special status:

> I had something more than my siblings had, too, because I had an aunt who really loved me. I would go home with her periodically, and she would take me places. She worked for a white family, and sometimes she would take me to work with her. I remember one day she took me to work and I met the little white girl who lived there, and this girl could read. She had these books and she was reading. I thought, "Oh, I would like to be able to read like that," but I didn't have any books. I used to tell my aunt how I would really like to have some books, and she would say, "Well, maybe one day you will get some." I couldn't understand how this little girl could have so many books and we didn't have any.

From Annie's example, as well as from the examples of others in the study, it appears that their special status as children opened doors for them that were not available to other children in the family. However limited the resources Annie's aunt could provide, she was able to expose Annie to another world: the world of the white child, where books were plentiful, and reading—a skill at which even the grown-ups in Annie's family were not adept—was easily mastered.

Steve, an artist and college art instructor, was another participant who indicated that he had been accorded special status as a child. He recalled the haven, both physical and emotional, made available to him as a young boy by his grandfather and his great aunts. By providing not only an escape hatch from an abusive family, but also an environment conducive to creative development, Steve's grandfather, especially, may have influenced his resilience and his emerging interest in art:

> I come from a very dysfunctional family, but my grandfather was very nice and docile. Every morning I would run downstairs to see him. He lived in our basement, and in his place was all this wood that he would collect from garbage that people threw out. I can remember at two and three years old being down there with a hammer, making stuff out of that wood. I think my grandfather was really smart because he would read all the time, and as I got a little older, he would talk about commodities and their futures. He would always say, "Watch what's going to happen here!" He was very nice to me and let me freely involve myself in creative play.
>
> I also had some very old great aunts who took me under their wings. I was the only male child at that time, and my two sisters were older. My great aunts and my grandfather thought I was the neatest thing. Then they all died, almost all at once, between the time that I was five and seven years old. That was really traumatic for me. It was terrible. But I think I had already gotten the idea that people could be accepting of you no matter how you were or who you were. I think I knew that was possible from my old great aunts and my grandfather. They liked me no matter what. That meant a lot to me.
>
> We moved from Chicago when I was seven, and in order to get away from what was going on in the family, both my sisters and I would go off by ourselves. I don't even remember my sisters until they were much older because they would retreat. I would either run away and read, or I would run away and paint. I played by myself the whole time I was growing up, and I feel that when I paint, I am doing exactly the same thing. I like people a lot but I paint by myself, and I also like the time when I am completely by myself. Both my sisters got pregnant and got married to get out of there. I would run away and draw or paint, just as I had done when I was little and I could escape to my grandfather.

As the first male grandchild in his family, Steve enjoyed a special status that was not available to his two sisters. With a grandfather and two great aunts who doted on him, he experienced unconditional approval that may have mitigated, to some degree, the horrendous effects of parental abuse. His artistic experiments as a young child with his grandfather's recycled wood are currently reflected in the art projects that he creates and the curricula that he designs using environmentally friendly and recycled materials. Steve's grandfather allowed him free reign in his artistic play, but sometimes he demonstrated his connection to and awareness of Steve by engaging him in conversations that communicated respect for Steve's ability to think. By the time Steve was seven years old and his great aunts and grandfather were dead, it appears that their loving intervention in his life had already affected his sense of self. He had been told, and he had believed, that he was loved and a special person. In addition, he had learned in his grandfather's basement apartment to value the solitude of artistic endeavor, a way of life that helped to sustain him throughout college and his adult life. His sisters, being girls, had found no comparable sanctuary, and running away to read presaged their running away, as pregnant teens, to get married.

Though Steve and his sisters were subjected to the same physical and emotional abuse, the enhanced quality of life that Steve experienced during his early formative years may have given him an educational advantage over his sisters. In addition to developing a love for what would become his chosen field and way of life, he knew for a fact that he *mattered* to someone. Almost everyone interviewed for this study related personal stories similar to Annie's and Steve's. Each emphasized that they had been more inclined to learn because somebody cared; that special status as young children helped to sustain them during later periods. Because they knew they were highly valued by someone, they had the confidence to overcome barriers to their goals. These participants seem to have accepted, as young children, that they were indeed special, knowledge that may have helped them to thrive.

Positive Naming

> I would look at my children and, based on their strong assets, I would name professions for them. In that way, I could highlight their gifts and give them something to work toward.
>
> — *Annie*

Closely aligned with being singled out as special is positive naming, which two-thirds of the participants discussed as significant forces in their lives. Interviewees who indicated that they were influenced by positive naming described a situation in which someone who cared about them or knew them well helped them to discover their potential. Positive naming is different from stating one's expectations of someone since implicit in an expectation is the charge or responsibility to carry out an action. An expectation is bound in the presumption of duty. Positive naming, on the other hand, seems prophetic in nature and carries no assumption by any parties involved that the one who has been positively named is being told what he must do. Rather, it is an affirming statement of condition generally based upon honest observation and assessment of the subject. It provides direction that is devoid not only of obligation that the direction be followed, but also of guilt if it is not.

Many of the study's participants attested to the significance of positive naming in their lives. For instance, Maria, a graduate of DePaul University, stated:

> I knew all the time that I was going to college and to DePaul. I always wanted to be an attorney even when I was a little kid because my dad always told me, "You constantly argue things. That's all you know how to do. You might as well make money at it by being an attorney." I used to argue the other point even if I didn't believe in it just for the sake of the argument. So I wanted to be an attorney.

As this example demonstrates, parents and others may direct children toward academic success simply by assessing their obvious strengths, aligning those strengths with a profession, and sharing their conclusions with the respective individuals. Maria's father clearly believed that his daughter possessed the critical thinking skills and the powers of persuasion necessary to becoming an attorney. By recognizing Maria's argumentativeness as a positive quality, he propelled her toward academic excellence while affirming her worthiness and her right to be exactly as she was.

Fred, a Baptist minister and college professor who overcame enormous educational setbacks before achieving academic success, also recalled several instances of being positively named, though not always in a specific way:

> When I was a little boy, everybody thought I was going to be a preacher, and . . . I used to stand on a crate and preach to everybody about drinking Dad's Old-Fashioned Root Beer.
> . . . My mother finally left the Penecostal church to join my father at the Baptist church. This was a much more education-conscious environment. . . . and they said, "Fred's going to be somebody one of these days!"
> . . . Mr. and Mrs. Brown were letting me stay at their house, and they

were feeding me often. They had a positive sense that there was something special in me. They never questioned that sense. In fact, they thought I was brilliant. I was fighting as hard as I could to make their dreams for me come true.

In their pronouncement that Fred was going to be a preacher, adults in his environment provided the young boy with a lofty professional objective. Certainly a preacher—especially an educated one—in the black community sixty years ago was at or near the apex of the society. The prediction in Fred's community that he would be a preacher coincided with the prediction among the educated folk of his father's church that he was going to be "somebody." Because Fred wanted so desperately to become somebody by becoming educated but had such difficulty achieving success at school, positive naming— along with the special status provided him by his landlords, the Browns—may have been the constant in his life that deterred him from academic capitulation. His discussion of the Browns illuminates the power that they gave him to persist in trying to succeed. Since they never doubted his ability or his impending scholastic triumphs, he was compelled and enabled to continue striving as a college student. As long as they believed in him and supported him, he believed that his own strength and determination would not fail. Fred recalled that not only did the Browns articulate that he was going to be somebody, their contributions toward that goal also took another form:

> They were both really good to me, and Mrs. Brown was downright inspiring. She would tell me sometimes, "You're going to be something one of these days." I owe her today for rent that I couldn't pay. She could have put me out many times. Many times Mrs. Brown knew that I was upstairs in my room with nothing to eat. She'd go out and catch some fresh catfish. And she'd say, "Fred, come on down here!" And I'd say, "Mrs. Brown, I'm not hungry, thank you." And she'd say, "You know you're hungry, boy! You'd better come on down here and eat these catfish!"

Although various factors emerged from the interviewees' stories as significant contributors to their academic success as first-generation students, nowhere in the cases was the power of a professor to change the life of a student more simply and dramatically demonstrated than through positive naming. It seemed to turn the force of negativity on its head and to create a new reality for the student. Many participants mentioned the key role that professors played in identifying, communicating, and affirming their nascent strengths and abilities. For example, Clara recounted the dramatic impact one of her college professors had on her life in this way:

> One of my teachers at Southern whom I got along really, really well with took a real liking to me. She told me, "You would be a great teacher." I had told her about my being an R.A. (resident assistant) and working my way through school and taking out loans, etc., and she told me that she wanted me to take her Foreign Language Methods of Teaching class. She explained that if I had that class, I could apply to be a T.A. (teaching assistant). I took the class. I applied for a T.A. and got it. With my teaching assistantship, I would be paid money every month in addition to having all my tuition paid. I went on to graduate school because of my teacher who told me that I would be a great teacher. . . . It wasn't until then, when I was teaching, that I felt confident in my Spanish, that I felt that I knew what I was doing. For the first time, I thought, "I am smart." I was in graduate school and I saw a lot of people who weren't in my position. Before, I would have thought they were better than I. But now I told myself, "I'm the one who is here in this position. They didn't get this position; I did!" I began becoming confident in myself. I began taking on the responsibility of the honor society that my teacher had started. I became the president of the National Honor Society for the Spanish classes. And for the very first time in my life, and this was in my first semester of graduate school, I got a 4.0 grade point average.

Along with special status and positive naming, participants indicated that the expectations of others—a characteristic discussed in the literature on first-generation students—also influenced them powerfully when they were young. The following two examples illustrate the difference between expectations and positive naming. The first is provided by Lorraine:

> I remember Mother's telling me that she wanted me to become a trained nurse like Miss Catherine. . . . I was around five at the time, so I grew up with that. And Miss Catherine would tell me, "You have to finish school, Lorraine, and you have to go to nursing school." I was all for it, and I was top of my class all the way up, even in college.

Lorraine's example illustrates a role that parents sometimes play in setting high expectations for their children. Lorraine's mother selected a role model for her five-year-old daughter. With the aid of the role model, she encouraged

Lorraine to accept her mother's aspiration as her own. In a case of positive naming, Lorraine's demonstrated characteristics would have been the major factor in her mother's selection of a profession to recommend to her daughter.

The less-personalized high expectations that Lorraine's mother held for her daughter may have been effective even beyond their influence on Lorraine's persistence and success in school. Though she became a teacher and a businessperson rather than a nurse, Lorraine remained interested in the health care field and spent a number of years in the employ of a physician.

Maria likewise described how her father's expectations influenced her:

> My dad had very high expectations. I can remember when I was in first grade and I brought home a C. He was extremely disappointed. He was like, "What is this? You could have done better! This is a C! I don't want to see one of these ever again!" I got the C in PE (physical education). It didn't matter to him that it was only gym. I still remember that. My dad was so mad! I decided I would never bring home a C again.

This example of high expectations differs from positive naming in two important ways. First, it does not name and, second, it conveys an explicit responsibility to carry out an action. An effective motivator for Maria, it demonstrates the intention to deter development of poor attitudes toward any aspect of the school curriculum. From the perspective of Maria's father, if a course was part of the curriculum, then it was worth doing well. Maria integrated her father's high expectations of her and went on to earn many scholastic honors.

However subtle their differences, special status, positive naming, and others' expectations emerged as important factors that may have enhanced the educational opportunities of many of the participants in this study. Also, it appeared that the attitudes toward learning portrayed by significant adults in the interviewees' early lives were central to laying the foundations for their academic successes. It is to this topic that I now turn.

Parental Attitudes Toward Knowledge

> In my family, there was a desire for learning. My mother had never been to school. My father finished fifth grade. My family did not have the understanding that they were going to do whatever they could to make

sure their children got to college. My parents' idea was, "Do whatever you can. If you can't do it, we can't do anything. If you fail the entrance exam, come back home and farm."

— Chang

In *Beating the Odds: How the Poor Get to College*, Levine and Nidiffer (1996) found that a heterogeneous group of college students reported an almost unvarying story of how they decided to attend college: a mentor influenced them to do so. While the same was true for many of this study's participants, they identified an additional component of their educational conditioning that I refer to as "pre-mentoring." They defined pre-mentors as individuals from their early lives who originally inspired them to value reading, knowledge, or education. With only one exception, the study's participants reported that they were influenced early in life, impressionistically, and deeply by the parents or grandparents whom they most admired and who held knowledge, education, reading, or combinations of the three in great esteem. Similar to findings by Gandara (1995), this is a salient point since it speaks to the power of adults, whether literate or not, to influence the development of their children's and grandchildren's appreciation of learning and, consequently, their chances for earning a college degree. The following discussion shows how the parents and grandparents, regardless of the facility with which they could read and write, may have predisposed the participants toward valuing knowledge, education, or reading by valuing these things themselves.

Certainly the parents and grandparents of the participants proved to be excellent pre-mentors despite the fact that most had attained educational levels of fewer than eight years. In fact, both parents of only three of the interviewees had earned a high school diploma, and only seven of the interviewees had at least one parent who had attended high school at all. Eleven of the participants had at least one parent with an educational level below eighth grade, and at least five had fathers with only a third-grade education. Not surprisingly, only three of the participants had aspired all their lives to go to college, while two of the three had never doubted that they would go. They are two of the youngest in the study, and in each case, both of their parents had earned high school diplomas (See Table 2).

As children, most of these first-generation graduates had not contemplated the possibility of attending college with any degree of confidence, if they had contemplated it at all. Since their parents generally had low levels of education, their stories reveal a strong connection between a parent's educational accomplishments and a child's confidence that he or she will attend college. It appears to be a false assumption, however, that parents with little or no formal education are not the initial, primary forces to impart to their children an abiding respect for knowledge. The interviews that I conducted show overwhelmingly that parents and grandparents of the participants, often in spite of their own illiteracy, were the children's first role models for valuing education, reading, or knowledge. In fact, the interviewees repeatedly emphasized that this parental respect played a vastly important role in whether they would earn a college degree.

One example is provided by Alex, who explained that although his father was not able to help him with his homework, he "had an incredible reverence for education":

Every morning when I was growing up, if my dad was home, he would . . . buy . . . a newspaper. He always bought the *Daily News*, which had pictures, rather than the *New York Times*, which generally did not. Then he would come upstairs and look through the newspaper. . . . I did not know that my dad could not read until I was older, and I thought it was wonderful that he had modeled reading by buying the paper and looking at it. As I got older, he would sometimes ask me questions about the pictures and what they meant. . . . He was very curious about what was happening in the world. . . .

Table 2

Participant	Educational Level of Father	Educational Level of Mother	Parental Support for College	Lifelong Certainty of College Attendance
1	12	3	No	No
2	3	5	Yes	No
3	8	3	Yes	No
4	3	8	Yes	No
5	3	8	Yes	No
6	3	6	Yes	No
7	5	0	No	No
8	?	6	No	No
9	8	10	No	No
10	12	12	No	No
11	8	8	No	No
12	10	5	No	No
13	GED	12	No	No
14	?	?	No	No
15	3	8	No	No
16	12	12	Yes	Yes
17	12	12	Yes	Yes

In explaining his father's illiteracy, Alex went on to say:

His own father had been a terrible person who abandoned my grandmother and their young son in San Juan. My grandmother was destitute, so she went home to her brothers on the family farm. She was received as a servant, and my father was not allowed to go to school after he reached third grade. He never talked much about his early childhood, but he did tell me that his uncles worked him almost like an animal. When he was twelve years old, he ran away. . . .

My father wanted us to go through high school so that we could do better than he had, but no one in my family ever talked about college.

While Alex's father was not a mentor—in the sense of the term used by Levine and Nidiffer (1996)—who encouraged him to go to college, his father played an instrumental role in preparing Alex to seize educational opportunity by valuing reading as a window to knowing. The many contributions of Alex's actual mentors, the cultural opportunities made available to him through the New York City Public Schools, and the college counseling provided by his parish were powerful and direct forces in his decision to go to college. But Alex's inclination to be open to educational mentoring undoubtedly flowed from the value that he placed upon education prior to his mentors' influence, a value learned from his unlettered dad.

Another study participant, Dorothy, told a similar story when she described how her earliest educational inspiration came from her mother:

I remember when I was a little girl my mother always encouraged me and would give me pens and pencils and I would draw something. She would say, "Oh, look at you writing! You're going to be a writer some day." She'd say things like that, and that really helped me focus on reading and writing when I was in school, because even when I was just drawing lines, she thought I had potential.

My mom and dad are my grandparents who raised me as their own daughter. They'd been brought up on a farm and had no education beyond sixth grade for my mom and third grade for my dad, so they could read and write some, but they knew how to do other things. Most of my inspiration for going to school and focusing on intellectual pursuits came from my mom. She enjoyed reading, and when I got old enough, I would get her big print books and we could share reading.

She appreciated me bringing homework home. Even though she may not have understood, she was always there supporting me and very proud of all the awards I got. She told me I could do more and I really believed that I could because she believed in me so strongly. I really had no idea that I couldn't do more until I got into the real world . . .

A clear case of positive naming, Dorothy's example also shows her mother as a pre-mentor whose parenting strategies included the use of encouraging words accompanied by modeling. As was true of Alex's father's actions, Dorothy's mother's reading spoke volumes to the child. Both pre-mentors communicated their value of reading by engaging in it as a valuable exercise. By so doing, they seemed to prepare the way for the education-related mentors who would later enter their children's lives.

Closely related to the pre-mentoring roles played by the interviewees' parents was the tendency of the participants to synthesize as children the education-related values demonstrated by their parents and to emulate those aspects of their parents' behaviors as adults. The following excerpts suggest how strongly the participants identified with the pre-mentoring qualities of their parents and how they mirrored those qualities in their aspirations, their actions, and even their professions.

Fred's early inspiration came from his father:

My father was from a family that had been in the north for two generations. He was a fairly educated fellow who had gone to high school. He had not attended college, but he had had great aspirations of doing so. I remember him when I was growing up as a reader. I remember him going to his bedroom to read all the time. He had this northern speech, which was really different from my mother's southern accent and vocabulary. At that time, there still existed a schism between northerners and southerners, even among African Americans. Northern blacks sort of looked down on those southern blacks who felt inferior. . .

My father had dreams of becoming a history teacher, and he had an academic air about him. . . . When I had to go back home and bury my father, that act seemed to catapult me into a manhood that I had not experienced before. I had admired my father so much . . . and I had believed that there just was no question that he could not answer—he was just that smart. Then he died, and I really felt that his spirit became my spirit, and I gained this great ambition to accomplish all that he could not accomplish. To a certain extent, I feel that I am whatever I am as a fulfillment of my father's aspirations.

Ken is a humanities and philosophy instructor who loves music and literature, as did his father:

> My father was a very intelligent man without the education. My sister said he actually bought the set of Great Books that was in our house because he was going to read them. My mother couldn't stand him reading books all the time, and the books, in their nice black covers, just sat on the shelves and got dusty until I discovered them.
>
> My father was musical, and he played the accordion when he had too much to drink, which was very common. He played the accordion, harmonica, and the piano simultaneously. He was a very musical man. It was very sad when I went back to see him in Sweden just before he died, and I tried to get him to play the piano and the accordion and he couldn't do it anymore. He couldn't remember how to do it.

Clara, a foreign-language instructor who loves to travel, was inspired by her father:

> When I was little, I remember my dad went back to school and was taking GED classes. He was studying about a lot of things. And when we had questions about directions or history or anything, we would ask my dad. He had been throughout the fifty states. He would bring up the map and show us all this stuff about people, places, and how to get to different locations.
>
> At sixteen, I bought my own car, went to Florida with my best friend, and did things that no one in my family had ever done. No one but my dad had traveled, and now me. But he hadn't been to Disney World or seen the Epcot Center. I worked hard and saved up my money and went on a trip to Europe with my high school. I liked Spanish because we got to talk about other people's cultures. That was a first for me in terms of classes—learning about other people of the world.

Arlene talked about her mother and grandmother as primal forces:

> When you look at me today . . . in large part you are seeing my grandmother. . . . When I consider the role model to go beyond what I was, I can look to my mother. . . . She left grade school by sixth grade, but what my mother accomplished was to me proof of what a woman can do. . . .
>
> . . . She would go out and speak at schools and to various community and civic groups. . . . the subject matter of her talks was called Indian lore.

She also hosted . . . a television program here in Chicago on Channel Eleven called *Totem Club*.

I admired my mother tremendously, and I said to myself that one of these days I would like to have a show on Channel Eleven. I was able to accomplish that. . . .

The preceding examples provide vivid illustrations of the significant effects that parental attitudes toward knowledge or learning had on the lives of the interviewees. In addition to becoming more disposed to appreciate education as a result of pre-mentoring, many of the interviewees also stated that they read voraciously during childhood, a habit that was in keeping with parental values and that has been reported as typical in the literature on first-generation college students. Apparently as young children, the value systems by which the participants would learn to play out their day-to-day interactions in the world were being formed. These deep impressions were woven in large part from examples set by the adults in their lives whom they most admired and would be readily and repeatedly retrieved as indelible clues to how the participants would infuse their lives with meaning. As the participants branched out from their families, other variables stemming from institutions outside the home advanced to command their attention. Concern about their identities within the context of their schools and communities was one of these variables.

Home, School, Community

"Get yourself a trade," was the strong message I got at home. At school there was no message at all. I just went through the grades.

— *John*

Contrary to what one might expect, parental interest in or respect for education or knowledge did not necessarily translate to parental support for college. The parents of fewer than half of the participants could be said to support their child's aspiration, either emotionally or financially, to seek a college degree. Also interesting were the shades or degrees of support among parents, schools, and community not only for the participants to attend college, but also for them to get the quality of education necessary for success in college.

A panorama of other issues and problems faced participants in this study as they endeavored to navigate the sociopolitical minefields of home, school, and community. These included non-supportive teachers, counselors, and administrators; parents who were unable to help with homework or other school concerns; class-based anti-intellectualism among family members; and racial and ethnic prejudice at school and in the community. How did these students manage, despite barriers of such great magnitude? Embedded in their stories are illustrative accounts of how they achieved success.

In addition to the students' helping themselves, their families, schools, and communities were supposedly working on their behalf—a widely accepted formula for a successful educational experience. Yet the interviewees repeatedly described situations in which the components of home, school, and community rarely, if ever, worked in any positive or integrated fashion for the benefit of the students. Instead, home, school, and community functioned most often in ways that were counterproductive and undermined the efforts put forth by the students. The study's case histories revealed that at any given point in the participants' educational experiences, one or more of those units was diametrically, and often intentionally, opposed to the good of the students.

Consider, for example, the case of Barbara, who was the first in her family to complete high school. As a child she had a very positive, supportive relationship with her teachers. She admired them, and still does, for their dedication to their role in the lives of children. Barbara recalled:

> These teachers thought I was smart, so while they didn't say, "You should go to college," school was a place where I could be successful. They would single me out for things. If there was a play, I would get the lead because they knew I would learn the lines. I got to hand out books. There was a contest of some kind when I was in seventh grade, and the prize was a book and going to hear a lecture by Edgar Rice Burroughs, the guy who wrote the Tarzan books. I didn't even know who he was; I didn't even know about writers' lectures. He was from Oak Park and he came back to lecture, and I went with my teacher to hear him. For me it was a peep into another world. What a wonderful woman my teacher was to do this. These women at my school—my school was a very old-fashioned, working-class school. . . . I think they devoted a lot of energy and caring. I don't know if they were affectionate particularly, but they really latched onto a kid who loved books.

This aspect of Barbara's history shows education working admirably and effectively, with caring, supportive teachers who provided her with experiences that were no less than transformational. Her doctorate in the area of the humanities, her role as a writer and college professor, her compassion for others, and her love of beauty and culture all have roots, she believes, in her elementary school experiences.

The role of the community in Barbara's life, however, was almost entirely negative. Racist and anti-education, especially for women, her community let her know that she didn't belong. Because her mother is Jewish, Barbara was terrorized by many of the eastern European kids in her immigrant neighborhood:

> Most of them would call me names, and I would find my coat with bad things written on the back. . . . There were no other Jews in this town so that I could find other people. What I needed to find were people who weren't anti-Semitic. And I had different ideas than they did on race relations, on all kinds of things. So I was considered to be peculiar, different, but not in a good way. And I never seemed to be able to talk that kind of small talk that you're supposed to be able to do.

Barbara was a smart kid and a voracious reader, as were many other of the study's participants. This was very helpful to her in elementary school but not at all helpful in her working-class community where "they didn't like smart girls." Interestingly enough, being smart did not help to ease her navigation through high school. She found that her high school teachers were less supportive than their elementary school counterparts. A large number of students in the high school were middle-class, and middle-class students were valued—Barbara was not one of them. She remembers not going to school some days because she didn't have anything appropriate to wear. Even though she was very active in high school, elected class president, and does not believe that anybody thought she was particularly dumb, she remembers a high school math teacher telling her, "You'll never go to college. Don't even try."

At the time that Barbara was receiving no encouragement from her high school to go to college, she was receiving even less at home. Throughout high school, she had followed two tracks, the academic and the vocational, because her father did not believe that girls should go to college and insisted that she learn a business trade. Because she knew that she would go to college if at all possible, Barbara spent her high school years doing twice the work of most students, as did some other of the study's participants. Holding down a job and taking two tracks in high school left little time for extracurricular activities, such as playing in the school orchestra, which she would have loved to pursue.

With her father, school, and the immediate community in opposition to Barbara's educational goals, her chances of getting into and succeeding in college were pathetically out of balance. Aside from her own determination, Barbara found limited support: a wonderful elementary school education; her mother as pre-mentor; special status as a young child; and positive naming. The latter two forms of support came from her grandmother, with whom she shared a room until she went off to college.

When the equation of student + home + school + community = academic success is applied to the other participants in the study, one sees stories similar to Barbara's. Different parts of the equation subtracted from the rest, and students got by with whatever assets they had or could muster. For instance, Ken spoke about his high school experience in almost the same positive way that Barbara described her time in elementary school:

> I took sophomore English with a man named Mr. Snow who I remember in great detail. I can remember whole pieces of that class. First of all, he gave us an outline of English grammar, which I still remember. And we used to diagram sentences and break things down. Then we read *Macbeth, Idylls of the King*, oh, whole passages, and all of a sudden I discovered literature! It was just incredible.
>
> Mr. Snow and his wife used to sing around the town, mostly show tunes. . . . We went to his house and he had a grand piano and he was a pretty cultivated man. He and just any number of high school teachers just opened the world up for me. That was a transformation. I had good grade school teachers, but everything was sort of proletarian, sort of ordinary. My high school teachers sort of made my life come alive. And everything else followed from that.
>
> Mr. Snow opened new worlds for me by example, by being worldly, by being well versed. He held up Wiley's book about advertising. He said he'd read it last night. I looked at my girlfriend. "He read the whole damn book last night?! Gosh!"

The lack of familial support for college that Ken experienced was almost a replay of Barbara's. Ken explained, "At home, regarding college, don't even mention it! They had no idea about it whatsoever. It was expected that I would get a high school diploma and go to work."

Maria, on the other hand, found outstanding familial support, and when a boy in her sixth-grade class called her a "spic," she felt that her school responded appropriately. But the community from which the boy came, and to which Maria and her family were relative newcomers, was not supportive:

It was a Caucasian—Irish, German, Polish—neighborhood. It wasn't really comfortable when we moved into that neighborhood because after that boy called me that name, I had to ride my bike in our back yard or I had to ride in the alley. My parents didn't want me riding out front because they were afraid that people were going to say things. We suffered from stereotypes because they would hear, "Oh, they're Hispanic," and they immediately thought negative things. Until they saw the type of people and type of family we were—that we weren't there to cause any type of harm to anybody. Then it got easier. We were sort of accepted, but it was different in the beginning. . . .

My dad said, "I thought that moving would be better, and now I have to keep them enclosed in their back yard." I couldn't walk to the corner by myself. I was never sent to the store by myself. If I was going to a friend's house, my dad would drop me off and pick me up. I couldn't stay over at my friend's. Girls who are twelve and thirteen always have slumber parties. Well, my dad would let me stay until eleven or twelve o'clock, and then he would come and pick me up. He didn't feel comfortable. He was afraid for my emotional safety. In the old neighborhood, he had worried about my physical safety.

While community was the weak link in Maria's experience, it was among the strongest in Alex's world. It was in the community that he found help with his schoolwork, help that his family could not give him:

I noticed that Max and Amy would help their children with their homework, so one day I mentioned to Amy that I was having trouble with math. . . . She invited me to come over . . . at a certain time. The Korn children would be doing their homework, and either Max or Amy would help me with my studies, too.

. . . They were raising their kids to go to college, and they started asking me questions about whether I wanted to go to college. They knew my academic weaknesses, and yet they seemed to see no reason why I should not go to college. They acted as if wanting to go to college were as natural for me as it was for their own children. . . .

Alex's words illustrate his willingness as a child to take a risk by approaching, completely on his own, an educated couple to seek help with his homework. This represents a proactive stance exhibited by the participants in almost all the life stories. For instance, Grant described how he overcame a debilitating stutter and improved his chances of getting a good education in part by assessing, completely on his own, the comparative quality and degree of his knowledge about school subjects:

> I must have been seven or eight years old and probably had the condition beforehand, but I remember, as I sit here, being in third or fourth grade and having a speech problem that made it difficult for me to ask a question. I would hesitate, pause, and stammer, "Do-do-do-do-do." I didn't realize until later, looking back, what caused it. At the time, it was a problem for me. People would ask me questions, and I wouldn't respond for fear that I would stutter and stammer and couldn't respond. People would say, "Why doesn't he answer? Does he not hear me? Can't he understand?" Then when I did answer, with the combination of events, they probably said, "Well, this guy doesn't have it all." I was sent to special ed. I stayed there for two or three days, and they sent me back to regular class. I was bounced back and forth between special ed and regular classes for three or four times. Finally, I guess the regular class teacher couldn't assign me to special ed permanently and just accepted the fact that I was slow. I didn't question their decision. I figured they knew what they were doing. They were adults and in control.
>
> I suspect the stuttering and stammering problem slowly went away. . . . I surely couldn't have had it in junior high, seventh and eighth grades, not a whole lot. Then around eighth or ninth grade, I started to realize that I could deal with whatever people presented to me. And once I realized that I could answer correctly and present reasonably well, the stammering slowly went away.
>
> By the time I was a senior, I had started to analyze why I had stammered. I realized that I had feared being counted a fool. So rather than speak out and remove all doubts, I would just remain silent. People perceived the silences as slowness. Then, although I hadn't relinquished my fear of communicating with people—I still didn't talk a whole lot—at least I was able to get rid of the stuttering and stammering. I went from high school to engineering school.

Showing uncommonly independent thought, Grant began to consider the mounting evidence that he was as intelligent as anyone else and came to reject the prevalent expert assessment of his capability. The negative names such as special ed student, slow, and one who "doesn't have it all" slowly lost their power over Grant under the scrutiny of his reasoning skills and his mounting academic prowess. Grant's analysis of the situation and his conclusion that the school authorities were wrong about his intelligence was likely enabled by the stance taken by the special education staff—who were also authorities—when they validated his intellectual normalcy by rejecting him as a special education student. In addition, they actually had won the battle with his classroom teacher on how he was to be labeled and served, and that meant his teacher was wrong and they were right. This may have been an affirming action even though Grant would be treated as slow for years. Such subversive affirmations by educators were not uncommon in the participants' stories. When viewed against the backdrop of the powerful educational systems and incongruous wrongs that were being subverted, these counteractions of "creative noncompliance" (Fliegel 1993, 55) appear inconsequential. However, they may have mitigated the negative effects that schools had on some of this study's participants. In turn, the students' enhanced self-concepts may have augmented their ability to recover from those and other educational barriers that would be put in their way.

Alex seemed to illustrate this point by telling about a speech therapist who assured him that his lack of fluency in English did not mean that there was something wrong with him. This was an important revelation since it opposed several negative reinforcements that Alex was experiencing in school at the time. With his identity under attack by authority figures who criticized his ethnic group, affirmation by the speech therapist was a signal that those teachers who spoke negatively about non–English speaking people could be incorrect in what they were saying:

> I started kindergarten around this time and sometimes heard teachers make negative comments about me or other Puerto Rican people because we did not speak English well. . . . There were no special programs for those of us who did not speak English, and we sank or swam on our own. . . . Groups of us were sent to speech therapy three times a week because we were not fluent in English. But the speech therapist was very nice and recognized full well that we did not have speech problems beyond an inadequate knowledge of the English language.

Interventions in the participants' lives, such as those related by Grant and Alex, seemed to make persistence in school a little bit easier simply by strengthening, however incrementally, students' perceptions of who they were as individuals and of their suitability for being taught. Still, as Alex's and Grant's examples also show, gaining access to a class where a student would be given excellent instruction was not always easy or possible for this study's interviewees. Ken discovered during elementary school that if he was not learning from his teachers, he could learn from other students who seemed to know more than he did just because of their middle-class status:

> One reason my mother always hated schoolteachers is that I was doing very badly in math and my teacher, who was a very domineering woman, made my mother come in and, just because she was an immigrant, sit on the dunce stool which my mother was obviously very familiar with. The teacher directed my mother, "Sit down here!" I really hadn't started to emerge at school. But we lived in a Jewish neighborhood in New York and all those kids seemed to know so much more, to be so much sharper because they had a middle-class environment. So I learned a lot from them. For instance, one kid asked me, "Well, are you going to go out to the country?" I said, "Yeah." He said, "Which county do you live in, Nassau or Suffolk?" I said, "What? County?" I had never heard the word before. I had no idea what he was talking about. I learned "county" from him. Then one time we were supposed to paint pictures of Arabs, and I had to ask him, "What's an Arab? I never heard of that." These kids were painting camels and people in the headdresses. I started looking at that, and I said, "Gee. . ." They had me paint sand because I had no idea what was going on.

Ken found that learning from advanced students was hardly possible, however, if he was not in class with them. He spoke of the difficulty he experienced when he had to spend a year in a lower track. His example clearly illustrates a strategy shared by many of the study's participants: When school did not advance their learning, they simply took it upon themselves to find other ways of learning as best they could:

> In my junior year, for one reason or another, I was not put in an advanced English class. I can remember only one story from that year, and I remember it well. It was something about a marriage in Louisiana where people made all this noise outside the married couple's cottage. Shivaree is what the custom is called. That's all I can remember from the whole year. I mean, I learned nothing from class, and everybody there was sort of out-of-focus. But being put in advanced classes with my background, not having had the advantages of some of these kids, was a wonderful opportunity for me to learn. The honors kids were some of the brightest in the school. My experience is one example of a tremendous argument for getting people with a lot of ability in classes with other people and getting them exposed. De-

mocracy does not require leveling where we waste human potential. And economics could stand a little bit of leveling out. . . . My junior year, I had to do my learning on my own. I just read everything I could from the public library.

In Jerry's case, the inadequacy of high school resulted in independent and specialized learning that influenced his desire to go to college to study aeronautical engineering. He recalled:

Adamson High School was grossly easy. I was out of school at twelve-fifteen. I had school for just four hours a day. I was not athletic, and I was very shy, a little egghead trying to hide it. I started going to local libraries and plundering the shelves. I got very interested in model airplanes and began building gas-model free-flights, which were very unusual. I began designing them. When I was seventeen, I drew up plans for one that won a lot of meets. People are still building that model airplane today. I had been building little rubber-band types before I saw a gas model flying and went crazy over it. I bought a kit, but I soon quit making the kit models and designed my own. I think that's what set me up to become an engineer. I started selling the plans after a while and earned a tiny bit of money. People saw me flying my plane and wanted it. Some parts are hard to make, so I started making kits to sell. I still have the plans. They are on tracing paper, in India ink. They are almost sixty years old.

In every case history, the interviewees discussed their tendencies to do their best to achieve their goals. By trying to make the best of a bad school situation, Jerry not only learned independently, he also developed a lifelong interest in aviation and began deliberations about college and a major course of study. The participants in this study are goal-oriented people who vigorously sought whatever they wanted. They were single-minded in their pursuit of a college education, and setting and keeping clear goals appear to have been a commonly beneficial behavior. By utilizing strengths as schoolchildren derived from both current and previous experiences at the time, they successfully combated inadequate degrees of support from home, school, or community. To a person, they possessed intentionality similar to that expressed by Steve in the following excerpt:

When I was in school . . . I wasn't very athletic, and my father just couldn't stand it. My brother was perfect in all these sports, and I was just . . . I'm so cross-focused, I can't play anything with a ball, and I had no interest. And I thought I was supposed to be good in athletics. I used to get beat up by my father constantly, constantly, constantly. And then I'd get a good grade on a test, and I'd get beat up at school because I'd ruined the curve. There were some times when I wouldn't get everything done as well and as fast as I should, and even though teachers liked me pretty well, they'd say, "Come on, Steve! Get your work done!"

I was so slow at reading and it was always a struggle for me. I would be in gym class and one time the teacher was so mad at me, he took a basketball and yelled, "What's the matter? Are you afraid of the ball?" And he threw it at me—boom!—and hit me square in the face. He was brutal. . . . I'd go to school, and it was pretty much hell, and I'd go home, and that was always hell. Even my older sister had become controlling. She couldn't control the situation in our house, so she tried to control other people. I tried to keep the peace, but I realized that I couldn't. I realized that there would never be an end to the madness at school or at home, so I just became rebellious—not in a bad way. But I just said, "I'm gonna do what I'm gonna do." And I did. I started really figuring out how I was going to do the things I thought were important, like going to college. No matter what anybody else thought, said, or did.

Strengthened undoubtedly by positive experiences such as the ongoing benefits of his special status during his early childhood, Steve was able to assert some control over his own life. However, what others thought, said, and did as role models actually was very important to Steve and to the others in this study. As they considered their own conditions in life and their dreams for the future, they often looked to exemplary others for clues to achieving their goals. By what processes did they crystallize their aspirations and adjust their senses of self? How did they become aware of those processes and learn to apply them in their own lives? These questions form the basis of the following section on ascending cross-class identification.

Ascending Cross-Class Identification

Seeing people I knew going off to college had everything to do with my wanting to go. No counselors or teachers told me to go or helped me. I had to look at people from the social class above mine and figure out how to make the things they were doing happen for me.

— *Clara*

One cannot dream that which one cannot imagine. As "castles in the air," dreams are as vague as mists. To "put the foundations under them" (Thoreau 1854, 616), specificity is required. Specificity demands definition, delineation, description, detail. It necessitates knowing, and access to knowledge often proved difficult for this study's interviewees.

I believe that one of the most difficult challenges that the participants faced in their journeys toward college was knowing what they should aspire to become. Generally speaking, this relates only peripherally to the profession that one should choose. And applied specifically to the participants, it had far less— perhaps nothing—to do with personality. It had absolutely nothing to do with exchanging their own genetic blueprints, natural talents, or innate characteristics for someone else's. To the contrary, their challenge was to figure out how to become themselves.

In essence, to become themselves meant that the participants needed to shed those limitations imposed by their environments that inhibited the development of their natural potential. With this dross discarded, the participants would have better opportunities to identify and to shape the precious metal that was left and that comprised their true characteristics.

To accomplish this was not easy, and the following steps in the process of achieving ascending cross-class identification are presented in an admittedly overly simplified and overly linear fashion. First, the participants, often as young children, needed to recognize those limitations imposed by their environments as the obstacles to healthy development that they actually were: "I'm a second grader in a public school that provides few and outdated books. This hampers my learning." Second, the participants needed to generate at least a vague conceptualization of themselves as free of these limitations: "I realize that if I had the books that I need, I could learn a lot more. I can imagine myself learning so much more than I am now." Third, they needed to believe that their imagined freedom was deserved and was right for them: "I deserve instruction and books equal to those provided children at schools in rich communities." Fourth, they needed a means of learning in some detail what freedom was really like: "When I visited my rich cousin in a different state, I saw that he has books in excellent condition for every subject. He can study at home as much as he wants, and he's planning on going to college even though he's only in second grade." And finally, they needed a means to attain freedom: "I'm going to live with my cousin so I can attend his school." Ascending cross-class identification is a primary process by which the participants appeared able to accomplish these tasks by freeing themselves from some of society's limitations.

In an earlier section of this chapter called "Special Status," we encountered

Annie as a child whose aunt introduced her to the world of a little white girl with a lot of books and the ability to read:

> I couldn't understand how this little girl could have so many books and we didn't have any. I would go home and try to read the one book that we had, an old Bible, as best I could. There were so many words that I could not understand, and, of course, my mom and dad couldn't really help me.

As countless other examples from the participants' stories show, Annie clearly recognized that the standards under which black people in her community lived were unjust limitations. Though she was from an extremely poor southern black family and, as such, the antithesis of the middle-class white child whom she met, she experienced ascending cross-class identification. Simply stated, this means that Annie imagined the integration of many books and the ability to read into her own lifestyle. This was remarkable since she experienced cross-race as well as ascending cross-class identification in the segregated south of the 1950s where even young children understood the implications of apartheid. In her identification with the little white girl, Annie refused to accept the implications of their racial difference. Thus, she exemplified those rare individuals who somehow do not internalize the corrupt implications or customs of the society in which they are born and raised. Instead, Annie seems to have adjusted her self-concept by bringing it into alignment with the reality of the Other, the little white girl with books.

Closely connected to Annie's identification with the Other was her remarkable intention to transcend the purpose of reading fiction for pleasure and to use reading as a vehicle to a transformed self-concept, as we see in the following passage:

> Now, I remember that one of my teachers gave me a book. . . .There was a story in the book about a woman who worked hard and did her job every day, and her husband was always complaining about the work she was doing. So she told him to stay home and do her work and she would go and do his job. He took her up on this, and she could do his job, but he couldn't do hers. And I thought, "There has to be another job that I can do. I don't want to do this job for the rest of my life."

For Annie, reading was also a source for research on what her transformed self should be:

I used to pray as a child. . . . So I said, "Lord, I know there is something else out there for me to do. I can't live like this for the rest of my life." And I thought that through reading, I would find help to change my life. I just wanted to do something different.

As the preceding passages illustrate, Annie resolved to use reading as a means of providing some details to an imagined life without the educational, social, and economic limitations of her experience. Annie's deliberate search through her small world of literature for ways to change her life is extraordinary in a young child, perhaps more so than the realignment of her self-concept after meeting the white girl. As an indicator of her character, I believe that intention, which marks Annie's deliberate search for ways to change her life, is far superior to coincidence, which resulted in the realignment of her self-concept. Both may be causal in Annie's subsequent matriculation and success at college.

Certainly causal through ascending cross-class identification were Annie's meeting a college student and the record keeping responsibilities she was given by her teacher:

I knew that I could do something different with my life when I was twelve years old. . . . I met my first-grade teacher's brother, who was in college at the time. I had never heard of college. I knew my teachers had to have gotten training somewhere, but this was the first time I had direct knowledge of college. And he made it sound like a terrific place to be. He was going to be a teacher. I remember telling my mother I would like to be a teacher.

Another important thing that happened to me was that in seventh grade, my teacher let me keep attendance. He put me in charge of the register because he thought I had good penmanship. . . . I would record the children's names, days present, days absent, what have you. That was fascinating to me. I would do all this recording and take it to the principal's office and he would send it to, I think, the superintendent. So I felt certain that I wanted to be a teacher. . . .

In these examples, Annie used ascending cross-class identification to gather information about college and about teaching that would help to put the foundation under her dream of changing her life. Similarly, Barbara talked about an opportunity for ascending cross-class identification provided by an elementary schoolteacher who took her to Oak Park, a middle-class town, to hear a lecture given by Edgar Rice Burroughs, one of Oak Park's famous native sons:

> I remember thinking at the lecture that the whole audience was middle-class, a group of people that I had never had anything to do with before. These people had time to go and listen and had bought the tickets to do so. My teacher probably made almost nothing in salary. And she had two tickets because I was too young to go by myself. The prize was given for reading a number of books, and she must have known that I would be the winner and that would be a meaningful experience for me. If they are still alive, those teachers, I should go back and thank them all, but they weren't young then and that was a long time ago.
>
> I think I was a little bored by Burroughs' talk, but the ambiance and what was going on around me were important. . . . Oak Park's library was a very handsome building of the type that I wouldn't have seen anything like it at the time. It is a Frank Lloyd Wright building. There were three bronze busts of three important people who came from Oak Park. The main, central one was Burroughs, flanked by Ernest Hemingway and Frank Lloyd Wright. . . . I take my students on architecture tours, so we go to the Wright buildings. I was very impressed by the houses in Oak Park when I saw them with my teacher, the first time I had ever been there, even though I didn't know who Wright was at the time. But the houses! There are reflections of Oak Park in this house where I have lived for so many years.

In this first exposure to the middle class, Barbara observed some of the significant differences between the way of life that she knew and the privileged existences of these Oak Park residents. As a college professor of the humanities, Barbara takes her students to see the Wright architecture in the Chicago area, and in her home she surrounds herself with Wrightian influences. Yet she attributed to serendipity a more immediately direct influence on her ability to go to college.

Just as most of the participants in the study gave considerable credit to luck, coincidence, or God for opportunities to experience ascending cross-class identification, Barbara attributes to luck an intervention from the larger community that helped to expand her horizons and firm her resolve to earn a college degree. Barbara's stroke of fortune came in the form of boys, students from the University of Chicago, who introduced her to another world:

> I went out with one who was actually from Oak Park, and he took me out to eat at a restaurant that had tables with real tablecloths on them. And I

pretended that I wasn't hungry because I was afraid I'd do something wrong, so I just watched him. And then you pick up what you do at those restaurants, and when you get older you can—well, now I can eat in restaurants. . . .

I knew I wanted to be in this new world—the old one didn't fit—but I was very uncomfortable with it for a while. I remember even pretending. One of these boys took me to a concert of classical music, which I needed in order to do some kind of report in a music class. A girlfriend of mine came along because she was in the same class. We chattered throughout the concert instead of listening to the music because I knew that if I listened, I wouldn't have anything to say about it because it was not music I had heard before. The Oak Park boy took me to a performance at the Shubert, to a Gilbert and Sullivan operetta, thinking that it wouldn't be so sophisticated it would be over my head, and I thought it was wonderful. I was so glad that I could appreciate it. I was able to see that there was something there although I was afraid of it. I didn't know enough to be confident that I wouldn't trip up all over myself somehow and not know what to do. These guys were helpful in ushering me into a place, a way of life, where I could be comfortable.

Barbara's example, replayed time and again by other participants, illustrates the powerful motivation derived from ascending cross-class identification. From reading and from her trip as a seventh grader to Oak Park, Barbara knew that there were alternatives to the way that she lived and the world that she knew. Her exposure to the students from the University of Chicago gave her not only a prolonged view of that new world, but also initial experience in its navigation. And as new learning so often does in our lives, it made Barbara uncomfortable. Reverberating throughout the literature on first-generation college students and in most of the participants' stories is the premise that straddling two cultures is difficult (Gandara 1995; Lara 1992; Levine and Nidiffer 1996; London,1996; Rendon 1996; Rendon, Terenzini, and Upcraft 1994).

With this in mind, it is interesting to note that since there were many middle-class students in Barbara's high school, ostensibly there were ample opportunities for her to identify with and to gain exposure to the middle class long before her introduction to the University of Chicago students. However, she did not. This may suggest that two factors are crucial to the transformation of self as a result of ascending cross-class identification. First, transforming one's self requires information about the Other that may not be readily available to the outsider. As Weber (1968) points out, membership in a status group requires a particular style of life designated by badges such as habits of consumerism, clothes, vocabulary, and social conventions. Membership, then, requires knowledge of what these badges are and how to attain them, as well as the wherewithal to do so. While superficial identification with the Other is easily achieved, in order to integrate the new identification, one must begin to know the Other. Only then can one effectively begin to adjust and align one's self-concept.

The second point about ascending cross-class identification is that in order to know the Other, one needs exposure to the Other's world. Unlike the middle-class students at Barbara's high school, the University of Chicago students welcomed Barbara into their world and provided her with guided tours. Perhaps Barbara saw them as more desirable hosts since they knew the world of the university, a world that she longed to enter. Still, no matter how helpful the University of Chicago students were, her excursions were uncomfortable because she was a tourist and not a resident. It would take time before she achieved Weberian (1968) certification. In fact, she went to junior college where the application process was not necessary before she got the nerve to apply to the university. "My high school must have had advisors," she stated, "but . . . I was one of the working-class kids who didn't fit into the group that was going to college." She was so afraid of the application process that she did not tell anyone—not her family, not even her University of Chicago friends—that she had applied to the University of Chicago until she had been accepted and her financial aid had been secured.

Welcoming exposures to a new world seemed to be the force that tipped the balance in Barbara's favor by strengthening her ability to adjust and align her self-concept. This exposure allowed her to begin to know and to internalize what her transformed self should be. Because her exposure was kindly, her degree of fear and loss of dignity during the process must surely have been diminished. Under less fortunate circumstances, her exposure to a different world could have been accompanied by derision at her every misstep from those who already belonged. In that case, a permanent retreat may have been her response. This is very important because it underscores the need to provide low socioeconomic-status first-generation students with welcoming exposures to better worlds. In a case such as Barbara's, where the equation for a student's entry into college and subsequent college completion breaks down, exposure to a new world may be the major contributing factor, other than the student herself, in the student's academic success.

Fortunately for many of the participants in this study, wonderful people who would be pivotal subjects for ascending cross-class identification stepped forward in their lives. For instance, among other interventions, Alex recalled the role played by the Coveys in helping him to conceptualize a different life for himself:

> I got the idea that I wanted to earn a college degree from several interventions in my life. One was that I had been . . . sent to camp outside New York City. . . . When I was eight, I went to Ma and Pa Covey's in Pennsylvania. That experience opened my eyes to a whole new world. Pa Covey . . . was a writer for a newspaper. . . . She had been an English teacher.
>
> There were lots of books at Ma and Pa Covey's house, and every night, Ma Covey would read . . . to Robert and me. And when we sat down for dinner, they always talked about things and asked our opinions. . . . The table was set with dishes that matched, and everyone had a fork, spoon, knife, and napkin. This was new for me since at home we never used both a spoon and a fork. . . .
>
> The Coveys . . . were well off. They were educated and they could do whatever they wanted to do. For example, every year we would go to New Jersey to the seashore. . . . I remember thinking that some day I wanted to be able to do those things for myself and whatever family I happened to have.

The Coveys also illustrated by example how Alex could aspire to change his life by earning a college degree. They aided in the crystallization of his plans by providing knowledge of how he could finance a college education:

> Just how I would get to go to college was suggested to me one summer when I was at the Covey's. They had a niece . . .who was working and paying most of her own way through school. Ma and Pa Covey told me about how they had worked their way through school, too. . . . Here was living proof that you did not have to be rich to go to college. You had to want to go to college, and you had to work to stay there.

Alex also discovered the masses who enjoyed middle-class status. He spoke of his participation in a music program that offered free tickets to New York City public school students:

> On days when I had a ticket to a performance, I would take the bus or walk across Central Park to the Met or to Symphony Hall after school. . . . I marveled at the audiences of white people who could take off during the day to go to the opera or symphony. For the most part, I saw no minorities

in the audience or on the stage, but I did get to see Marian Anderson once, I think at Symphony Hall.

In these and in many other examples from their stories, Alex, Barbara, and Annie exemplified the histories of most of the individuals interviewed for this study as they experienced ascending cross-class identification. They learned through the process of ascending cross-class identification to recognize aspects of middle-class life that they desired and believed they deserved. Through their associations with the Other, they used ascending cross-class identification to conceptualize important specific information entailed in becoming free from the shackles of underprivilege. With a basic appreciation for their own personalities, genetic blueprints, natural talents, and other innate characteristics, they could begin burning away the environmental legacies of educational, economic, social, and mental disenfranchisement to uncover their true selves. In this manner, the interviewees prepared themselves to enter the educated middle class by earning a college degree.

4 | One Heart, One Love

Of my father's three sisters who lived to adulthood, none married well. When the eldest of the children, Lucille, left secondary school, she went to teach in a little town near Wilson, North Carolina, where she met and married a good-looking, no-good man, effectively ending her teaching career. Aunt Lucille was notorious within the family for her lack of domestic acumen, which seemed just fine to her handsome, shiftless husband and her two children. In her existence, so far-removed from our own, she struck my siblings and me as living a happy, bohemian life. We had the impression that Aunt Lucille's one household skill was playing the piano, and we swore that we wouldn't eat her cooking even if we were starving to death.

Aunt Ruth Ann's marriage was far more disastrous than Aunt Lucille's. Her husband, an alcoholic who never held an honest job, openly earned his living by selling bootleg liquor. Even though they lived within a few miles of her parents and many other relatives, none of Aunt Ruth Ann's family, except an occasional brother, ever visited her. If her brothers stopped by her house, they left their wives and children in the car. Her clientele was the underbelly of society—men and women who drank their wages, let their children run wild, and visited the bootlegger's house rather than church on Sunday morning, after having been there on Saturday night. I knew Aunt Ruth Ann well because she, unlike her husband, was welcome in her family's houses. She did not seem to resent us for our unforgiving attitudes toward her way of life. My mother always said that Aunt Ruth Ann was one of the nicest people she had ever met.

Of my father's sisters, Aunt Eloise seemed the closest to us although she lived the farthest away. By the time I was born, she was divorced from my cousins' father and living and working in Baltimore. My cousins lived with our grandparents, so Aunt Eloise would come home a lot to be with them. She was a steady presence in all our lives, and when she came home from Baltimore for the last time, it seemed fitting that my father, who was the closest to her in age, would be the one to go to the city and bring her back.

Someone had to bring her back. Aunt Eloise had become so ill that she could not travel by herself, and we all thought she was going to die. I remember one Sunday during her illness, when the extended family had gathered at my grandparents' house, Aunt Eloise asked to see the children. Two at a time, we were ushered from our quiet play outside into the sickroom where her bones of a face spoke to us and her sticks for arms reached out. One of my grandfather's hunting dogs began a mournful howling from the backyard, and my father came out of the house to run the dog off with a stick of stove wood. Even we children knew that a dog howling for no good reason is a harbinger of someone's death.

When Aunt Eloise recovered, she moved to Scarsdale, New York, where she became the live-in maid for a rich Jewish family. She raised the two children in that family, a cockeyed compensation for not having been able to raise her own. On Thursdays she would take the train to Mount Vernon, a working-class community, where she would shop and visit with a woman she had met at church. When her daughters and nieces began graduating from high school, she rented first a room and then an apartment in Mount Vernon, so that they would have a place to stay when they came to the city looking for work to help pay their way through college.

Over our college years, Aunt Eloise helped to find jobs for nine of her family's daughters, all of whom earned college degrees. We would take the bus from Edenton, North Carolina, to New York City's Port Authority. From there we would take a cab to Grand Central Station where we would board the train to Mount Vernon. Although exhausted from an eighteen-hour bus ride and anxious about our new situation, we would head to our jobs on the day of arrival if we had a position lined up. Otherwise, we would apply at the employment agency and wait and pray for a humane family to hire us.

The most difficult aspect of my entire college experience was feeling like an alien in upstate New York. I had never been away from home before I graduated from high school, and the last thing I wanted to do was to go and live as a servant with strangers whose environment provided no opportunity for me to meet or speak with anyone on equal footing. I drowned my homesickness in hard work, laboring from the time I got up in the morning until I went to bed at night. I never had time to read, and even though I often spoke by phone to my aunt and cousins, I lived a soulless, disconnected existence.

In retrospect, I can see that I must have been an unsettling and unsatisfactory maid. I worked for one family for three summers, and I knew that they were amazed by the quantity and quality of work that I could do. They did not know that my uncomplaining attitude toward my ceaseless work was an antidote to my heartbreak at being cut off from affirmation, validation, and appreciation of my ideas, my personality, my self. They did recognize, however, that I was not completely happy, and to their credit and discredit, they cared. They cared that I did not commit to them emotionally every day. They wanted to see that my life with them was as fulfilling for me as it was for them. They did not seem to understand that I would naturally perceive them, and my life with them, as alien. They were good people, but they had no idea that for the communion required by my heart and mind, their world lacked community.

If I shut down emotionally when I went to work as a live-in maid, I shut down physically when I went off to college. My older sister had just graduated, and I had seen how financially draining those four years had been on my parents. I had a four-year academic scholarship, and I was terrified that my grade point average would drop below a B+ and I would lose the money. My weight dropped from 102 to 97 pounds. More seriously, from the time I entered college in August, I had no menstrual period until I came home for Thanksgiving and sought medical intervention. I had anemia, low blood pressure, and a sinus infection. Among other medications, our family doctor prescribed birth control pills, but he did not identify them as such to me. I quickly learned that if I took one every other day, rather than once a day as prescribed, I could drastically cut the cost of my medicine by making a month's supply last for two.

I had also learned, once the women in my dorm had gotten to know me, that a few of them had hated me at first sight. And they could say exactly why: They thought I was spoiled. I cannot say that I blame them, however poor their judgement of character, because I looked spoiled. I was wearing a new gray dress with black piping and black pumps, and I was carrying around a teddy bear that my brother had given me as a going-away present. Both my parents had brought me to college to help me settle in and had gone through the entire admissions process with me. We were ushered to the front of all the long lines, and often right into the offices of the administrators in charge, so the registration process was greatly expedited for me. Naturally attractive, my parents looked tailored and prosperous and seemed to navigate the campus with relative ease. Some women later admitted that they had envied and hated me for seeming to have everything that they did not.

While my parents had neither education nor affluence, they did have experience. Since my sister had recently graduated from the same college, they had gone through the registration process many times before. They moved my things into my dorm room, unpacked my clothes, and made my bed, cutting out a lot of work for me on that hot afternoon. They left me with a large stash of food and one of my mother's coconut cakes. Of my three roommates, one was my first cousin and best friend. By all outward signs, I was all set.

My first encounter with academics occurred on the second or third day on campus when students took standardized mathematics and verbal placement exams. We were given the verbal exam first. Before the math exam started, I was summoned to a room of seven or eight professors and administrators who said that I had earned the highest score on the verbal exam ever recorded at the college. They indicated that a couple of them, as well as the college president, were alumni, and still I had done better. In characteristic fashion, I did my very best on the mathematics test, and I wound up in advanced math and English.

My advanced math class was comprised of juniors and seniors who were math and science majors with one exception other than me, a freshman majoring in chemistry who had studied under our professor in a high school bridge program. I did not understand even one of our professor's demonstrations of advanced calculus. To me she was a whirling dervish who ran from one end of the chalkboard to the other making numeric notations and erasing the whole jumble before I could copy it down. The university had assigned each freshman an upperclassman mentor, but mine was an English major who knew little of math. So I asked the freshman in my class to tutor me, and on the first test we both got D's. I had to do better, but how? Even if the juniors and seniors in my class had looked approachable, I knew from their comments that they were faring poorly, so I went to plead with the professor.

I explained how hard my parents worked, that they were in the fields under a blazing sun even as we spoke, that they had a stretch of at least fifteen years when they would have a child in college, and that for eight unbroken years, they would have two children in college at once. I told her that my parents had sent my sister to college for four years and two summers, and that my other siblings were not likely to get scholarships. I explained that the prospect of losing my scholarship because I could not get a C+ in math was extremely difficult for me, and I asked for any help or suggestions that she could make.

My professor began to draw parallels between my life and hers. She had come from a family so poor that attending college had been completely out of her sphere of possibility. "I went to college late in life," she said. "It was my husband who sent me to college." She told me to keep working as hard as I was and not to worry. At the end of the term, my tutor got a D in the class, exactly what he had earned; and I got a C+, a gift outright.

If the compassion of a less-than-spectacular female professor was my salvation during my first semester of college, the lechery and vindictiveness of a brilliant male professor was almost my doom. His impact forced me to appreciate the difference between the supportive, familial-like relationships I had enjoyed with my high school instructors and the predator-prey aspect of some faculty-student relationships on the college campus. He taught a course in world civilization, and his infectious interest in ancient peoples, traditions, and times transported the untraveled student such as I to ages past. He had a practice of asking a different student at the beginning of each class to provide an oral review of the lecture from the previous session, and one day he asked me to review my notes. I was an excellent note-taker in those days, so it seemed reasonable that thereafter he most often chose me to provide the oral review. I became very uncomfortable, however, when he began detaining me after class and repeatedly requesting that I meet him at his office. I was an A student in his class, so I simply refused his requests. When he tried to hire me to dust his office, I told him that my parents did not allow me to work. Because I found him very offensive, I added that I would never visit his office.

My grades arrived while I was home for semester break, and I learned that I had received a C+ in world civilization. On my return to school, I went to the professor's office. I quietly stated that my parents were decent, hard-working people and so was I; that he could affect my family and my future by putting my academic scholarship in jeopardy; that I had earned an A in his class; that lowering my grade to a C+ had been unfair; and that I wanted him to change it immediately. I was wearing a heavy car coat against the damp chill of the winter day. The professor's office was too warm, and I was trembling and perspiring. But I did not remove my coat, sit down, or cry. He said to me, "Don't be so upset . . . I told you that you would come to my office . . . And, yes, I will change your grade."

Thus began my perilous journey over the white-water rapids of higher education. Not only were my parents far away, I hated the idea of looking to them to protect me in a world that they did not understand. How could they fight the elite of my university, and why should I disillusion them with what college was not? As a seventeen-year-old freshman, I learned very quickly that other female students were my surest source of protection and support against male authority figures. When I had to shove a male professor, overturn a chair between us, and run, I had only to get out the door because one of my female friends was standing sentry in the corridor of what the professor thought was a virtually empty building.

My family came to my college graduation with an entire home-cooked dinner in the trunk of the car, and after the ceremonies were over, we drove to a cemetery to eat. The setting was cool, quiet, spacious, and free—exactly to my liking.

I was wearing a black spaghetti-strap sheath, exceptional attire among the clouds of white dresses under our academic garb. "Why don't you want a white dress for graduation?" my mother had asked. "Aren't all the other girls going to have one?" I didn't care what the other girls wore. Besides, white dresses seemed a meaningless expense for so many poor parents who had made great financial sacrifices to put their daughters through college. My own education had been basically free, but my brother had been in college for two years and one of my sisters would be going that fall. Money was needed in my family, while a white dress that no one could see beneath a black robe was not. I decided to rebel against a financial hardship perpetuated by the victims themselves. We were not required to wear white dresses, and if strangers did not recognize me as a graduate once I had taken off my cap and gown, so be it. Of what worth to me, beyond the petting of my ego, was such recognition anyway?

I still feel that a more important rebellion, on behalf of female students, was required. Two women that I knew very well had been expelled from college just days before graduation because the college had discovered that they were pregnant. Each of these women had spent four years of their lives and their families' lives working toward graduation, only to be derailed by damaged condoms and intact libidos. I have inquired about these women over the years and know that neither of them ever earned a college degree. Had they been able to graduate, they would have been the first in their families to do so, and they could have lived easier lives. I have never been able to reconcile the severity of their punishment with their sin. I can imagine these women questioning their own audacity in aspiring to step outside the box of their uneducated families and predecessors by going to college. Perhaps they despised themselves for destroying their own and their families' dreams. They probably believed that through their mistakes, their families' sacrifices on their behalf had become unredeemed suffering. I know that neither of them had access to counseling or psychiatric help in dealing with their circumstances. Their fate was not uncommon for women, yet I never knew a male student to be expelled for any legal behavior of a sexual nature during all my college years.

Chapter 4
Access, Success, Egress:
The Collegiate Experience

Many of the first-generation college students in this study could not depend on their high schools to help them with the process of getting to college. Instead, they depended on their own resources or on their communities since their parents often knew less about the subject than they did. Most were blessed with the pioneering spirit, but for those who had never heard of a college entrance exam, had no understanding of where to get—let alone how to complete—college application forms, had no money and no concept of how to attain financial aid, and believed the message from others that they were not college material, the college-going process posed a serious problem.

Getting into college can be a frightening process for anyone, even those students who are given the best that their schools can offer in terms of academic preparation and college advising. Students who have the benefit of family members with college degrees, ample financial resources to cover college costs, and familiarity with the college milieu may still be insecure about the college-entry process. Many parents who send their children to elite high schools where they receive excellent educations expend additional funds on test preparation courses and private college counseling to give their children an extra edge in the college acceptance competition. Yet these students from privileged educational backgrounds find that during their senior year of high school, "April"—when they can expect acceptance or rejection letters from the colleges to which they have applied—"is the cruelest month" (Eliot 1952, 37).

How, then, did many of the first-generation college graduates in this study, those at the opposite end of the spectrum, not only gain access to college but also manage socially, financially, and academically once there? How did they navigate between the two worlds of home and college? What were those qualities that they and others displayed that aided in their success? I address these questions in this chapter.

Getting in the Door

> My first choice was the college of engineering. My second choice was surveying. They assigned me to English because my best high school English teacher had given me a good report. I loved him. He couldn't stand the torture by the students during the Cultural Revolution so he ran under a truck.
>
> — *Chang*

How did the interviewees in this study succeed in gaining access to college? For many of them, the routes to college entry were alternative ones. Creative, lucky, resourceful, resilient, and intentional, many of the participants frequently battled their own ignorance along with the indifference of others in the college-going process—and won. They were able to create for themselves the possibility of getting into college despite their fears that they had not been adequately prepared for the rigors of college academics, that they just were not smart enough to go to college, that they could not amass enough money to pay for college, and that they would not be able to figure out the maze of the college entry process.

In this section I explore two basic issues of college access that were of great concern to most of this study's participants: institutional support, or the role of the high schools in providing these individuals with the college counseling that they needed; and peer support, or the role that fellow students played in providing the participants with what the high schools did not. The case histories are rich with examples of how the interviewees successfully countered barriers to college entry.

Clara, who did not receive the academic advising in high school that one might expect, provides such an example. As she related, the idea that she would go to college came to her late in her high school career:

> The whole time I was growing up, we had to sit down and do our homework, but we didn't talk about college because my parents didn't have that kind of experience. College wasn't expected. Upper-class families had that idea. My parents didn't think along the lines of sending us away to school. We were made to feel that our homework was important, but we were never told to go beyond high school.
>
> I guess I never even thought about going to college when I was in high school until almost senior year when I realized, "Wow! I actually have somewhat decent grades, and I have to do this, this, and this to get into college." But it was almost like it was almost too late to be able to get in. I started to

look at my situation, and I found that I didn't really have the grades and I didn't have the money to go away to college.

Most of my friends weren't going off to college. I got along with all kinds of people so I did have groups of friends with no intention of ever going to college. But I also had friends who were from the popular crowd, and they were all planning to go. It was expected of them, and "What school are you going to?" was how they thought about it. I wanted to go where they were going and do some of the things they were going to do, but I hadn't done enough planning. In my school system, I didn't feel that I was directed or made to feel like high school was just a stepping stone and you go on from there. . . . I had no preparation or explanation about how to go through the process of admissions and choosing a college. When I actually had to go through it, I was really lost.

Clara was a working-class student who felt that because she was not a member of the middle class, no one at school ever advised or encouraged her to see high school as a stepping-stone to college. But noticing her middle-class acquaintances getting ready for college prompted her to assess her own situation. In a dramatic illustration of same-class identification, she noticed women much older than she at the restaurant where she waitressed who held jobs identical to her own in duties and in salary. She realized that her own future was mirrored in the present of many women in her own social class. She was deeply troubled by the probability that she would not be able to get a stimulating job with only a high school diploma. Then one of the kids at school mentioned that one had to take the ACT in order to get into college:

I found out that one had to take an ACT test almost after the fact and had to slide myself into a very quick date that was still available before we graduated. I hurried up and got registered. I took the test, and I got a nine! When I realized how badly I did, I didn't want to tell anybody because I thought that everyone would think I was stupid, and I thought that I must be. The score of nine told me that I was severely mentally handicapped. This made me feel like I was nothing; that I couldn't do anything. I thought, "Well, I can't even get into the community college with this score." At that time, the community college wanted a score of fifteen or higher. Then I said to myself, "But I'm not failing out of school, and I'm not on probation, but how come I'm so dumb?"

Then one of the teachers who had sponsored a trip to Europe that I had gone on told me about the ACT prep class held at night. I had told him that I had taken the ACT and had tested like a monkey and had gotten a nine. I knew that I read very slowly and my math skills were bad. I didn't have a strong science background, but at least after taking the ACT prep class, I was able to raise my score by six points to get into the community college.

Clara's example supports the finding in much of the literature on first-generation college students that good advisement is crucial to their success. Her example marks just one of the various degrees of dereliction of duty that participants reported having experienced at the hands of high school counselors because of individual or institutional race, ethnic or class bias. Indeed, Clara, Barbara, and others among the participants were so cut off from the college advisement process in their high schools that those processes may as well not have existed. Jorge, who attended a prestigious private high school, was closer to the other end of the spectrum, but still in need of intervention by a fair-minded professor who happened to discover how Jorge was being advised. As Jorge put it:

He asked me, "Where are you applying to school?" I told him and he said, "No! You belong someplace else. You go ahead and apply to Brown, you apply to Harvard, you apply to Yale because schools like those are where you belong." Now, I was aware that the college counselor . . . did not think that such schools were where I should have been looking. This English instructor just stopped me short. He said, "No! You belong someplace else." With that in mind, I applied to Yale, Harvard, Brown, Dartmouth, Bates, and Carleton. I went back and talked with the counselor, and he said the new choices were fine. The one word of advice he offered me was that given my personality, Carleton or Bates might be where I wanted to go because I wanted "to be the big fish in the little pond." I took that advice to heart.

Jorge experienced a change of heart, applied to Yale, and became a Yale graduate. While Carleton and Bates are undoubtedly excellent schools, it is noteworthy that the counselor advised an impressionable youth to select those schools over more competitive choices. In addition, the counselor's statement that his advice was to protect Jorge's own interests seems disingenuous at best. Even though Jorge had attended highly selective private schools his entire life, he would be the first person in the history of his family to go to college. On his own, he knew nothing of what to expect from college and was ill equipped, as were his parents, to evaluate the councelor's advice. He had no clue that his solid B+ average and SAT scores of 680 on the math section and 690 on the verbal should have prompted higher expectations from his counselor. The counselor's statement that Jorge wanted to be the big fish in the little pond may have conjured up images in Jorge's mind of being far out of his league at an Ivy League college. The difference between Jorge's case and Clara's was the degree of malfeasance committed by their high school counselors. Neither student was adequately served.

Both Jorge's and Clara's experiences suggest a means by which first-generation college students manage in the world of academia. They make connections with others who will help them to arrive at and survive in college when those whose job it is to do so fail to carry out their duties. Often help comes from other students whose experience becomes the template by which the first-generation college student's path is drawn. Their role is significant, and the data attests to the benefit that they bring to their peers (Rendon, Terenzini, and Upcraft 1994). Indeed, some of the participants reported that their peers provided the only help that they received in maneuvering the complex process of college entry. Without that help, success in getting into college would have taken the participants a lot longer, if they had achieved success at all. After finding that information from their high school counselors, advisors, and teachers about the college-going process was protected and that they were not privileged to share it, many of the participants saw their peers as their major source of information. Ironically, those students who most needed help with getting into college often received the least. Clara explained how this "least help" enabled her to get from the community college to the university:

> When I got ready to leave the community college, I had a friend who was going to Southern. He helped me to do the application and learn whatever I was able to learn about the college-going process. His parents hadn't gone to college either, but somehow they seemed to know more than my parents ever did. He helped me through a lot of the questions I had. I didn't understand that banks could sell you loans. There were informational meetings on the different floors of the dorms that my friend told me about, so I would go to the meetings on my floor and then turn around and go to the meetings on the same topic on his floor. I had a double chance to learn. I became an expert on financial aid so I could help other people who were like I had been.
>
> When I decided to go to Southern, it was only because I knew someone who was going there and I thought I could afford it. I had worked for two years saving money while I went to CLC part-time. I sold my car and everything else that I owned, but I only had enough money to get me through one year. And I thought, "What am I going to do? I can't go back home now. I've quit a very good job with benefits—a good job for not having any

education—and if I go back home, people are going to think I'm a failure. I'm going to feel like a failure, and I can't be a failure." So I started looking for a way to manage. I found that I had enough credit hours to apply to be an R.A. at the dorm, so I tried to get a job and they actually hired me. That way I could manage. If I hadn't had a friend who went to Southern and who helped me, I wouldn't have been there. I kind of felt like I was following that person at the time.

While Clara's friend could not offer expert advice for getting into Southern, at least he had a year's experience more than Clara, who had none. Her story underscores the positive role of peer mentors and advisors in the participants' college-entry experiences. But in terms of leveling the playing field for these first-generation college students, peer mentors fell far short. It is no wonder that professionals are hired to help students manage the maze of getting into college.

When Jerry, another participant, decided to go to the university, no one at school or anywhere else advised him on anything. No one in his community inspired him to go to college, and he was acquainted with no college graduates. He decided with a high school friend that they would go to study engineering, even though he had no clear idea of what engineers did. His idea to study engineering sprang primarily from his involvement in a special interest that he happened upon, the design and building of gas-powered model airplanes. At the university, he joined a fraternity right away, which was, he believes, a very positive thing:

I joined a group of young men who were learning to manage by handling the finances and food and maintaining a mansion of a home. We worked together. They taught us manners. We wore jackets to dinner every night. We opened dinner with a prayer. We sang songs at the end. We were taught table manners by the pledge master. We learned how to meet and greet people, how to treat a woman. If you're going upstairs, she goes first. Going down, you go first. You hold the door. They told me how to part my hair and act decent. I learned a lot of social graces I never would have learned for a long time. It was a great polishing experience. The guys who were in the fraternity with me are dying off now, but they are still friends.

As one of the oldest participants in the study, Jerry benefited from an opportunity that may not have been readily available to low-income, first-generation college students entering the university over forty years later—students such as Clara, Jorge, and Maria. It has become expensive to join a fraternity or sorority, and their wholesomeness seems to have diminished. Yet the necessity and benefits of bonding with peers recurs in the life stories from the oldest to the youngest of this study's participants. Once they had gained access to college, confronting issues of identity within the sociopolitical context of the campus and of the home environment became critical concerns for the interviewees. To answer these concerns, the participants endeavored to construct safe passageways for themselves between the culture of home and the new culture of college.

Cold Comfort Zone: Entering the Culture of College

> The time that I first started going to college was the most traumatic time of my whole life, and I didn't know if I was going to survive it. I would have accidents. I broke my arm, I broke my leg, I crashed the car. These things just kept happening to me, but then things changed. I can almost tell you the minute when someone said, "You should set limits between yourself and other people."
>
> — *Steve*

Writers such as Gandara (1995), Levine and Nidiffer (1996), London (1996), Rendon (1996), and Rendon, Terenzini, and Upcraft (1994) have explored the transition to college of many first-generation college students. They, as well as others, have found that factors such as family, peer, and faculty support are crucial to the success of first-generation college students. The interviews that I conducted produced similar findings and also appeared to shed light on the complex issues of identity, family loyalty, and the need to belong, or "belongingness," in the college-going experiences of this study's participants. In this section I examine the concept of belongingness or the student as "resident" rather than "tourist."

The interviewees in this study stressed that establishing a comfort zone within the college environment was a key component of their academic success. However, they suggested that the ability to feel comfortable at college required a student's personal reconciliation of his or her identity as a college student with his or her identity as a representative of home. This did not mean that the student had to retain the same cultural icons and traditions in each setting. Rather, it meant that he or she recognized and accepted the differences in customs, conditions, experiences, and badges that existed between the two cultures. Thus, by becoming a resident, or one who is at home in one's surroundings, the student could avoid the dislocation and gawkishness of the tourist, or one who does not belong or is just passing through. While these roles were most frequently played out in the non-academic experiences of the interviewees, the degree of comfort that students felt in the total college environment may have had a commensurate effect on their academic achievement.

A few people in the study were not new to straddling two cultures, but all were new to straddling the new culture of college and the culture of home. The complexity of breaking away from home as London (1989) depicted it often seemed more complex in the impassioned telling of some of the participants. Yet many of them realized that a key to successful biculturation was recognizing and accepting the different attributes of both cultures. Annie provided a vivid example of the dichotomy between the culture of college and the culture of home:

> I grew up poor. I went to Tuskegee and started living with people who were upper–middle class. . . . Except for leaving home and going to Tuskegee, I took my first trip out of the county with these people. I stayed in my first hotel. . . .
>
> When I first went to their home, I hardly knew what to do because I had not been accustomed to going in to a bathroom to brush my teeth. I had brushed my teeth standing on the back porch. I grew up going outside to use the toilet. Their whole lifestyle, the living experience, was totally new to me. But the kids had to do chores and stuff, even though their father could give them anything. Like my dad, he made them do things.
>
> I first got to know about other cultures through baby-sitting. The husband in the first family I baby-sat for was from Zimbabwe. I was exposed to African culture at their house. I ate African dishes. Their house was the first place where I had ever eaten out of a silver spoon and at a table set with china. . . .
>
> Getting to be around people from other parts of the world taught me that when you're with people of other cultures, you can adapt. And when I go back home with my family and get that fruit jar and that tin plate, I can adapt. . . . While I would listen to them at dinner, I would ask questions. And the next day the wife would congratulate me on the questions that I had asked. I was learning a lot just by contributing to the conversation.

In this aspect of her passage from the culture of home to the culture of college, Annie maneuvered successfully as a resident of both the lower class and the upper–middle class. She lived in zones of comfort in both worlds. Two reasons for her success seem to be key. First, she simply enjoyed the beauty in her new surroundings. A well-appointed house, scintillating dinner conversations, excellent food, and the affirmation of being included may have enabled Annie to appreciate her new environment and to improve educationally and socially at the same time.

Second, that she was encouraged to exercise her voice, to be heard as well as seen, was immensely validating for Annie. That her employer congratulated her on the questions that she asked during dinners affirmed her intelligence and her worth as one who contributed to the conversation rather than simply learning from it. Annie's employers did not treat her as if she were an outsider or inferior, and she, in turn, neither felt alienated nor exhibited signs that she perceived herself as not belonging. She was free to learn whatever she could without fear of being thought a fool, just as she was at home. In her statement that she could adapt to the fruit jar and tin plate at home, Annie proved that the Wolfeism (1942), "You can't go home again," is not necessarily true for those who *want* to go home again. This point was demonstrated repeatedly by most of the interviewees who did go home again as often as they could.

Other participants seemed to turn Wolfe's (1942) adage on its head with the acknowledgment that it is those who are left at home and rooted firmly in the old world who are immobilized. They cannot meet with familiarity the family member who is a college student in that student's new environment. Entering the culture of the college has given the first-generation college student flexibility, however uncomfortable it may have been initially. But it has limited the freedom of loved ones who have little or no hope of joining the collegiate society through ascending cross-class identification. Their previous freedom to meet on common ground has been canceled until such time as the student re-enters the culture of home. Any meeting as near equals must take place strictly on the student's terms. This is generally understood, if not articulated, by students and families alike, and for the students it may cause both guilt and grief. The study's participants seem to have diminished such pain for themselves and for their families through understanding their own senses of vulnerability as first-generation college students.

In part, that understanding entailed distinguishing the relative likelihood with which different family members might switch their status in the college environment from tourist to resident. It is extremely difficult for one who is firmly rooted in the culture of home to enter the student's new world through ascending cross-class identification because the internalization of information necessary for transformation cannot occur without a basis for believing that one can become the Other. And in the families of many of the first-generation college students in the study, such adjustment and alignment of self-concept for parents, especially, was almost impossible. However, even much older siblings of some participants did make the trek successfully from home to college graduate, following the trails blazed by the participants.

For most of the participants' parents, the idea that they, themselves, may have become educated was a dream beyond possibility. Sadie, for instance, described her father as a brilliant man who only got as far as third grade in school. He had basically taught himself to read and write. When people from their community needed to apply for social security, they would get her father to write the necessary letters for them. Even though her mother had an eighth-grade education, had grown up in a middle-class family, and had married down by marrying a sharecropper, Sadie gave full credit to her father for influencing the intelligence of his children:

> My father came along at a time that was not conducive to his pursuing his education. He was very good at math and would read and discuss politics and all those things with anybody. Our teachers at school learned to respect him because he was articulate and could expound on social and political issues. He and my math teacher became good friends over the course of a year.
>
> I read a lot as a child. There were *Time, Life,* and *Look* magazines around our house. My father would subscribe to these magazines, and back in those days, they wouldn't put you in jail if you didn't pay for them, which was often the case.
>
> My father always wanted someone to go to college, and when I went, every now and then, as a total surprise, my father would come to visit me at school. I wouldn't know he was coming. Someone would announce over the intercom, "Sadie Green, your father is here!" He would be sitting in the lobby. I would go out and see him, and we would chat. Every now and again, he would give me ten or twenty dollars or whatever.
>
> My friends knew my father's nickname was Slick, and they would laugh and tease me about Slick's coming to visit unannounced like that. Later they said they were kind of envious because their parents never came to visit them. The only time your parents came to see you was, maybe, at graduation. You would take the bus to school and back home again at the beginning and end of the semester. My father came for my graduation. I was proud of that. In retrospect, his visits had been enough to tell me that he was proud of me. At the time, because I was young and stupid, I did not appreciate that.

It could be argued that Sadie failed to appreciate her father's visits not be-cause she was young and stupid, but because she loved him and saw both him and herself as vulnerable in a society whose rules he did not understand. A foreigner to Sadie's world, her father may not have comprehended that etiquette in her society was based on practicality and required him to plan his visits. He seemed not to understand that taking an unannounced trip to visit a college student might be much more of a risk than traveling two miles on Sunday to visit his neighbors unannounced on the next farm. With no real concept of the subtle events in the life of a college student or the badges of belonging, such as appearance and language, he was without the information needed to fit in for even a very short while. The college had occasions, including graduation, set aside for outsiders such as parents when judgments of them as Other could be suspended. At all other times, without an invitation, they would enter the collegiate world at their own risk. If they did not portray the characteristics that would mark them as belonging, discreet derision would not be off-limits.

To assume that Sadie was ashamed of her father would be, I believe, an oversimplification as would assuming that her father was cashing in parental collateral to impose himself on the college setting. Both assessments would cloud the real issue, which concerns identities made vulnerable by not belonging. Across all cases the study's participants revealed a need to achieve a sense of belonging in the college environment.

In the new world of college, these first-generation students were vulnerable not only in the ways of new people in new surroundings everywhere, but also in terms of the shifting sands of identities in flux. They were acquiring and processing the information that they needed to become authentic members of the college society. Their identities were being adjusted as they learned and began to gain assurance in their new ways of being. Acquiring the badges of college students raised their personal collateral and shifted their self-concepts from the extreme of inept imposter, or tourist, toward the goal of authenticity, or resident.

This shift was sometimes a slow process. Before they had made considerable advancement, the students may not have acquired enough personal collateral to withstand the devaluation sustained when someone with whom they closely identified, who had none of the trappings of belonging, was interjected into their new environment. Some students may have felt embarrassed by a family member who clearly did not belong, guilty about their newly emerging cultural identities as college students, and ashamed of their desire for a college education—which would increase their difference from their families. But as Sadie indicated, when taking the longer view, the result of such discomforts was validation. In every case, when interviewees spoke of visits by family members who did not belong, at least in retrospect they saw the experiences as important, affirming, and a source of pride. At this stage, the interviewees had achieved a much better understanding of their multifaceted sense of vulnerability as first-generation college students.

Many participants spoke of the angst of seeing their parents in settings where they were vulnerable. Dorothy described the reactions of her parents to the college environment during graduation:

> My parents came to my graduation when I got my bachelor's degree. I was very proud. And there's something that I remember to this day. It touches me. My mom was a shy person, and there was this big crowd and somehow she got separated from Dad, even though they sat together. I found her. She said, "Don't leave me!" I said I wasn't going to leave her, that she should stand right there by that post until I found Dad. Some of my friends came to my graduation, and the mother of one of my closest friends came. And they saw me, and that was nice. I didn't have other family there. My graduation was very special.
>
> When I got my master's, I had a very unusual reaction. I got my hood and all that and just didn't go to the ceremony. I think I didn't go because for whatever reason, my dad didn't want to go, and I knew that if my dad didn't go, my mom wouldn't go. So what would be the point of my going? So I just said, "Okay. I won't go." At first I was upset about their not going to the graduation, but they'd seen me walk for my bachelor's, so that was fine. If they had never seen me get a degree, I'd have been much more upset. Maybe my dad was afraid of the crowds.

Dorothy clearly voiced most of the participants' understanding that their parents were tourists who may have been as afraid of the crowds when they began their infrequent forays into the college arena as the students had been upon first arrival. Of course, as aspiring residents, the students had far more at stake. Their searches for zones of comfort and belonging were searches for an identity, and they were played out in different ways within the college milieu. But their parents' discomfort as tourists was painful for the students, too, and prompted their efforts to allay their parents' fears and their own guilt for assuming a new identity as college student. They began the process of clarifying for themselves and demonstrating to their families that they had not abandoned the culture of home but were becoming dual residents by also acclimating to the new culture of college. In most cases, they could not expect their parents to venture onto campus very often, but on those rare occasions when they did, the participants endeavored to make their visits as culturally familiar as possible. For instance, when Clara's family came to her campus for her graduation, she planned an outing to a Cubs/Cardinals baseball game—an event her whole family would enjoy. By diminishing the cultural distance between home and college, this study's participants were able to lessen the discomfort of their visiting families and friends. By so doing, they enhanced their own levels of comfort and belongingness within the collegiate environment. In the following section, I consider their efforts to acclimate to college life outside the classroom.

Purpose, Process, and Place: An Agenda for the Informal Curriculum

> The university gave me a work-study position where I could work for twenty hours a week to pay for my room and board. If I worked thirty hours a week, I could earn money toward my tuition as well. For me this was incredible good luck.
>
> — *Alex*

Every fall, thousands of college students flock to the nation's campuses ostensibly with a single purpose: to claim scholastic success. For some, especially for those whose families have established a tradition of college attendance, the experience may be a somewhat familiar journey. For others, especially for many of the first-generation college students among the throngs, the transition to college may require immense sacrifices augmented by prayer, faith, and luck. Since getting in the door may have been so difficult for the latter group, one might expect them to focus far more strongly on the formal curriculum than on any other aspect of the collegiate learning experience. The stories of this study's interviewees, however, reveal an almost equal value on certain facets of the informal curriculum. Specifically, many of these first-generation college students had dual purposes, processes, and places for the most important learning that they would do. Their primary purpose was, of course, to earn a college degree using the formal curriculum as process and the classroom as place. The discussion here concerns the participants' second, but almost equally important, collegiate agenda: the discovery of self and others through the informal curriculum.

Life outside the college classroom, as depicted in the literature as well as in the participants' stories, was a forum for continued learning. As the individuals I interviewed were able to lessen the dissonance between the culture of home and the culture of college, they felt increasingly able to direct their attention to the pressing business of integration into the college environment.

Beyond the objective of determining who they were and how they would fit in, they were beset by additional questions of identity. What did they bring to the enrichment of the informal curriculum? What did they most need to learn from that curriculum? What time management strategies would they apply to their involvement in the informal curriculum? The daily events of their lives outside the classroom revealed interesting and varied rituals of "being" and "becoming." For most, the non-academic scene was the arena for discovering who they were and how they fit within the mosaic of college life.

For Jorge, as was true for others in the study, life outside the classroom was a journey toward self-discovery, a journey entailing his recognition and internalization of his ethnicity as personal, social, and political dynamics. Since Jorge had attended highly selective private schools with only one or two Hispanics prior to college, when he arrived at Yale, he had not known very many Puerto Ricans outside his extended family. Right away Jorge began hanging out with the Puerto Ricans on campus. There were only about a hundred, and the number was about evenly split between mainland and island Puerto Ricans. He became good friends with the whole Latino crowd, as well as with others from the various racial/ethnic groups. But he found the island Puerto Ricans to be a strange breed: "They had no idea what a minority was because they were all coming from the upper strata of society on the island. They came with money and were a nice, happy, pampered bunch." Jorge perceived a definite tension between the island Puerto Ricans and the "wild-eyed, urban types" with whom he identified.

Jorge also spoke of an Asian roommate with whom he shared a mutual and passionate hatred. As he told me:

> We almost came to blows on more than one occasion. I was just getting into my cultural identity, and he was everything that I thought somebody from an ethnic background should not be. He was very "white." As a student, he did well; his folks did well financially. He was a nice, good, solid, conservative Republican, and I . . . well, I was just in the process of transforming myself into a semi-radical mainland Puerto Rican from an urban environment who had spent summers and weekends in the inner city, even though I had never gone to school there. My Asian roommate wasn't really like the people I had known from Francis Parker (the prep school where Jorge received his high school education), and if he was, I didn't notice their bad qualities until I saw them in him.

Jorge was a young man who was adjusting his self-concept to fit his perception of "semi-radical mainland" Puerto Rican even as he was maintaining and cultivating friendships with members of other groups. And even as he was openly critical of and hostile toward his Asian roommate who was not ethnic enough, Jorge was being called "too white" himself:

> I remember getting very upset at the time with one of my Latino buddies. . . . I remember getting so angry with him because my roommates wanted to go out one night and do something, and I already had plans with some other friends. My buddy said, "Why don't you go hang out with your white friends, then?" I let him have it! I told him that the fact that he had no life in his college shouldn't put him on my case. In truth, I was the most social in our bunch; I have always worked all sides of the crowd really well. And one thing I am never hassled about is skin color. Sometimes I wonder about that. I think I have a sense of regret about that. I absolutely do have a sense of regret about that.

The necessity for Jorge to defend being too white to Latinos was balanced by the necessity for him to defend being "too Puerto Rican" to whites:

> Some people had a problem with me because they thought I was too Puerto Rican. They thought I was rabid about my ethnicity. One guy at one point said to me: "I don't understand why you're so Puerto Rican, why you have to be so . . . you have to throw it out there. Look at your friend, Freddie." Now, the guy speaking to me was white. Freddie was a Puerto Rican from the Bronx. He was dark, hip-hop dressing, the whole works. And this guy says, "Besides, Freddie looks more Puerto Rican than you do."
>
> I just kind of shook my head. And I was immensely saddened because being Puerto Rican doesn't have anything to do with how anybody looks. It's a state of mind. It has nothing to do with race. It is absolute ethnicity. And he had no concept of that. I didn't even bother responding beyond, "you just don't understand." I didn't want to get into it. He didn't understand at all. I could be anyone's spitting image and I could be absolutely Puerto Rican while that person wouldn't be because it's an internal thing. The kind of ignorance that this guy was expressing just sticks in my craw.

As Jorge's examples suggest, adjusting one's self-concept may require ongoing consideration of the perceptions, however erroneous, of others regarding what you should be. Should they be factored into the database that will make up your new self-concept? Should they be ignored? Should they be used as a springboard for educating others? Jorge's fair skin further complicated the identity issues he was negotiating during college. Specifically, Jorge was perplexed by the seeming inability of other intelligent people to understand race as a distinctly different construct from ethnicity. In the United States where the quality of one's life experiences may depend on the color of one's skin, Jorge expressed concern that the ethnic anonymity inherent in his whiteness may have altered his consciousness of who he is:

> I have a sense of regret about my skin color sometimes because skin color is something I just don't know how to deal with. And it's something I wouldn't have minded dealing with. I think I have a sense of regret from the perspective of loss of experience. I understand it in theory, but I don't have any practical experience with it except through osmosis and through group experiences on a couple of occasions. I mean, I was always the palest one in the bunch for the most part. But since the others looked so much more ethnic than I, there was enough visible ethnicity to cover me too, in some instances. Prejudice is not based on reason, and the bigot has no trouble extending his hatred to whoever associates with those he dislikes.

Experiences outside the classroom aided in Jorge's emerging self-identification and enhanced his sense of belonging, two factors that appear crucial to the success of college students (Astin 1993):

> In sophomore year, you go to live in your residential college with about five hundred other people. You get your own dining hall and various other conveniences. As a freshman, I was very much into the Latino crowd, and I went about with my circle. Sophomore year is when we began to disperse a little bit even though the Latinos, both the Puerto Ricans and the Mexicans, all knew each other and got along well. We also knew the African Americans who were active in the African American cultural center. We all formed a pretty tight group, actually.
>
> Sophomore year was an odd year for me. My roommate and closest friend left midway through the year because that place was "killing" him. But I had a couple of really good friends, Latinos, from the freshman class. During junior year I became much more active in the day-to-day life of my residential college. One of the football players, a senior, and I had been in a couple of classes together my freshman year. In the dining hall he would call me over, and I would go and sit with him and his friends. We used to hold court during meals. I started to hang out with them, and, once football season was over, every Friday became a big party day in their room. These were white guys, but there was an African American guy that I am really

close to still. He and I would watch sports together, and I met a lot of his friends through him. By junior year, I was definitely steady in Pearson, my residential college. I had my crew, and I loved it.

While there was much for Jorge to learn from non-academic life, he suggests that he had much to contribute to the informal curriculum on the subject of valuing diversity. It is important to note that the impact of the informal curriculum upon Jorge's issues of identity may have been compounded by other factors stemming from family and home and relating specifically to his status as a first-generation college student. This was true of many other participants in the study and should not be taken as an indication that other such issues did not exist.

For Arlene, the informal curriculum proved crucial to her awakening identity as a Native American. Arlene had grown up on a reservation, but her family had "protected" her by keeping her ignorant of her people's traditional ways:

As if the magic of the church were not potent enough to banish Indian beliefs . . . I got the message that there were two kinds of Indians: the good ones who were Christians and the bad ones who practiced the traditional ways. . . . were pagans. . . . I knew and was interested in nothing of substance about my culture.

Arlene explained that the wealth of information that she learned from her Native American peers at NAES (Native American Educational Services, a Native American college with a campus in Chicago) became an invaluable and personalized part of her curriculum. As one with practically no knowledge of the history and traditions of Native American people, hearing the personal histories of her college friends gave Arlene an immediate base of information about herself, her history, and the many nations of her people. Arlene pointed out that life outside the college classroom enriched and corroborated what she was learning through the formal curriculum:

At NAES, I would hear about the government run boarding schools for Indian children in the States and in Canada. . . . [M]y best friend Joan . . . went to a boarding school . . . when she was four years old. She shared with me how she became very ill around one Christmastime. The people in charge of the school put her in a room that was dark, and she was still there the next Easter. . . .These exposures to real-life experiences . . . that are part of our history became part of my curriculum. . . . The knowledge that I received from my colleagues was as great as what I learned in the classroom.

. . . I learned about taking part in powwows and eventually thinking, "I'll be darned! That's the grass dance!. . . . I know this! I know that!" It was quite a springboard for me to begin to realize that . . . many Native Americans were torn from their families but were still able to maintain a strong spiritual link to the traditional ways.

Also important to Arlene was the bonding that took place among the students. She described their relationship as family-like. The students had much in common, as many were of nontraditional age, were divorced, had children, and were the heads of their households. Through the informal curriculum, Arlene gained the opportunity to immerse herself into Native American culture by attending traditional events with her peers. She was absolutely intent on learning all that she could about herself and her people. She became a virtual sponge, absorbing everything that she could and building community with her acquaintances in the process. "I've been trying to learn what I can about the traditional ways," she stated. "In terms of learning, I have no time to lose because during so much of my life, I learned practically nothing about my people."

For many of this study's participants, the informal curriculum provided opportunities for affirmation and validation through bonding with the faculty. For example, because Sadie had worked for a year and a half before going to college, she saw herself as an older student and felt somewhat removed at first from her classmates. But she made friends with an English professor who welcomed her into her office for informal talks. Another professor actually visited Sadie in her dorm room, sat on the floor with her, and through a discourse of equals, enhanced Sadie's sense of self and affirmed her worth as a member of the college community. When Sadie first traveled by plane, her English professor gave her spending money because she knew that Sadie was almost completely without funds. Later, when Sadie was able to pay her back, the professor would not accept the repayment. She asked Sadie to do the same for someone else someday. Sadie indicated a commitment to living by that credo.

Several of the participants spoke of their connections with others through extracurricular involvements as helpful in giving them confidence and in establishing an identity for themselves on campus. Clara became president of the Spanish National Honor Society as a result of a heightened self-image. This improved her self-concept even more. Grant became active in school politics when he was in law school. He had been shy as a child, but as vice-president of the Student Bar Association, he had to talk. His peers had pushed him into the role, but he found that he had an affinity for all the social and political duties that the position demanded. Barbara was active in the NAACP and worked on voter registration. Others participated in various activities that enriched their lives and forged bridges between themselves and others.

Sometimes the participants' connections with others took on the flavor of rebellion. Accustomed to the excitement of life in the city, Barbara was caught in a flood of lights as she crawled back in the dorm through a window at ten-thirty from an evening of small-town fun. She was actually brought to trial by the university senate. John left Berkeley during the Vietnam War demonstrations of the 1960s because the political unrest was too disruptive to his studies. He recounts spending a couple of weekends locked up on a concrete slab in Sacramento where the authorities would take Berkeley students who were simply walking home from classes on Friday afternoons. Sometimes his classes were held on Haight Ashbury. The Berkeley experience introduced him to some of the students who were involved in the anti-war demonstrations and with whom he later connected at the hippie commune, The Farm. Alex played an active role in the 1960s Civil Rights demonstrations in the south. He spoke about the sense of community and the seriousness of purpose that were part of his involvement:

> Everyone I knew was involved . . . in the Civil Rights movement. . . . Hundreds of nicely turned-out college students would approach the ticket booth at movie theatres and ask for a ticket. . . . Their requests . . . were always refused unless I or a white-looking black was the one asking. We would buy a ticket, go in, stay a little while, and come out and join the line again. . . .We wanted to show that skin color can fool anyone foolish enough to make decisions based upon it. . . . that sharing a theater with someone who is black poses no harm. . . . that we weren't tired and we would keep coming back until justice was served.

How did the students make time for learning from the informal curriculum? Everything in their lives was arranged around their classes, the top priority within the formal curriculum. As the top priority in the informal curriculum, work was coordinated with classes before time was allotted for any other activity. More pervasive than any other pattern in the out-of-classroom experiences of the participants, work gained supremacy by being absolutely necessary to the financial and, by extension, academic survival of most students in the study. John learned carpentry and how to lay linoleum and carpet, skills that he later used to help support his family. Clara was a research and teaching assistant which enabled her to help other students learn to navigate the world of the university. Arlene was a development officer in the area of her anticipated degree. All of the participants worked, and most reported that their work experiences were important far beyond providing them with badly needed money. Grant worked to earn extra money for flying and violin lessons. Later he worked from six until nine in the mornings as a flight instructor before going to his job as an intern in patent law at Westinghouse. While working for Upward Bound, Sadie learned that she could be a teacher and a leader. Annie's work as a nanny enabled her to live with educated, kind, financially secure people who changed her life by ushering her into another world. Steve worked at many jobs, sometimes three or four at a time. He recalled one job that was especially significant:

> In my second semester at the community college, I had an instructor who just didn't think I was going to make it as an artist. I would think, "Maybe he's right!" But there was a woman whose daughter I had gone out with in high school, and she was an artist. She said, "Come over and I'll teach you how to paint." She had these very generic-looking clown paintings. I would sit with her and she sort of mentored me. She said, "Well, if you're gonna paint these things, you're gonna enter 'em in shows and you're gonna sell 'em." She took me around Chicago to all these places where she had her paintings hanging on the walls of these restaurants. And she mounted my stuff on the walls! She'd say, "Get all these framed up!" I didn't even know *how* to paint. I'd stick the brush in the tube of paint. I didn't even know you put paint out on something. She showed me how to do it. And she said, "If you're gonna do it, you're gonna make a living off of it." I remember we went into some real divey bars and places like that, and she'd hang my paintings on the walls, and her stuff was down there. I started selling paintings, and that's what I really put myself through school with. I did art fairs. That was almost like being a street peddler. If you talked to people and asked if they'd do art fairs, they'd say, "Well, then you'd be seen as no good. You can't be serious about your work if you're doing art fairs."

> I had that problem all the way through graduate school. I had to do it. I had no other choice because that was the only way I was going to make it through school. When I finished graduate school, I went to the college art association, and there weren't any jobs at all. I bought my house at that time off the money I had made off my paintings, and I paid it off in four years.

Chang provided another example of academic-discipline-related work. When he came to graduate school at an American university, Chang needed to find work to support himself. On a professor's recommendation, he was given a position as a teaching assistant in the English department on three day's notice. He did not understand English as spoken by the students, especially when they used slang. His courses were hard, especially literary criticism. He had not studied Freudianism. He had not read deconstructionists such as Derrida, and he had no concept of why "a center is not a center."

Chang never went to bed that whole year before midnight and never got up later than seven in the morning. He ate dinner at midnight. Every Sunday he would cook a week's supply of food and put it in the freezer. He would prepare chicken legs and snow peas and would augment this fare with the eastern noodles that you simply put in hot water. His wife and young son were in China. When he got to see them again two years later, his son had forgotten him.

Yet Chang realized that as the third person in the history of his village in China to go to college, he was extremely lucky. He related that many of his friends had gotten too deeply involved in the Cultural Revolution and their lives had been wasted. In their zeal to follow Chairman Mao, they had killed many people. Chang recalled an extremely intelligent friend who was imprisoned and forced to spend all his waking hours writing a self-criticism. Falsely accused of multiple murders, day in and day out he was forced to write the lies that comprised his self-criticism. One day he decided to resist and gouged the sharp pointed pen into his eyes. The inky piercings blinded him.

As was true of many other participants, Chang felt that the chance to work in order to earn college degrees and to change the educational, social, and economic status of future generations of his family was a gift of great worth. Even with his singular voice and his specific experience, he encapsulated the spirit with which most of the participants embraced both their coursework and their jobs. His words seemed to say for all of them, "This is why we worked and why we studied":

> I got the chance to compete at college, and I knew I could, but I sometimes felt it was unfair that I was chosen over my colleagues to sit for an exam. I owe something to them and to my family. My older brother didn't have my chances. My mother was very sickly, and he had to miss a lot of school to go to the city and stay in the hospital with her. My parents were poor, too poor even to come to my graduation, and I was off working, teaching, during that time anyway. My classmates at college would talk about their

families and how well they were doing, and I knew that my family was not doing well. So I thought that maybe I'm the person to change things for my family.

Because I had so little money, I felt pressure from other students when they wanted me to go to town, to the parks, to have something to eat like pot stickers or something. I didn't have money to do these things. I would try to avoid going with them. Now, I think staying behind all the time was good because all I could do was study. I look back now and I can say that I did better because I was studying. Of the eighteen students in my class, I was the best.

Life outside the classroom seemed to provide the participants with important experiences in the discovery of self and others through various types of work as well as through other aspects of the informal curriculum. These experiences seemed to form not only rich extensions to the formal curriculum but also platforms for the developing social consciousness among the participants. Almost universally, the marks of the informal curriculum on these first-generation college students appeared indelible, figuring prominently in how they would both work and play long after their college days had passed. In most cases, the interviewees reported that the benefits of learning from the informal curriculum abetted their classroom experiences, the subject of the following section.

The Professor as Change Agent

> My professors did other things that I found life-changing. I remember
> one time Syracuse had a workshop. . . on aesthetic ambiguities. . . .
> [P]rofessors gave me a lot of freedom to experiment. . . . I try to do just
> pure experimentation at least six to eight weeks a year. Much of that
> practice came from my experience at the Syracuse workshops.
>
> — *John*

The single most important measure of whether students are successful in college is their success in the classroom. Far more important than how well they have adjusted, what they have learned, or what they can prove they know, the grades that students achieve symbolize the degree to which they are academically successful. Since first-generation college students from low socioeconomic backgrounds are almost universally afraid of failure, it is easy to imagine the trepidation with which many of this study's participants mounted the unrelenting scales of competition in the college classroom.

Many had previously experienced reasons to be afraid. Gaining access to college had been an enormous battle. Reconciling the culture of home with the culture of college had severely tested their mettle. Establishing themselves in the society of the college had, at times, seemed unattainable. And since most of these factors could not be dealt with in linear fashion, their tectonic jostling might have rattled the equilibrium of the Sphinx. Needless to say, the participants in this study were not sphinxes. Yet they all earned bachelor's degrees, and some even earned graduate and professional degrees.

The participants reported a variety of college classroom experiences, both good and bad, which presented strong evidence that specific variables positively influenced their college success. Factors such as the intellectual and personal connection between professors and students, dialogical teaching, professors' transformative power, the students' belief that their professors believed in them, and the intentionality of the students themselves were all stressed as instrumental in the success of these first-generation college students.

A recurrent theme in the interviews was the positive effect of intellectual as well as personal connections that professors were able to establish with this study's participants. For these students, interacting with their professors, especially in small classes, transcended the classroom experience to form the basis for friendship long after the classes were over. Ken spoke about the excitement of discovering like-minded individuals among his professors who presented, fully fleshed-out, the skeletons that were his emerging ideas:

Most of my classes were seminars in philosophy with nine people in them. I got to know my teachers well. We were welcomed in our teachers' houses. Two years ago, another philosophy instructor and I went to hear one of my professors from William and Mary speak at Roosevelt. He took us out for breakfast. After all those years, the relationships don't break down. They are just wonderful people, wonderful teachers who did new and different things for me. All of a sudden, here were people who thought the way I did, who were putting forth in the classroom the same ideas I was beginning to develop on my own. The world just kept expanding.

I also had a wonderful professor, David Jenkins, who taught me William Butler Yeats. He was an eccentric bachelor who, not being married, had lots of time for students. I would be sitting there eating ice cream, and he'd say, "Hey, come on, I'm going to the airport. Come along for the ride." He had an old Austin that he could barely fit in. He was this great big lanky man who helped us to uncover the genius and beauty of Yeats' work. William and Mary was just a wonderful experience because of the professors. I couldn't have chosen a better school for me at the time.

Ken's example, which is representative of many others in the interviews, stresses the impact of professors who help their students to stretch intellectually but also to develop zones of comfort within the college milieu. Affirmation, validation, enfranchisement, a sense of belonging, and excellence in education are only a few of the benefits for students that most of the interviewees attributed to professors who made genuine connections with them both as students and as individuals.

Jorge provided another example of the involved professor's contribution to the academic success of an interviewee. He spoke of a tough professor at Yale who awakened his identity as a Puerto Rican, underscored the importance of social and civic responsibility, urged the students toward moral agency, and assessed them in a meticulously fair way:

What really helped to shape me from those years was a professor, Manuel, that I had during my freshman year. . . . He was vicious! We had these monstrous casebooks, and we had to read five hundred pages a week for our once-a-week seminar. You would come into class and Manuel would start firing questions at you, left and right, and you wouldn't know where he was going to go next. And those were specific little questions, so you had to have done the reading. I loved that class! It was hell . . . but we loved it! The entire course was based on the status of Puerto Rico which had developed over time. That Manuel was Puerto Rican made all the difference in the world in terms of his teaching the course. . . .one of the first things that we did was read an article he had written on the subject. We had three very large casebooks of decisions and opinions. . . . Then Manuel came back my junior year and taught another course. Most of us in the class had taken his first offering . . . The majority of the students were Latinos. . . . because of the subject matter.

But Manuel had a lot more than subject matter to offer. . . . He taught us that there is a definite sense of rightness and that the responsibility to make it happen lies with us. He said that Puerto Ricans comprise 2 percent or less of the Latino population and that we had to make sure we figured out what to do and that we did it well. I learned a lot from Manuel; I learned a ton from him. More important than what I learned academically, Manuel fostered my learning about my cultural identity—who I am as a person and who I want to be. I am very grateful for Manuel's example. . . . I still have a copy of the recommendation that Manuel wrote for me. . . . He worked us hard, and he . . . praised the brilliance that he saw in us.

From both Jorge's and Ken's examples, there is the clear message that professors who can offer common ground on which they and their students can meet intellectually are, in effect, extending a bridge to their students. They are meeting the students on the expanse and engaging them intellectually and, perhaps, in countless other positive ways. From his professor's influence, Jorge grew academically, politically, and personally. Dorothy, in much the same vein, not only grew academically in a creative writing class, but also emotionally as she came to understand and value the respectful critiques of Cyrus Colter, a famous author and professor who compelled her to strive for excellence:

He said to me, "I think you're more like Toni Morrison. You're not good with plotting, but your descriptions are quite vivid. You may want to re-think some of these things." He was really hard on me. I got a B. I thought I was going to get a C. He gave me an incomplete at first so I could finish the piece I was working on. Then he wrote me these long, two pages of comments on my story. He filled two pages of legal paper. Those comments are my pride and joy. It amazed me that he would give me that kind of attention. There was the disappointment, though, that he didn't really like my writing the way he did some people's.

He let me know that I could take criticism and not dissolve. Being in class sometimes felt like a totem pole deal where other students were climbing all over you to make their work look better. He was tough! Egos would fly! People would clash! It was a wonderful experience.

Just as the effectiveness of a professor at connecting with and engaging his students was reiterated in most of the case histories, their pedagogical styles were also important to the academic success of the interviewees. Dorothy emphasized the power of dialogical teaching on her survival in academia by first relating the conditions under which she had previously defected from the isolation and emptiness of college life: "I didn't know what I could be. I was very much lost. The university subtracted from me. There was no closeness. By the time I left, I had no idea what I *could* do."

This was a bleak and different perspective from which Dorothy had origi-nally contemplated her possibilities. She had believed that she could achieve whatever she wanted to achieve until she entered the "real world of higher education." She entered the university as an English major, but as an African

American, she quickly discovered that she was an anomaly in the department. She had graduated from Lundbloom Technical High School on the south side of Chicago where most students were of color. But in courses at the university such as Shakespeare or Milton's *Paradise Lost*, she was the only black student and found herself socially isolated on the campus. Her dreams of becoming a teacher or writer were replaced as her priority by her sudden concern with social status and racial identity.

As the only black in the classroom and as one who had no connections with others on the campus, Dorothy felt that she had to prove herself. She stated that she tried to make sure that she had read every extra assignment so that she would be ready in the classroom; but the coldness and alienation consumed her confidence, and once in class, she could not speak. She described sitting in huge lecture halls with five hundred other students while trying to understand history and finding the small group sessions with teaching assistants inadequate to foster real communication. She indicated that no white student ever tried to cross the divide between them, and she had no student support system because she never made friends with any one. So one day, after she had been on the campus for a year and a half, she asked herself, "Why am I here?" Not finding a substantive answer, she dropped out.

When Dorothy resumed her college career at Columbia College, the structure of the classroom and the dialogic teaching style of her professors proved crucial to the transformation that she experienced:

We sat in a room with people and actually looked at them. We sat in a circle. The teacher . . . was relaxed . . . and accessible. . . . Connections with students were much easier to make. Classes were small, and sometimes the same people would be in different classes. I was delighted by that. It really helped me.

I guess I decided I had a voice at Columbia because I wanted to become a writer and I didn't like having the professors indicate that women didn't matter because we weren't being taught at Harvard or being tested on the GRE. I thought that belittled me as well as the great writers like Toni Morrison. . . . I still have a hard time defending myself, but when other people are affected, I can leap, as they say, to the fore.

At Columbia, the professors helped to create an atmosphere that was conducive to change. The atmosphere made me feel free enough to express myself in class, and my views were validated by students and faculty. . . . I could talk to and be friends with faculty and peers. I was able to value myself as a person and as a student. I could say, "I don't like this; I don't think this is fair."

Professors were facilitators. They involved all of us, and it was so nice to be taken seriously. . . . Even if your professors didn't like what you had to say . . . you still had a forum from which to say it. You weren't in those huge lecture halls where the people who were already outspoken sat at the front with their hands raised, and the shy rushed to the back, and nobody ever tried to get them to integrate.

My experience . . . shows the power of professors to help a student become who that student really is. If you are too quiet, then . . . you are not talking about those issues that are of real concern to you or recognizing that people value the contributions that you make when you talk. In a setting where you are really encouraged to do that, what happens is that you begin to become who you really are.

Another factor that greatly contributed to the college success of many of the study's participants was the power of professors to aid in transforming their students. Many of the participants talked about the professors who changed their lives by being the role models whom they emulated in their professional lives. Clara, a teacher, provided one example of the transformative power of a professor whose methodologies Clara re-creates in her own classroom:

My teacher who sort of saved me taught Latin American Culture and Spanish, her third language. I modeled my classroom after hers because I liked the way she set up the classroom so much. I thought it gave people who didn't know how to do very well in all areas a chance to get credit for the hard work that they were successful at doing. She divided the points you could earn in class into 50 percent for exams, 20 percent for quizzes, 20 percent for homework, and 5 percent each for attendance and participation. If you weren't great at taking exams, you could do well in the other areas and, perhaps, build your confidence. If you had confidence, you could do better on exams. I didn't always test well, but in small chunks and in projects, I would pour my heart into everything I did. On the big exams, I didn't know how to focus because I didn't have the study skills, I think. I would still get a decent grade in her class even if I didn't test up to what my potential was. She gave me credit for all the things that I did well. I really liked that. I thought that I might have many students like me with test anxiety, and they might not make it on the tests and would just feel stupid when they're really not. I wanted to give them a chance. My professor was the biggest person in my life.

While one might correctly expect that participants who became teachers would model exemplary instructors from their student days, it also appeared true of participants in other fields. Maria, who holds an accounting degree and works for a social service organization, put to excellent use the teachings of her freshman English professor at DePaul:

> She always allowed us to write about something personal. She thought people were most effective when they wrote about personal things. She felt that you are going to catch the reader's interest with personal writing because the reader wants to know about you. It is so true. . . . when I have to do an annual report, when I have to do a write-up for the newspaper, for funders, I always attach a case history about one of our clients. It gives them a flavor of the kinds of things we do. . . . It has what the client's gone through and how we were able to help. Even when board members or others come out to visit, I take them out to see clients and they can see firsthand how we use the money—"This is who we lent it to, and this is what the person has done."

In addition to those referenced in the preceding excerpts, many other professors whom the participants encountered in the classroom were invaluable agents of positive change in their students' lives. In fact, some of the participants, such as Clara, credit one or more of their professors with being the single most significant factor in surviving their college experience. Barbara gave an account of how her professors' presentations and courses of study were so dynamic and interesting that she became intellectually involved in the classroom against her will. She explained that, at the time, she had never taken herself seriously as a student. In her background, there were certain behaviors that were off-limits for girls, and becoming intellectually involved with ideas was one of them. Barbara had not thought of herself at the time as a very intelligent woman who was pretending to be less astute. Rather, she had thought that she was smart enough to get her degree, but really not very smart, and that she should not bring attention to her intellect. She had been afraid that if she were seen as an intellectual threat or challenge to anyone, she would increase her chances of making a fool of herself. She provided a clear illustration of a positive self-concept that was "in the closet," held back even from her own consciousness by the conventions of her background:

> I pretended that I wasn't really interested, that I just wanted to get the degree. But that wasn't really true. I was fascinated by the courses and the work that I was reading and doing, but somehow I couldn't freely admit to

that. I remember knowing one woman who was a colleague of my husband—already in graduate school—who took herself seriously and got a T.A. She was the only woman I knew who had one. They didn't give them out to women or to blacks. They only went to white guys. I kind of disapproved of her. There was something very masculine about her. I thought at the time, "Who is she?"

Professors who connected with and engaged Barbara in the classroom may have generated her metamorphosis from non-serious student to serious scholar. By contrast, Annie talked about the negative effect of a professor whose approach to teaching was without connection with or engagement of his students. In fact, the professor was presented as an extinguisher of enthusiasm for a subject, rather than the involved instructor that Annie needed:

The teacher was very knowledgeable. . . . But his teaching style and my learning style did not match. He'd tell me answers but wouldn't show me the process. He'd stand there and lecture. . . . When the teachers were involved with the material and let us have a lot of practical or hands-on experience, I learned better. I would talk to other students to see if I could learn from them. I got a D from that math class, and I had loved math before. My grade wasn't because I couldn't understand math. I just didn't get the help that I needed from that teacher.

Annie felt that by using the straight lecture mode and by failing to demonstrate the process of solving math problems, the professor had failed at his job. The cost to Annie was not only an unsatisfactory grade but also the loss of a subject—since it had been rendered incomprehensible by her professor—that she had loved. When Annie could not get the help that she needed from the institution, she sought help from her peers, a strategy that was often reported across the case studies. Even when such interventions did not meet with the desired degree of academic success, most of the participants were able to analyze their circumstances and to determine where the real cause of the problem lay. By objective isolation of the problem's cause, the participants could devise a realistic battle plan to achieve a solution. By ascertaining that the cause of the problem was external to herself and rightly fell under the province of the professor, Annie was spared the lowered self-esteem of thinking the D in math meant there was something wrong with her. Analysis appears to have enhanced Annie's resilience, a causality repeatedly demonstrated in the participants' stories.

Such intentionality seemed to work in similar fashion for Maria who spoke about a professor who did not use a dialogical or student-centered approach to teaching. Maria had to take his class three times:

> I had to take a cost accounting class three times because my professor was just a total jerk. He was very cold. He presented the material very quickly. He didn't have "any time to tutor you. You either get it or you don't. It isn't difficult stuff." He knew I had taken the class twice, and I went to him and said, "I'm graduating. I've taken this class twice. . . . Please cut me some slack." And twice he gave me a D. I'm not the first person he did that to. Even if I took it in the daytime, he was still the only professor teaching it. When I enrolled in the class the third time, it was a TBA [to be announced] and I had no idea it would be him. I said, "I'm not dropping." He knew it was my third time and I was stuck. He did other women the same way he did me. He doesn't teach there any more. He didn't even have tenure. . . . Even if you said, "Can you repeat that, please?" he'd say, "Well, we don't have time for that right now. We're gonna move on to . . . and if you have questions, you can ask me later." And I needed the question answered *before* we went on.
>
> He was very intimidating. You were afraid to ask questions because he'd already told you he didn't have time for that. How did he expect us to go on to the next material if we couldn't grasp the first? Once I asked, "What's the sense of going on if we don't know how to calculate *this* to insert *this* in this cost analysis?" He said, "You can save your remarks for someone who cares or wants to listen to them." Then I was fuming because I was paying for the class and wasn't getting anything out of it. It was humiliating to have to go to him after class and ask for his help.
>
> The third time I took the class, I could have taught it for him. . . . I was successful because it was the only class I was taking. I had notes from the first and second times I had taken it. I had done all my work the first two times, but the fact that I knew what to expect and what types of tests he gave and the repetition made it doable. There was *no one* I could talk to about how that professor was. They were just gonna say, "You're taking cost accounting," like I was expected to fail. I was asking myself what was wrong with me that I couldn't grasp cost.

According to Maria, that she was a woman in the predominately male accounting department was the major reason the cost accounting professor treated her and other women with such disdain. Her problem with the accounting professor, she indicated, was certainly not that the subject was difficult. To the contrary, it was that he had discouraged communication and un-

derstanding to the point that she just did not understand the necessary procedures. "If you have to work with formulas and you've no idea how he's getting
this particular number, how are you going to plug it in?" Maria asked rhetori-
cally.

As was true of Annie, Maria seemed to have analyzed her situation and
found that the professor's lack of connection with his female students and his
unwillingness or inability to use a more student-centered, hands-on approach
to teaching were major barriers to her success. In spite of her professor, her
own powers of analysis and intentionality, qualities displayed repeatedly by
the study's participants in academic as well as other settings, appear eventually
to have resulted in her success. Two successive D's had made Maria doubt
herself, but by analyzing her predicament and isolating the reasons for her
unsatisfactory grades, she seemed able to identify and execute a solution. At
the same time, by objectively placing the blame for her situation squarely upon
the shoulders of her professor, she appeared able to retrieve her sense of
worth.

Most of the participants in the study credit outstanding college professors
with enhancing their academic success by generating intellectual and personal
connections, involving the students in the learning process through use of
student-centered or dialogical instructional approaches, and transforming students by means of illustrious example. Augmented by the students' own intentionality, these professorial qualities may have propelled the interviewees
much closer to their educational goal of college graduation.

5 | My Job Description

As a seventh-grade language arts teacher in the integrated public schools of a working-class city in Illinois, I began observing every day the fruits of the district's tracking system. Most black students could be found in the lowest level classes, including special education, while most whites were in the higher level ones. Four years later, as an English teacher in the district's high school, I taught basic, as well as regular and general-level English classes. Then Honors English for juniors was added to my schedule. Honors and regular English served a mere sprinkling of minority students, while basic and general English served few white ones. This was 1972, and I was the first black English instructor in the long history of the district. I had to repeatedly explain my role at the high school since everyone assumed that I was a newly hired special education teacher.

Deeply troubled by a system of segregation so entrenched inside the schools, I went to graduate school to earn a second master's degree, this time in educational administration and supervision. I hoped that as an administrator I could exert greater influence on the policies and practices that seemed to support educational inequality for low SES students in general, and for black students in particular. Through their parents' and grandparents' migrations north to escape deplorable life conditions in the Deep South, these students had become strangers in their native land. Their standard English skills, both spoken and written, as well as their mathematical skills, closely resembled those of their poorly schooled parents whose roots were in Mississippi, Alabama, Georgia, South Carolina, Florida, and Arkansas. What had been the effect of the Civil Rights movement on the lives of these children whose integrated public school experiences had been far inferior to my own segregated and vastly unequal ones? The world was moving rapidly forward and leaving them farther and farther behind.

Few of my basic and general-level students seemed to understand the future implications of their present educational circumstances. In discussions of social ills, they stated that they had never experienced discrimination, relegating injustice to occurring only in the south. Though barely literate, they most often indicated that professions in law or medicine would be their chosen fields because they wanted to make a lot of money. As class projects, we began examining what these and many other professions entail and the preparation they require, along with the services and salaries they provide. My students tried hard to assume success-promoting behaviors—equating orderliness, politeness, and quiet, rote practice with primary evidence of scholastic attainment. "Give us some English, Miz Rod," they would tell me, referring to fill-in-the-blank exercises in their grammar books. Their idea of English reflected all their years of lower-track classroom exposure. They believed that busy work comprised the core of learning. They had never seen an English class of regular or advanced high school students since their only untracked classes were physical education, home economics, and wood shop. Yet most were natively intelligent young men and women whose academic talents lay buried.

I remember my first class of provisionally promoted students who were expected to pass math and English exit exams at the end of the first semester in order to become freshmen. On the first day of the semester, I challenged the class to master the skills needed to pass the English exit exam in nine weeks instead of eighteen. They vowed to be ready in six weeks. At the end of six weeks, they each wrote a letter to the central office administrators showing off their new skills and stating their and my belief that they were ready to pass the qualifying exam for freshman English. They received a response from the director of curriculum who agreed that based on their letters, they were ready, congratulated them on their achievement in so short a time, and informed them that unfortunately they would have to wait the additional twelve weeks before earning credit as freshmen. Though disappointed, the students spent the rest of the term improving their critical thinking, reading, and communications skills. The fact that I had done most of the writing assignments along with them convinced the students that if I could continue to learn something from the curriculum that I offered, they probably could, too.

While the few minority students in higher-level classes escaped the mind-numbing curriculum of most basic and general tracks, they remained vulnerable to the whims of racist teachers. One year, for the first time in the history of the school, a black student was voted homecoming queen by the student body. The counselor and faculty in charge of counting the votes were discovered in their plot to change the tally. And like the student tracking system that was supposed to benefit all students equally by allowing them to advance at their own pace, other district policies worked to promote the very evils they claimed to cure. *The Adventures of Huckleberry Finn* was banned from the curriculum under the guise of protecting black students. At the time, former, current, Anglo, and minority students of mine argued the benefits of studying *Huck Finn*. While the administration could not counter the students' arguments about their own experiences, the district could and did dismiss the arguments as relevant only to student experience in *my* classroom. In other classrooms, the district contended, the study of Twain's classic undermined the self-concepts and racial pride of black students. With its typical flair for avoiding systemic improvement, the district—instead of devising and implementing nondiscriminatory teaching practices—at best excised one out of a million possible opportunities for classroom malpractice by the faculty.

I went into administration to change teacher quality and student achievement by throwing a monkey wrench into a corrupt system. I would be the major decision-maker regarding which teachers to hire for my department, effectively ending the automatic replication of then-current faculty members. Working within the constraints of the district's teacher evaluation policy, I could reduce the baby-sitting approach to teaching reserved for lower-level classes. As the departmental supervisor, I could nearly eradicate comments such as one made by a highly respected white male instructor to a black female who was combing her hair: "Stop carding your wool!" I could advocate for poor students and their uneducated parents who had no easy access to legal recourse against unfair treatment by the school. And I could model holding the students to higher standards, fully expecting that they could meet them. I decided to fight the beast from within its belly because my influence would be greater than from one little appendage, a classroom. When I joined the faculty at a community college, I lasted one year before I went into administration there for similar reasons.

An enormous problem for students wherever I have worked has been the question of identity, the students' own sense of who they are and the categorizations that others have placed upon them. At the high school where I worked, no matter how academically stellar the mostly white honors students were, they attended—on counselors' advice—state universities, "fit destinations for the children of working-class parents." I told my best students to apply to the best colleges in the nation, and they did with great success. I taught them to write outside the parameters of the five-paragraph theme, and over the years several of them became winners of national writing awards. As a college administrator, I changed the complexion of the college by diversifying the faculty, the curriculum, and pedagogical approaches in my division. I created an uproar on the campus by promoting the dismissal (unheard of at the time) of a tenure-track faculty member who had become a detriment to students and to the college. I advanced the cross-pollination of courses and faculty from the predominantly white main campus with the predominantly minority downtown campus. I encourage students—the largest nonunion group on campus and the least powerful—to insist that the college work for, instead of against, them.

As an employee of a community college, I understand that our tenuous connections with four-year colleges, universities, and the communities that we serve must be strengthened by our own efforts to demonstrate who and what we are. We suffer, as do our students, from an inferiority complex as the last chance-opportunity for the academically underprepared, and we bemoan the fact that university professors seldom make us the subject of their research. Such research, we believe, would cast the community college, including its many first-generation students, in a more favorable light. The unadorned truth is that community college faculty and administrators must accept the responsibility of conducting such research themselves. If educational quality in the new century converges around the results in academic achievement that schools can produce, more than any other educational institution, the community college must substantiate its effectiveness. Similarly, we must demonstrate congruence among our philosophies and practices: Who, what, why and how do we teach? Who, what, why and how do we assess? What outcomes do we achieve, and what is their value? At all levels of the educational spectrum, from preschool through graduate school, truth and fairness in these matters will define the drama of the new activism. I intend to play a role upon its stage.

Chapter 5
Paying Back:
A Sampler

Since one of the questions that guided my research concerned the impact of the participants' previous experiences on their roles as social or educational activists, I expected to find information on the participants' lives before college graduation that might relate directly to their activist lives after college. What I did not anticipate, however, was a seemingly common relationship between the participants' identity issues and their contributions as activists. The finding seems to be very significant in every case except one, where it is merely less so. In essence, the activist efforts of all participants appear to address, either directly or indirectly, the problems, issues, and solutions that are part of their self-concepts.

More specifically, I set out to identify experiences in the participants' lives, both prior to and during college, which may have had an impact on their academic success in college. In conjunction with isolating those experiences, I hoped to learn about their imprint on the participants' decisions to become educational or social activists. A further benefit would be any illumination of how those experiences affected the ways in which the participants lived their lives and influenced others as agents of change.

With these ideas in mind, I profile six activists from the study by providing brief biographical sketches and allowing them to describe their activism in their own words. Next I identify themes that appear both common across the interviews and germane to the participants' activism. These themes may suggest the influence of pre-college and college experiences on the participants' decisions to become activists and on the forms that their activism has taken.

The final section of this chapter speculates about the participants' risk-taking tendencies, bringing the book full-circle by linking these tendencies to special status, positive naming, and ascending cross-class identification, qualities about which the book began.

Engaging Activism: Profiles of Six First-Generation College Graduates

You have to pay your dues. You have to pay back. I've always felt that I have been given this great opportunity and I owe somebody— I think it's this amorphous, universal kind of thing—this good life that's been given to me. I don't think it was a person that gave it to me, but it was fortune. I had good fortune. Therefore, I should pay back.

— Barbara

Grant

My intent was to conduct all of the interviews for this study more or less on the participants' home turf, but I had a problem with my schedule and wound up interviewing Grant in Chicago. He was coming to Chicago for a convention and, being aware of my scheduling difficulty, offered to be available to me for a few hours during his Chicago stay. This helpful gesture, I learned from secondary interviewees (persons who know the participants or their work), is typical behavior for Grant, a graduate of the University of Michigan and Georgetown University School of Law. Grant is an attorney who practices in Washington, D. C., and he was happy to help me with my research and to save me time and the cost of a plane ticket.

From the blazing heat of a late summer day in Chicago, I entered the cavernous lobby of the hotel where I was to meet Grant. There were hundreds of people, mostly African Americans, who seemed to be relaxing over drinks, making dinner plans, meeting old and new acquaintances, and discussing the events of the day. They were impeccably dressed in expensive business suits, and in the air-conditioned comfort of the lobby, they were impervious to the sweltering heat outside. They were lawyers in attendance at the National Convention of the National Bar Association, and Grant had delivered one of the day's speeches. I remember thinking at the time that every black kid in Chicago would grow in self-esteem if they could just look at this crowd and visualize what they could become under certain conditions. As I made my way to meet Grant, I thought about how different from these posh surroundings his beginnings, and my own, had been.

Grant was born in 1948 in Grand Rapids, Michigan. His parents had relocated there, his father by way of Chicago from a hard life as a sharecropper in Alabama. His mother had been born in Arkansas. During his childhood, Grant had been impressed by the stories his father told him about teaching himself to read and write during the 1930s; about working for ten cents an hour in a factory and living in a rooming house where he paid $1.55 a week for his room and dinner; about the struggle of blacks in the South and how the inequities there had motivated him to leave. He had gone to Muskegon to work in the machine shop or the glass factory or the aluminum factory for Chrysler's Army Tank Division. He taught Grant, the second of four children, many lessons including "the value of a penny, a dime, a dollar, how that value fluctuates with the times, and how the time when you could get a good job without an education was in the past."

When Grant was a kid attending the Grand Rapids public schools, he was bounced back and forth between his regular classroom and the special education classroom because he stammered when he talked and was viewed by his teacher as having a learning problem. This view was not softened by his keen interest in mathematics or his ability to solve math problems rapidly and without use of pencil and paper. Grant determined as a teenager that he had been afraid to speak because he had been insecure in what he knew. As he grew in confidence by observing that he could deal with whatever people put in front of him, the stammering slowly went away. His interests expanded to science and art. He set up a chemistry laboratory in an unused kitchen at home and won an art scholarship for freehand drawing when he was sixteen. He decided to go to engineering school, however, and relegated sketching to a pastime for twenty years.

Grant went to engineering school because he wanted to deal with gadgets and objects rather than with people. In engineering, he did not have to talk to anybody. He loved to create contraptions, and he was good at it. But he began looking at people who were fifteen to twenty years ahead of him, and they were not what he wanted to be in fifteen or twenty years. So by his senior year of undergraduate school, Grant was certain that he did not want to become an engineer. He went to law school instead.

"How the hell did someone like you end up in law school? You never did like to talk!" his former roommate from undergraduate school asked him. It was an important question. This former engineer who did not like to talk has held positions at several prestigious law firms, the latest of which is a billion-dollar-a-year operation that he heads. "I can learn to talk just like you did," Grant told his former roommate, evincing an intentionality that is prevalent throughout the case histories. "I had a problem with it," he told me, referring to law school. But active participation in school politics forced him to talk, and he discovered a proclivity for talking and an enjoyment of it.

Grant also discovered luck. With no money for an apartment in Washington during his graduate school days, he lived with his father in Baltimore and commuted by train to his classes at Georgetown. Within the first three weeks of law school, he happened to sit down on the train by a man who was a law student at night at the University of Baltimore and a Westinghouse employee by day. He told Grant of a job opening at Westinghouse, and three days later Grant was hired. His education was paid for by Westinghouse, and he had a job with the company after graduation. He went into private practice after graduation, however, because the job with Westinghouse would have required living in Pittsburgh. Neither Grant nor anyone else in the study stayed in jobs or locales after graduation that they believed would not make them happy. "I just didn't like the area," Grant said of Pittsburgh, "so I left the company. I went into private practice with no clients, no job, no money, no nothing. . . . I starved for six months."

Grant has not starved since that time. He is a very successful lawyer, a social activist, and the owner of an art gallery. And like everyone in the study, he said that while the nature of humans is to want more, he can live without it:

> I could have a Jaguar, a Rolls Royce, a fancy airplane, but I'd just as soon provide a facility for the artists and do some electronics stuff. I put one of my artists through college. He came to me from prison, out of Ohio. He came and showed me his work when he'd been out of prison around two months. He still had post-prison syndrome and was trying to find a niche in life again. He needed help. He was self-taught as an artist while in prison. I said I thought maybe he could make something out of himself as an artist and that I would finance it. He had gone to Howard University for maybe a year. He killed another student. I think he killed someone in the heat of passion over a woman. Then he spent twelve years in prison.
>
> At my suggestion, he took a couple of courses at the Corcoran Museum during the summer and passed them with flying colors. Then he went to Howard, and I spent $10,000 to $12,000 per year for four years to finance his college education. Last year he graduated, and he is now in graduate school studying art. We had a couple of art shows when we had his artwork exhibited, and a number of his family came. I suspect he wanted to show them he was making it. We sold his work and he got money for it. His folks came and looked at his work, but I think they were not ready to accept him.
>
> When he was in school, he would come and talk to me about some of the problems that he had with the other students. He was ten years older than they were, and the story was out that he was an ex-con. People whispered about him. He developed a complex over it after a while, but he stuck it out.
>
> During the 1980s I graduated in income beyond the real struggling phase, and I had time to understand and appreciate the struggle of black people

and the need to preserve their ways of life and the culture, beliefs, spirits, and principles by which they have lived. My motivation was fortified by the motivation of institutional America not to recognize it. So it was a reactive force—"Okay, you asshole, you don't like it, so here's more of it"—not directed to any one individual, but to America as a whole. I'd had some experiences myself with denial, discrimination, unfairness. It all added up over forty years of my life, and I said, "You're going to do something about this!" I also felt the need to provide guidance and role models to young people in the arts.

No art gallery makes money, but it gives me the chance to present an element of society that represents us truly, many of whom were denied access elsewhere. We have art from at least fifty countries. My interest is to have global representation of mostly black people. Right now there are at least a couple of hundred pieces from Africa and another couple of hundred from other parts of the world. We have black artists who are among the most respected in the world, and we keep the door open to emerging artists. Loads of school children, and others, can come through here and see what black art is about.

Jerry

On a brisk autumn morning, I drove to the town where Jerry's business sprawls on the banks of the Fox River. The old brick buildings are refurbished and beautiful, lending an aura of hope to the rest of the working-class community. There is a park on Jerry's property that is open to the town's residents for picnics and leisure. A graduate of the University of Illinois, Jerry is the owner of an engineering company. Before our interview, he took me on a tour of the business, rushing to make sure I met everyone before they went to lunch. "Everyone" was over 300 employees who appeared to love their boss and their work. I talked briefly with a number of them who praised Jerry for his ingenuity, willingness to take risks, pride in their work, and compassion. He, in turn, praised them for almost those same qualities. "That beautiful machine shop," he said, "its effectiveness, cleanliness, everything grew out of John's (an employee) creativity. He was given the latitude to make something work, and it did. People appreciate being treated like responsible people on the job."

Jerry, who is white, was born seventy-four years ago in Chicago. His paternal grandparents came from Germany where his grandfather fought in the War of 1870. His father was a very intelligent man who completed eighth grade in his native Chicago. As an adult, he ran a logging operation in Wisconsin before World War II. He told Jerry about his involvement in facing down Communists at that time because they were trying to make people feel dissatisfied with America. "They were members of the International Workers of the World, or Wobblies," Jerry told me, "and they had a violent encounter with my father."

Jerry is as politically concerned as his father was and spoke emphatically to me about the need for a good moral and economic plan for America. Seven years ago, he started a not-for-profit organization on the premises of his business with the objective of teaching people how to run for and get elected to office. A strong advocate for school vouchers, he explained that public school children, especially among the poor, are pawns of educational bureaucrats. "Those poor children do not become prepared to help the country, because they can't help themselves to become educated contributors to a morally and economically sound society," Jerry stated. "The public schools are bringing up ninnies," he said. "You can't run a country with ninnies."

Jerry's own education seems to reflect his views on, and activist work in, public education. When he was in elementary school, his parents tried to give him a Catholic school education, but he ended up going back and forth between Catholic and public school. With five children to raise, his parents just could not afford the nominal tuition. The youngest of the five, Jerry started first grade but was quickly moved up to second because his sister had taught him the alphabet and a bit of reading. When he went to Catholic school for third, fourth, and fifth grades, he was put back a year because his skills were so poor. Then the family moved and could not afford Catholic school anymore, so he went back to public school where they moved him ahead again. He felt that he was not learning in the public school, but he discovered reading.

There were books in the house that the older kids had in school. Jerry read *Ivanhoe* when he was a little kid. He read *The Iliad*, *The Odyssey*, Robert Louis Stevenson, *A Tale of Two Cities*, and *The Book of Knowledge*, a one-volume encyclopedia, from cover to cover when he was in grammar school. High school was grossly easy the first two years, and school was out at twelve-fifteen in the afternoon. He developed a creative outlet, building and later designing gas model airplanes. This interest probably led him to become an engineer. He started making and selling his own airplane kits. He stated that antique clubs still fly his prize-winning plane, the *Swoose*, designed when he was at Oak Park High School. At Oak Park, he felt he received an excellent education in eleventh and twelfth grades.

Jerry seemed convinced that in many public elementary and secondary schools, education means money in the pockets of the adults with very little going to the kids. He stated that educational, social, and economic change must take place at the legislative level. While Jerry explained that most of his activist work is conducted through his political organization, he has become a fervent advocate for public school choice in Chicago. He described his activism in this arena through the following example:

> St. Elizabeth's is an entirely black Catholic school in Chicago with 410 students. It is a plain old building without graffiti and with contemporary cast-off furniture. Most of the teachers are black, and there are a couple of nuns. It is in a tough neighborhood, right near the Robert Taylor Homes. The children, if you listen to popular opinion, are not supposed to be educable; yet St. Elizabeth's is doing a fine job with them. When I first went there, I saw 410 kids who looked like happy little kids. They sat in orderly rows in classrooms sometimes; other times they sat in groups. They laughed at little things. They seemed free and easy. There was no rowdyism. And I learned that they graduate at close to the national average in spite of coming from the Robert Taylor Homes and from families that live in that area. They go on to high school, and a lot of them go on to college. Many of the black movers and shakers in Chicago come out of settings like that, and not from the public schools. Some are so natively intelligent that they could make it anywhere, but why should they have to? And there are a lot of kids who are really smart and haven't found themselves yet. There are kids who aren't as smart, won't join Mensa, maybe wouldn't profit from college. Who knows? But the usual spread of talent is present in those kids from the area in and around the Robert Taylor Homes. And all of those kids deserve a good education. I've come to believe that you can make or break education in the first three grades. . . .
>
> I became an advisor—that's a fancy name for the guy who helps them get money because they do not have enough—to St. Elizabeth's, and I went to the eighth-grade graduation a year ago. The graduates were a bunch of kids who looked happy and like they knew what they were doing. The graduation came off with nothing that wasn't first class about it. This is success at a third of the cost per pupil in the public schools. At St. Elizabeth's it costs $2,365 per pupil, and in Chicago [public schools] it's around $7,000. I asked this black man who is an advisor what percent of the students they put out for disruptive behavior. He looked puzzled and said, "I don't know. Not many." So I asked Sister Carol. She said that in the last ten years they have expelled four students. They take anyone who comes unless they are severely disabled. Otherwise, they take them all. The public schools lose half of their students, who vote with their feet.
>
> I've been doing the St. Elizabeth's thing for six or seven years now. I get

money from my business. The personal money that I make, I put back. I don't have a lot of cash on hand, and I don't have a lot of stocks. But I live well. I'm a rich man. I've got freedom . . . and all the things that I need. I give a few thousand to St. Elizabeth's every year, but what I do there is at best anecdotal. The majority of my money I put into the political process. That's the best way that I can think of to make sweeping changes to help students and families and the country. It is the electoral process that politicians will respond to, not the sound of sweet music.

Maria

My experience driving to Maria's office for our interview was a metaphor for her earlier days. I was lost and alone in my car with no one to help me read the signs and find my way. I anxiously maneuvered through the busy Chicago streets to arrive at Little Village, a Latino enclave on Chicago's near west side. I was relieved when I saw that arching the main avenue was the Little Village sign. A coup against Levittowns everywhere, house fronts bearing the distinct tastes of their owners lined the street. In the center of the community, houses gave way to businesses of various types. A bridal shop; a record store; a restaurant; a laundromat; and clothing, appliance, shoe, grocery, and furniture stores paid witness to the everyday needs of communities everywhere. Following Maria's precise directions as carefully as I could, I parked and discovered that I was, miraculously, in front of her office building. I felt set free, shedding the fear that always grips me when I venture alone to an unfamiliar area.

Maria understood. The poised, articulate, risk-taking, twenty-nine-year-old Latina business advisor I met had not so long ago been terrified at the prospect of finding her way during college orientation. She had worried about whether she would get lost, whether people would be friendly to her, whether she would be late. She had been to DePaul University before her orientation trip, but her father had dropped her off. For the first time in her life, she had taken the train by herself. Her mother had told her how and where to take the train, but Maria had been very unsure and frightened; she had resorted to asking directions in order to find her way. Once at school, she had to walk up eleven flights of stairs to get to her psychology class because she could not find an elevator that worked. She did not know where to sit in the class, which met in a huge lecture hall. Her mother was at work in a factory just three blocks away, which was reassuring, but neither of her parents had been able to tell her anything about college, which was not.

Maria told me that she never wanted to be dependent again, that her dependence on her parents earlier in her life had been disconcerting. Yet she deeply valued her family life. She was as proud of her parents as they must be of her. And they had done everything that they could to protect Maria and her younger sister.

Maria never learned how to swim because her father would not let her go to the park or to the public pool where she might learn to swim. When she and her sister complained, he put a pool in the backyard and said, "You want to swim, you can swim here." Maria's mother was the intermediary who influenced her husband to allow Maria to date her only boyfriend whom she later married. She never lived among her extended family because they all lived in Hispanic neighborhoods. Maria's father had been one of ten children from a very poor family, and he intended for his children to have the advantages that he had lacked. Maria never attended a public school, was given access to a new car when she was sixteen, and always knew that she was going to college. "Hard work pays off," Maria heard from her parents—a maxim that they demonstrated in their lives and that Maria, in turn, demonstrated in her own. None of the participants in this study lived fairy-tale existences, and Maria was no exception.

When Maria was growing up in Chicago, her parents worked hard to provide their two children with educational opportunity and a safe environment in which to live. At about the time Maria turned nine, her family moved from their home in a changing neighborhood to an area where most of the residents were from ethnic European backgrounds. Life in the new neighborhood seemed a cruel joke since Maria and her sister could not play on the sidewalks or in front of their home for fear that the neighbors would harass them. It was a tough time for the family. Maria's parents had moved farther from their jobs so that the children would be exposed to a better neighborhood and better schools. A classmate at Maria's new school had called her a "spic," and the reception that they received from the neighbors was disheartening. In spite of these hardships, when Maria graduated from eighth grade, she was valedictorian and took almost every award that the school gave out. As she accepted the Principal's Award, she heard her father say from the audience, "They were worried about this Hispanic. Well, this Hispanic just cleaned up all their awards, and what are the parents going to say now?"

For Maria, hard work had paid off, and with few exceptions, it has continued to do so. In her work for a not-for-profit organization, she provides business loans to people, helping them make their hard work pay off. She is able to act with a degree of independence. When a potential client comes in to ask for a loan for a business venture, she establishes a relationship with the person and determines her response to the request. If she believes in the person and feels confident that he or she is going to repay the loan and that it may transform a life, she will work hard to sell the idea for the business to the committee. Maria explained:

> If I believe in you, I'm going to do everything in my power to convince that committee to give you that loan. I can offer that comfort, and I really, really like what I do because I'm giving back something to the community. The clients don't go through anything alone. Whatever that business goes through, I go through, too. They need somebody to believe in them. Two of my directors think I would be phenomenal in the banking field. Maybe I would, but right now this is what I want to do.
>
> There is this comic book illustrator, an African American, who had a comic book designed and illustrated in ink and everything. It was ready to go, but he didn't have any credit. He was extremely honest with me from the beginning. He wanted to go to the comic book convention, and he explained the price he thought he could get for selling the comic book. He was asking for a small amount of money, but he couldn't secure a co-signer. I got him the maximum you can get on a non-co-signed basis. He published his first comic. Now he teaches at Kennedy-King College, at the Duncan YMCA, and he is coordinating the first comic book convention for African Americans at Malcolm X College.
>
> He still works full-time for the Miles Square Health Center, and he was recently awarded a contract with a pesticide company that's doing work in a Chicago Housing Authority project. The company wants to promote pest control without aerosols and baits and pesticides. They want to create this little booklet that they can pass out to residents to help them learn the new methods of pest control. My client was raised in the projects and is mentoring one of the kids from the projects who is artistically inclined. My client had approached Marvel Comics, but they told him that he doesn't have any talent because they saw who he was rather than his artwork.
>
> In truth, he's incredible. He is on his third loan. He's paid me back three times, on time, all the time. I've hooked him up with a client who has opened a comic book shop, and his work is going in that shop. He has been featured on *Fox Thing in the Morning* and in a couple of the newspapers. He was quoted, too, at the comic book convention. All of his books have historical information as a basis. They are not all blood and guts. They are educational and are done from a multicultural basis.

Jorge

With a great deal of humor and not a hint of hubris, Jorge, a twenty-eight-year-old Latino and graduate of Yale University, told me that his parents' IQ took a quantum leap upward, or so they thought, when he received his bachelor's degree. He elaborated:

> They felt that they had learned through osmosis and that the conferral of my degree was a part of them—which I thought was really interesting. I tease my mother about it all the time. My parents achieved, almost instantaneously, this increased base of knowledge, this increased pride, this legitimization. We have a comic household; things are not right if two people are not teasing somebody else, so I can remind my family of their enhanced status through my degree and they don't mind. They are convinced that they had the right kid at the right time.
>
> As far as going to school was concerned, I was always in the right place at the right time.

While Jorge, as well as most of the study's participants, attributed much of his good fortune, especially regarding his schooling, to luck, clearly intention and design—his own and his parents'—were contributing factors. His parents sent him to a local parochial school for kindergarten. Noticing his academic exceptionality, his teacher suggested that he go to an elite private school the next year. Jorge skipped first grade completely, and went from kindergarten to second grade in a new school. Luckily, he left that school after eighth grade since it closed its doors the very next year. By that time, Jorge was safely ensconced in one of Chicago's elite K-12 private schools. During his senior year of high school, the lucky intervention of an English teacher in his college search process resulted in his going to Yale. While there, he was fortunate to have an incredible visiting professor as an instructor during both his freshman and his junior years. The professor, a Puerto Rican with a bachelor's degree from the University of Pennsylvania and a law degree from Yale, changed Jorge's life. Now through his work as an administrator for a not-for-profit social service agency, Jorge changes the lives of others.

Jorge has held two jobs that have enabled him to do the type of work he loves. He shared the following comments about one of them:

> I went to work in Chicago for the Latin American Chamber of Commerce as a small-business developer. My job entailed sitting down with people who had businesses or wanted to start them. I would help them obtain

financing for their businesses, or if they were at the idea-development stage, I would help them determine whether the ideas they had for a business were viable. My job entailed all aspects of business formation. All my work was pretty much focused in the Latino neighborhood in Chicago, particularly in the Logan Square/Humbolt Park area. Most of my work was external rather than internal to the organization. I could see that I was creating tangible value outside the institution and actually in the communities themselves. I could see the measurable impacts on people's lives as well. When someone who owns a jewelry store is on the edge and you help them get a $20,000 loan which will carry them for another year and a half, you know they are going to be able to continue to make their car payments, continue to feed their family, and continue to serve the community. It's a win/win situation for everybody involved, and I loved it!

I also found that sitting down with someone and taking their business idea out to the end and showing them that it is not viable is a very valuable function. It stops them from sinking their resources into something that just isn't going to work. It puts them on a different track so they don't lose everything they have. I also dealt with the perception of people on the street, in the community, and among the small-business owners that it should not be so hard to get money when you know that your venture is going to work. I dealt with their frustration at running into this stone wall that is the banking system time after time and finding, over and over again, that they can't get financing either by hook or by crook. That particular reality came as a shock to a lot of people. They didn't seem able to comprehend it, and understandably so, because they had been working and putting everything they had into their businesses, yet they were not worth anything to a banker. Having to deal with that kind of dejection on a pretty regular basis helped me to see clearly the necessity of putting my shoulder to the wheel and pushing with all my strength.

One of the biggest things I learned while working at the Latino Chamber of Commerce is that even in a situation where you have very poor management, an organization can continue to flourish if it is providing valuable service to its constituents. I learned that I have a definite affinity for working in the community. If I came home upset about my job, it was never because of the people I had to work with, the work I had to do, or the people I was serving. It was always because of the people I had to answer to.

When Jorge began his current job, he was twenty-six years old. He was the executive director of a new social service agency with himself as the only employee. There were no offices, and he was working out of a home. With the help of added staff and a board of directors, he was able to build the organization from the ground up. In two years, they had put half a million dollars on the street in the form of loans that went directly to the people who needed them.

When Jorge was in college, he experienced an awakening as a Puerto Rican. He says now that he knows he will be happy in his life as long as he can help Latinos to strengthen their families, their communities, and themselves.

Clara

When Clara, a twenty-nine-year-old white female, was a child, she greatly admired her grandmother who lived with the family and went to work everyday—unlike Clara's mother who stayed at home. Her grandmother encouraged Clara's independence by paying her to do small jobs that she could manage. Clara's grandmother would let her peel apples for homemade pies; her mother would never have allowed such a thing, afraid that Clara would cut herself. Clara first learned about bilingualism from her grandmother, whose native language was Polish. She would talk to her friends and tell Clara stories and sing songs and nursery rhymes to her in Polish. Clara's grandmother, a factory worker, seemed independent and knowledgeable about the world. Clara valued and began emulating her grandmother's qualities.

When she was old enough to work, Clara began buying most of her own clothes, and she bought a stereo and a car. As a college student, she tried very hard not to ask her family for financial support. She explained:

> One time when I was in a bind in college, my parents took out a parents' loan for me, but I paid it back for them right away so they wouldn't have to worry about it. They did that only once. They would give me the shirt off their backs if they knew I needed it, but I knew that I didn't want to put the other kids in danger. If my getting help would hurt the family, then I had no right to ask for it. My parents had done as much for me as they could. It was up to me to do the rest.

Clara's work ethic seems to have translated into helping others to help themselves. As a graduate of Southern Illinois University and a college instructor, the positive experiences of her life have joined forces with the negative ones to make her a stronger and better person—for herself and others.

In the small town of her childhood, Clara experienced the stares and unenlightened comments of the citizenry as they observed her Caucasian parents and their multiracial children. Like her parents, Clara is white, but her siblings, all of whom are younger, are Native American and Asian. At times Clara would be asked to explain her relationship to her sisters and brothers. A heavy child, she also experienced cruelty from other children because of her weight. Her self-concept suffered, and she became very shy. In high school, a Spanish teacher let Clara make a presentation in the teacher's office because she was too intimidated to speak in front of her class. By the time Clara graduated, she felt that she could do two things well, sing and speak Spanish. Clara earned bachelor's and master's degrees in Spanish and now teaches at a community college. She collaborates with her Spanish teacher from high school to carry out joint activities among high school and college students. Of her activism, Clara stated:

> I got involved in doing a lot of things in the beginning because I needed to supplement my income. Now that I am working full-time, I have the luxury of volunteering. It is not that I don't need money, but I can make enough to pay my bills. I had a grant-funded position that allowed me to go out into the community and do things with people who weren't at the college yet. I worked with the fire department. When I got involved with the Latino Club, I brought in the fire department to train the Latino Club members in CPR. Then the Latino Club members began helping the fire department to give classes to Spanish speakers to certify them in CPR. Last year we took twenty-five members of the Latino Club to a leadership conference at the Hilton in Chicago. We are going to a conference this month at Northern Illinois University. I think my being younger makes it easier for me to make a connection with the students. They've really taken me in like one of their own. I feel like I'm part of their club and part of the community.
>
> We've brought all kinds of speakers to the college. We met Dr. Hector Rosaldo Flores, a pianist and medical doctor, at a conference and brought him here. Dr. Antonia Novella, ex Surgeon General is someone we want to bring here. Edward James Olmos will be at the conference we're going to this month, and we want to have him for Hispanic Heritage Month. The students are really excited.
>
> One of the things I brought to the club is the idea that you don't have to just put up with what people tell you. People can say no, but you can find a way to get a yes. I tell the students that they can make a difference. They wrote to Gloria Estefan asking her to come here. Before, they never would have done that. I wrote to Vice-President Gore. They saw me talking to congressmen at a conference like I'm someone important. Well, I told them

that we're all important, and if I can do a thing, so can they. I tell them that they're as good as the President, as anybody. That no one is higher up or better than they. That others may just have a position of power, but their power can be a resource for the students. The students just got a response from Gloria Estefan saying that she is on tour, but she will consider their request when she is not on tour. We don't want her to sing; we want her as a speaker, so the club is writing her back to see if she can come for Hispanic Heritage Month. Today the club is meeting with some people to talk about a college tour. We've been talking about different ways of using our voice.

There is no way I would have guessed two years ago that the president of the Latino Club would develop the leadership skills that he has now. When he came on a trip to Mexico that I sponsored, he took a position where people were looking up to him and asking him questions. His family is in the area, he speaks Spanish well, and he was a fountain of information for everyone. I told him that I wanted to see the same person in him when he got back here that I saw in Mexico. He decided to run for president and he won. He is doing very, very well.

There is so much that can be done at the college and in the community. I would like to start a Spanish-language National Honor Society here. I volunteer to teach people at a Catholic church two nights a week. I need to establish an exchange program with the University of Guadalajara where I sponsor the summer courses. I need some more time!

Fred

I entered Fred's church on a Sunday morning and settled in a pew near the back. I had no choice in the matter—though my seat suited me just fine—for the church was packed. I had come on a fact-finding mission. I had identified Fred as a black leader I would like to interview, and visiting his predominantly black church when he was preaching, I thought, would tell me a lot about him. I came armed with paper and pen for unobtrusive note-taking. I scanned the program, noticed the children and adults—males and females—in the congregation, and marveled at the number of women in the pulpit of this Baptist church and their active role in the pre-sermon rituals. Then the choir marched in singing "God Is Already Here," and all my intentions of taking notes were blown away by the sheer force and beauty of their voices.

Fred is a sixty-year-old minister, educator, and artist whose drawings adorn the walls of his office. He is an artist, too, in the way he creates the literature that is his sermons. As he exhorted his congregation on their responsibilities as persons made in God's image, I wondered how they could ever lose sight of their beauty and potential for greatness. Even though I live quite a distance from Fred's church, two Sundays later I was back to hear another of his sermons.

During the first week that I sought to arrange an interview with Fred, he was in Washington, D.C., with some other ministers to meet with the President of the United States. A short time later when he was available for an interview, I learned far more about him than I had been able to glean from two Sunday sermons. He related to me a striking interpretation of Plato's allegory of the cave. It may be that the enlightened person in Plato's allegory has a parallel in Fred and that the story encapsulates the essence and the challenge of his activism. Fred explained the allegory:

> Everybody's watching the shadows on the wall. I offer my own rendition of that situation. The person who's watching those shadows as he breaks the chain on his neck can turn around and see something different from all the others who are looking at the illusion on the wall. And finally he goes up, and he notices that the configurations on the wall are configurations of people walking with pitchers on their heads. He goes further up, and he sees that there's a light shining on these configurations. He goes on up a little higher, and he sees that the light is actually an opening in the cave. He goes outside, and he's a whole lot smarter than anybody else. He sees that the sun is shining through the opening, casting light against the people against the wall. Well, that kind of enlightenment poses a dilemma because the real task is not to *tell* everybody but to get them to see. And that's what makes preaching so hard. You see hundreds and thousands of people out there looking at shadows, and you know that the shadows are only reflections of reality. It takes a lot of patience to work with people when you're looking at people and they're looking at shadows that they think are reality. At the same time, you know because of your enlightenment that there is a cause-and-effect relationship to everything that is occurring.

Fred was born and raised in Ohio, his father's home, but his mother was a woman of little education from Bessemer, Alabama. Her family had migrated north just ahead of a lynch mob that was after her brothers. In her background, a "smart nigger" was a "dead nigger," and she admonished her sons to be good boys at school. But Fred remembers her as possessed of a raging anti-intellectualism. "My mother disdained education to such a degree that as a child I couldn't even ask her a question. She'd say, 'No, don't ask me that!'"

Fred failed first grade and struggled through school, desiring to be as intelligent as his father who had a high school education and a great love of learning. He flunked out of three or four colleges and served a stint in the Marine Corps before beginning the journey of success. This journey netted him a B.F.A. degree from Kent State and M.A. and Ph.D. degrees from Vanderbilt University.

Fred's journey of success required his coming to grips with the fragmentation in his life. He began a quest of self-discovery that led him back to the beginnings of his people as slaves in America. He went back to uncover those forces that had shaped his mother who, in turn, had shaped him. He understood how the slave mentality could keep black people fragmented and in ignorance over a hundred years after slavery was over. Fred's goal as a preacher and professor is to promote wholeness in himself and in others. He does so through his broad-based activism involving his church congregation, student motivational activities, care of the homeless, tutoring services, support groups for graduate students in the thesis and dissertation stages, feeding the hungry, and local, state, and national politics. He teaches that we should not be intimidated by models of achievement or immobilized by our imperfections; rather, we should work diligently toward our true potential, achieved only through wholeness:

> People look at things that I do to help people become who they can be, to realize their potential and get rid of their hang-ups. There are various programs that we run from the church that affect getting people fed, that affect politics, that affect economics, that affect social opportunity. They are all one thing. All that I do has to do with an essential philosophy which I learned. Wholeness, that which is whole and one within itself, has power to do anything that it wants to do. A whole bird will fly and soar. A whole bee will do that which bees do normally. A whole human being will do that which is sufficient or efficient for its being. A whole race, a whole nation, is indivisible, is awesomely powerful. And wholeness will manifest itself in all aspects, so one has only to live by that simple principle and all else happens.

> The Bible is replete with magnificent models of manhood: from Adam to Abraham, Isaac, and Jacob; from Job to Joshua to Jeremiah to John the Baptist and John the Revelator; from Moses to Malachi; from David to the twelve Disciples; from Peter to Paul to Sampson to Shadrach, Meshach, and Abednego; and on and on until the perfect man, namely Jesus Christ. These men are more than magnificent models of manhood; they are manhood under the divine unction. They are manhood representing its most redemptive potential possibility. Yet they are manhood inclusive of its most

mundane and often miserable representation of human degradation, dehumanization, and disappointment.

We need to be honest when we read about those heroes in the Bible. Adam was a perfect man, but Adam failed, and he fell. Abraham was a blessed man, but he was also a polygamist who married his half-sister, attempted to sell her into prostitution, and abused his other wives. Yet God took Abraham and used him as the father of our great heritage of faith. Moses was a murderer, and after that an outlaw. Yet he became the liberator of Egypt. Noah, an alcoholic who was caught naked and in a drunken stupor, was found out by his sons, almost wrecking the history of humanity. Nevertheless, God used Noah to make a whole new world. David was caught in adultery but became a man after God's own heart because he repented. Nobody knows what that thorn in Paul's side was all about, but we can speculate that Paul was struggling, and God saw fit to turn this persecutor into a liberator. And Jesus, the quintessential perfect man, became the most notorious and wanted gang leader in history. He was hunted down as a gang leader. And afterwards, they infiltrated His gang, bought off one of His gang members, and assassinated Him as a common criminal. If you had read the Roman paper at the time, not the Christian paper, you would have seen that they did not report that Jesus was a timid cream puff hanging on a cross somewhere, but that He was a gang leader who they had had to root out and run down like the criminal they perceived Him to be.

Yet when we read the Bible, we see niceties about these heroes. In truth, they were not perfect men; they were men like other men out there right now. Let's get the truth out. Let's talk about reality when we talk about men of the Bible. How can biblical heroes be instructive models for people of today if we're going to make them look like sissies rather than the strong but imperfect men that they were? They were strong men with weaknesses, and they overcame them by the grace of God.

No biblical hero is of historical significance because he simply lived and died, never made a mistake, or never did anything wrong. Like us, they existed somewhere between the fallen Adam and the new, resurrected Adam. All of us are fallen men. What happened to us? How did we descend to our current state of woundedness? We were created in the likeness of God. We were created whole. Just as God didn't make Adam weak, a murderer, a liar, God didn't make African American men lazy, ignorant, loiterers on street corners, jail inmates, womanizers, woman abusers. He made all of us honorable, powerful, respectful, in His image. Being whole, being one with God, is our ultimate potential. It is my goal. It is where I should exist. My life, my struggle, is in that direction of wholeness through grace.

These excerpts reflect only a few of the activist efforts of only six of this study's participants. While the activism of each participant is different from that of the others, central to the activist projects of them all is their overriding concern for the quality of life for others. Each life story presents an inspiring man or woman who strives mightily to identify and alleviate areas of concern in their own lives, but more so in the lives of their fellow humans. In many of the cases, the radar used in detecting needs and the standards for treatment seems to relate to the participants' pasts. This is not to suggest that the participants see their past experiences as reflections of the present day or their present day as paeans to perfection. To the contrary, they appear to be tireless workers rather than proselytizers. And their activism seems meaningful and on target because they are genuinely interested in or personally knowledgeable about it. Time and again, their stories suggest that understanding hardship leads to discovering a way out of it. The perseverance, resilience, and generosity of the men and women in this study unveil, many times over, ways of breaking generational chains of poverty, ignorance, and relegation to the lowest tiers of society. As such, the study suggests a guideline for replicating educational, economic, and social success, especially among first-generation college students, those least likely to achieve it.

Why Activism?: The Compulsion to Love

Jesus didn't set out to perform a miracle by walking on water. He had to get someplace, so he did it. He wasn't even thinking about a miracle. He wanted to get to the other side, and there was an urgency to get there. Most of the extraordinary people I've met in life . . . don't think about being extraordinary.

— *Fred*

One of my objectives when I began this study was to determine the imprint of academic success-enhancing pre-college and college experiences on first-generation students' decisions to become activists, as well as how these experiences affected the ways in which they lived their lives. Based on the interviews that I conducted, I identified two factors common across all cases that had a direct bearing on the participants' decisions to become activists and on the nature of their activist endeavors. Quite simply, and not altogether surprisingly, positive and negative experiences from their pasts seemed to play a major part in determining the participants' activist roles. It seems that the interviewees' more difficult experiences may have compelled them toward activism, while their more positive experiences may have informed the design of their activist programs.

To illustrate this point—but at the acknowledged risk of applying too facile a gloss over the participants' lives—I examined significant concerns or events, both positive and negative, from the participants' past experiences. Grant, for instance, faced educational discrimination during his youth as the result of a stammer when he talked. He was also deeply influenced by his father's accounts of his life as a black person in the south. Both Grant and his father needed a fair chance, and no one made those chances available to them. Like almost everyone else in this study, Grant decided that he would be available to curb the degree to which others endured hardships similar to his own or similar to those of people, such as his father, whom he cared about. His own interests and areas of expertise—engineering, art, and the law—influenced the design of his activist program. Thus, in the example of his activism that is quoted in the preceding pages of this chapter, Grant intervened in the life of a deserving black male who had served time in jail and was discriminated against because of his criminal record. Where else would this artistically gifted ex-con have found the chance that he needed?

Similarly, Jerry's contributions to St. Elizabeth's Catholic School are one example of how he helps poor children to receive a good education, which would not be the case, he believes, if they were attending their neighborhood Chicago public schools. In Jerry's own school experience, he had been unable to get an uninterrupted Catholic school education because his parents could not afford the tuition, and he spent years receiving "poor instruction" in the Chicago public schools. He tries to prevent the duplication of his experience for poor Chicago school children of today. By investing a large part of his income in his not-for-profit organization, Jerry seeks to exert a positive influence on America's moral and economic development. He is fervent in his patriotism and invokes the memory of his father in violent confrontation with the Communists who "were making the people dissatisfied with America." In the design of his activism, Jerry looked to his own experience and that of his father for the template that he would follow.

The patterns of activism of the other participants profiled in this chapter are as readily detectable and as consistent with their pasts as those of Grant and Jerry. Both Maria and Jorge are involved in helping others, mostly Hispanics and other minorities, to develop and maintain businesses to counteract the lack of opportunity generally available to those groups by society's traditional lending institutions. As Puerto Ricans, both Maria and Jorge were raised somewhat on the periphery of a Puerto Rican identity, and their meaningful work as activists on behalf of the disenfranchised may void to some extent their own negative experiences—and the experiences of those they care about—as a result of their ethnicity. Similarly, the discrimination that Clara encountered as an overweight, working-class student would have been effectively altered by intervention of someone like herself. In Fred's case, his mother's obfuscation about the worthwhile role of a black male in America almost ruined his life. His teaching and preaching wholeness and reality, as related in the preceding pages of this chapter, is clearly antidotal to his mother's and to his own previous condition of fragmentation and unenlightenment.

The participants whose stories are presented in Chapter 2 each selected a program of activism that would counteract their own difficult experiences or would replicate or enhance their positive ones. In the following quotations from their stories, the first alludes to past experiences that informed their activist programs, while the second refers to their activist endeavors. In the first grouping, for example, we see that Annie emulates the teachers who influenced her during her days as a student:

> The teachers that I had in grade school and high school are still my motivators for my work now. I know how I was helped when I was a child, and I just know that children today need our help. I know I would not be where I am today without other people. I do the best I can do in whatever I do, and I help whomever I can. . . .
>
> Like my mother, I love children, and that is one of the reasons I am so glad that I became an elementary school teacher. . . .
>
> I met my husband through having someone come into the classroom to enhance education for children. Many of the children in my district are very poor, and their parents cannot provide certain educational enrichments for them, so it is important for the schools to do all that they can. We had been studying sand in my class, and I contacted this glass blower from Abbott Laboratories and had him come in to demonstrate for the children. . . . I bring in various types of enrichment for students as often as I can. I also do classroom presentations for other teachers on my African travels and on other subjects in an effort to help children whenever I can.

Through storytelling about Native American cultures, Arlene counteracts the type of ignorance about Native American people that was, by the design of her family and of society, her unfortunate experience:

But my teachers, although they were Indian, taught me nothing about my culture. . . .

. . . In many respects, [my teachers] were as wooden as the carvings of Indians in headdress that once stood outside small-town general stores. . . . Storytelling, a major force in my activist work, brings me absolute joy. I do it naturally and everybody of all ages responds in kind, with joy. I tell my stories, I sing in Mohawk. Afterward, people come and talk to me. . . . I try to make my experience and what I have learned real for my audience. I like to invite them into the experience. And I try to keep learning, to keep getting better.

John's activist work with children shows him connecting with and encouraging youth in a way that never occurred in his own experience as a child or teenager:

I grew up by my own devices, pretty much on my own. My mom and dad sort of let me go. Whatever I did was okay. It was as if they forgot about me. Of course, there was discipline and there were rules and stuff. But they never really paid much attention to me. . . .

I'm going to open a store for teenagers because they need a sense of how to run a business. You are never taught in college or high school or anywhere else how to live a life as an artist. . . . If the kids had a store, they could show themselves the gestalt of the art experience. I'm hooking up with Hull House to make this happen. . . . There is one area about the size of my shop that they can part with at one o'clock in the afternoons. That would work out perfectly for the kids. They could operate the store from around one-thirty to seven o'clock and go through what a store owner goes through.

Lorraine replicates the service of helping those who are less able, just as others helped her:

I will never forget the time when I didn't have a dress or shoes to wear to a special event at Voorhees. My friend's mother had sent her two new dresses. One she wore and the other, brand new, she insisted that I wear. Another friend of ours had shoes that she said were too small for her, and she wanted me to wear them and stretch them to her size. So I wore my friends' finery feeling like a princess, not a beggar, because of their genuine desire to help me. . . . I think about those friends. I think about them all the time.

I could never forget the things they did for me when we were going to school, and I was poor and they were not.

I had to learn the labor laws, but it was worth it because it exposed me to the living conditions of other people. The job heightened my caring spirit for other people. I have always wanted to help others because somebody helped me. And I was able to help so many people. . . .

Even though many of the participants in this study play out their activist roles in multiple ways, in almost every case there is a direct connection between their own experiences and their programs of activism. But why they became activists is almost an afterthought as presented in their stories. In their sentiments if not in their exact words, these deeply empathic people became activists either because they wanted to do for others what someone had done for them, or they wanted to do for others what no one, unfortunately, had done for them. The interviews suggest, however, that examination of a few qualities shared by all the participants provides room for speculation that other factors influenced their becoming activists. These factors are considered next.

Audacious Dreaming: The Benefits of Risk

We pulled twenty-five women off welfare a while back, and I thought it was going to be real challenging to get their kids good day care and get the women training and a good job in exchange for their welfare checks. I thought I was going to get a lot of heat from their men and their families because they might not want that kind of change, but it seems to be working. . . . I'm pushing these reforms because I think they will help to put responsibility, dignity, and hope back into these women's lives, but it's real scary.

— John

In analyzing the interviews from this study, I found that several qualities of personality were common to the participants and appeared pivotal in their activism and the ways in which they lived their lives. While among the general population these qualities may suffer from overuse in theory and underuse in practice, they nonetheless were hallmarks of the seventeen men and women who participated in this study. Specifically, two qualities were repeatedly discovered in the interviews: a willingness by the participants to take risks for themselves and for others and a willingness to live a relatively simple life. Time and again, participants discussed situations that revealed their compassion and courage in responding with their energy, influence, expertise, time, and money to causes, often high-risk ones, for other people. The interviews that I conducted suggest that their willingness to take risks was an important factor in their decisions to become activists.

That the first-generation college graduates in this study took risks to enhance their lives and the lives of others seems almost too obvious to warrant discussion. Clearly, they had to take enormous risks in most cases to develop and execute the plans that would get them to college, help them to meet with the success required to remain at college, and result in their graduation. More demanding of explanation is *why* they were risk-takers in ways that departed so radically from their families' histories. In these pages, I seek an answer to this question by investigating the risk-taking tendencies of this study's participants and their willingness to live relatively simple lives. I then connect these investigations to the participants' decisions to become educational or social activists.

I begin by pointing out that responsible people weigh the probable consequences of their actions prior to carrying them out. If the losses and benefits of an action seem to warrant its execution, only then does the responsible person carry it out. But whether the anticipated losses and benefits are seen as warranting execution may depend on factors far removed from the degree to which the person is responsible. That said, I believe the participants in this study became first-generation college graduates in part because they were responsible risk-takers. Since others in their families may also have been responsible risk-takers, a question that presents itself is "What was it that made the participants' risk-taking net such different gains?"

First, while they may not have been either more or less responsible than their siblings or others in their environments, this study's participants were probably able to define responsible risks more broadly than were others. Thus, the risk of giving up a "good job" in the present in favor of earning a college degree and qualifying for a better or different job in the future may have appeared more responsible under the broader definition of the interviewees than it did to their families. Still, the risk was overwhelming for many of the participants. As Sadie put it:

> After high school, I went to New Orleans for a year and a half. My mom had died. . . . I had a job in a department store. I told my supervisor I was going to go to college and the response was, "You're sure you want to go to college?" I started in January, 1974. I left on a Monday morning, and it took

the bus all day to cover what is a three-hour drive. My luggage wasn't with me when I got there in the afternoon. I didn't have any money. . . I got registered, but I got in wrong lines. It was a tremendously hard experience. I was there by myself. It was a very traumatic experience for me. I knew I had left my little job. I had not achieved a great amount of success, but still I was living, making a living. But I wanted to go to college. I wanted to get a college education. I didn't know if I would finish. I'd say to myself, "If I can just make it through this semester, maybe I'll leave it alone." But at the end of the semester, something would enable me to go on.

If leaving the security of a job for the uncertainty of college was frightening, the forces that made college attendance a responsible risk for Sadie and for most others in the study were, indeed, significant. Evidence points to special status, positive naming, and ascending cross-class identification as the forces that influenced the interviewees' identification of a responsible risk and, by extension, their decisions to become educational or social activists. Consequently, I end my analysis with a brief discussion of those factors with which it began.

Special status people are often freer than others to take calculated risks to effect their own well-being. Having repeatedly experienced the benefits of being special, they form the expectation that fortuitous occurrences outside the norm may actually work for them. If they have been positively named, their confidence has been further supported, and they may have determined with a degree of faith a direction for realizing their potential. Since the power of positive naming lies in its credibility, students will believe their teachers' assessments that they should go to college, as Sadie did, and the threads of hope that their aspirations will be realized are automatically strengthened. This is one manner by which a foundation of reason and responsibility could have been added to special-status participants' calculated risks. Special status and positive naming may have enhanced the courage of the interviewees to take risks, and their risk-taking often paid off. It may have reinforced the belief that they could become not only first-generation college graduates, but anything else, including educational or social activists, that they set their minds to. Again, Sadie's words remind us of how the participants were willing to embrace the "Yes I can!" philosophy:

I went to New Orleans for two weeks after graduation and then went back to Alcorn and waited for the Upward Bound program to hire me for the summer. That's the only thing I wanted to do. It didn't pay much—just enough to get me to Bowling Green. I had finished Alcorn in three years. I learned from that experience with Upward Bound that I could be a leader and a teacher.

In graduate school I studied pop culture. I was the first African American female in the Department of Pop Culture to get a degree at Bowling Green. My department chair was very encouraging. He encouraged me to write papers, and I got my first bibliography of the cable industry published in a journal of public TV. I realized I could be a researcher at Bowling Green.

Another important component of the participants' foundations for responsible risk-taking may have been provided through ascending cross-class identification. By creating a source for critical information about what they wanted to become and, sometimes, how they could go about achieving that goal, ascending cross-class identification added substance and reality to the participants' aspirations. Armed with the information gathered through ascending cross-class identification, the interviewees could take risks that were much more informed than would have been the case if those same risks were taken by a sibling who did not share the participants' privileged information. In other words, while the participants' situations within the confines of their families may have appeared to be the same as everyone else's, in almost all cases they were, in fact, quite different with the advantages of different information and greater confidence falling to the participants. These advantages may have improved the interviewees' chances of achieving their goals.

Along with help from pre-mentors, teachers, community members and organizations, professors, peers, and others, responsible risk-taking on their own behalf worked for the participants in this study, and they achieved college degrees. The extension from risk-taking for their own benefit to risk-taking for others was a natural progression made easier by the fact that the participants, to a person, were compassionate people who preferred to live relatively simple lives. Since none of the seventeen were interested in amassing a great deal of personal wealth, they were free to give of their time and money to deserving others.

By way of example, Grant, a lawyer, is a contradiction of the easy conclusions resulting from stereotypical thinking about the way lawyers live their professional lives. As is true of every participant after college graduation, Grant is a risk-taker who refuses to do that which does not meet his standard of responsibility. He turned down a job after graduate school because he did not like the area where he would have had to live. He went into private practice instead, with no clients or money. He tacked his name up over the door and experienced six very lean months, doing the overflow work that his boss gave him. His cases included divorce, shoplifting, drunk driving, contract disputes, wills, probates, and estates. The other lawyers in the office represented the lowest of humanity. Grant took the financial risk of refusing to serve those clients:

> My clients weren't representative of the scum of humanity. There were five other lawyers in the office, and *their* clients were. We had rapists, murderers, bank robbers, everything going through the office. It was hard for me. And although I had certain people come to me who were murderers, rapists, and robbers wanting me to represent them, I refused to do so. My view was I refused or they needed to understand that it wasn't in their best interest to have me represent them. I'd say, "I can probably get you off with fifteen years on this one; maybe twenty; maybe the death chamber. If you're guilty of the crime, you're guilty and you've got to pay. It's as simple as that."

In the following example, we see Grant taking an informed risk out of compassion for innocent people whom he had never met:

> I was able to help a lot of people—sometimes not in accordance with ethical rules—but, nevertheless, help them. I remember a taxi driver who came to me in the late 1970s. He had told his wife to come down to the bank and sign on a $10,000 loan. That was a lot of money at that time. He had a deal that was hot, and he needed his wife to sign so their house could be secured for this loan. His wife was a homemaker who had no idea what was really going on, so he got the money and went and bet it on a horse. The horse fell down and broke its neck—didn't even finish the race. Now, the guy was in trouble. He came to me and said, "I'm in trouble. I borrowed this money and I've got to pay and I can't. And I'm going to lose my house. My wife and kids are upset." I said, "Here's what we're gonna do. It ain't right, but we're gonna do it. We'll file bankruptcy for you, but not for your wife. That way, she'll owe the money, but you won't. The house is in both names, and the bank can't foreclose on the house until she dies."
>
> The bank was pissed. The lawyers for the bank called me every name but God's child. They said that I was screwing up the system, using it, all kinds of things like that, and they were right. I took advantage of a loophole to save this man's house for his wife and kids. At that time, I was in private practice, and I felt good about what I did. But if I were to do that today, I would be kicked out of my firm.

Corollary issues, such as more money than one needs to live simply, appear to be far down on the list of priorities for everyone in this study. Again, Grant's voice is representative of the participants:

> Integrity maintenance among lawyers is normal, not different. My mother used to say, "Never treat anyone different from the way you want to be treated yourself." My father would say, "You have to earn your own living. You shouldn't be expecting handouts because no one owes you anything." From my mother, I got "respect other people," and from my dad, I got "work for your own living." These are two hard principles that are so deeply ingrained in me. Integrity means treating people with respect and not abusing a trust, and to me integrity is normal. People want to do right—inherently.
>
> There have been different opportunities that have arisen, and I've had to make a choice to be honest or to be rich. I choose to be honest. It brings further opportunity. I won't even give a second thought to taking someone's money because it's not in my program. I have had the opportunity to do so many times. I would gain in the short term and lose in the long. That doesn't pay.

Another voice espousing simple living is John's:

> I make a difference in my own life by living as simply as I can. Right now I'm trying to live on $5,500 a year. My costs are down to about $20,000 . . . and I try to live on a hundred dollars per week. . . . And the rest of my income I give away. I'm serious about the job description that I wrote when I was just starting out . . . that I wanted to effect social change and that would be my job. . . . When I was at Berkeley, I was particularly affected by something the professors used to say: "Artists are very poor but that's good because then they are living on the edge of a picket fence and they are always telling the truth. You have to tell the truth and money has to be completely out of the picture or very, very secondary."

Steve expressed a similar sentiment:

> No matter how well you do in art, there's always more to do. If you're ninety, you can still keep going because there's no limit. That's what my motivation is. I see people do things for money, but for me the issue is time and doing the stuff that I value. I can remember doing things because I liked what I produced, and then I found that I didn't care about the product

so much. It was a process, the doing, not the product or money that mattered . . . I don't have a lot of drive to make more money because I'm content. I'm easily content. I feel like I'm very lucky. I have all the stuff I want. . . . I have my cars. I have all the art supplies I ever wanted. I get time to do my artwork, and I get to help people out. I'm doing exactly what I want.

Jerry reiterated the preference, common among the participants, to live a relatively simple life:

I get money from my business. The personal money that I make I put back. . . . I live well. I'm a rich man. I've got freedom, a new Lincoln every two years, a nice home, though it's no palace. And I can do what I want . . .

The interviews that I conducted present the participants as imbued with a proclivity to take informed risks that have a pivotal effect on their academic successes, on their lives in general, and on their activism. Many demonstrated the willingness to take a calculated risk long before college, and in some cases this independence of action directly affected their chances of getting to college. Moreover, aspects of their calculated risk-taking to enhance their own educational opportunity was often reprised in their activist work. For example, when Chang heard that the schools were going to be reopened during the Cultural Revolution, he was in a remote area where he had been sent to work on a farm. He formed a study group with four other youths, and they studied every night and on days when it rained too hard to carry on with the farmwork. Even when they were working, the youths would discuss questions that they had about the materials they were studying. They used books borrowed from older students who were in school before 1966 and focused their study on science in particular, believing that scientific knowledge was not changing very much. For Chang, at risk was studying very hard for nothing and falsely raising the hopes of his friends that an almost nonexistent chance of their getting into high school would materialize. When they took the exams for admission to high school, four of the five were accepted. This was a tremendous accomplishment, for over 2,000 students had competed for only 800 possible seats in high school classrooms. This triumph has definite overtones in the Chinese school that Chang has begun for Chinese youth in his residential area.

John provides another striking example of risk-taking for himself that later informed his activism. Throughout his pre-college years, neither his family nor his schools seemed to care very much about his education. While his father seemed to prefer John to his older brother, neither parent connected with John in a meaningful way. No role models came forward from the community. Knowing full well that his family expected him to learn a trade and get a job after high school graduation, during high school John took the risk of studying architecture "under the guise of taking a trade." Having decided that he wanted to be an architect, he risked leaving home and girlfriend for Berkeley, California, where he hoped to enroll at the university. He earned the money to go to Berkeley, actually got himself enrolled, escaped the madness at Berkeley by dropping out of college during the Vietnam War demonstrations, discovered and traveled to San Miguel de Allende in Mexico to work and study with artists, finished his degree in San Diego, went to New York and aligned himself with the Art League because he had "heard that the art league would work you to death and really discipline you," and went to graduate school. These and other actions attest to John's propensity to take informed risks. As his case history indicates, his risk-taking college experiences were as varied as his current risk-taking activism, which includes his rehabbing an entire town, providing school children in a blue-collar town with an art mobile, and using proceeds from artwork to benefit the homeless and members of the old Negro Baseball League.

There was a great deal of evidence in the interviews that by meeting bias, ignorance, or insult with enlightenment, the participants often risked being judged as non-assertive. As they explained it, this, too, is an issue that demands to be addressed as the opportunity presents itself. For instance, Clara, who is white and comes from a family of two Caucasian parents and five multiracial adopted children, explained that reacting to people's prejudices with anger rather than understanding is counterproductive, wastes an opportunity for learning, and risks the perpetuation of ignorance:

A lot of times when I was younger, I'd go to the mall with my sisters and brothers and people would say, "Oh, are you baby-sitting?" And I'd say, "Yeah, my mom and dad went out so I got stuck with the kids." Then they'd look with their jaws kind of hanging. They'd blabber, "What? What did you just say? Is this your sister?" Then I would realize, and I would explain, "We're all adopted. That's why we don't all look the same." When my father died a few weeks ago, my sister had friends who came to the funeral, and they kept saying, "Well, where's your mother?" because they could see what my father looked like; he was lying there in the casket. And my sister said, "That woman over there with the gray hair. That's my mother." And her friends were like, "Wait a minute! We don't understand this!" My sister said, "Ohhhhh . . . we're adopted!"

When my father died, he was at the university with my youngest sister, taking her back to school. They had been getting ready to get on the elevator to take her things up to her room. The paramedics arrived and one of them said, "Well, who knows this guy? Who does he belong to?" And my sister was standing right there over my dad. She said, "He's my father!" Because she's Asian, they couldn't fathom that she had a familial connection. It takes us by surprise because we forget that we look different.

I grew up with my mom getting angry at people who reacted to us in a certain way. My brother who is Native American would get really, really dark in the summertime. My parents are pretty light, and I am too. So, we'd go to the grocery store, and if someone were staring . . . my mom would say, "What are you looking at? Do you have a problem?" She taught me to stand up, but I don't get angry because it's better to teach people that what they thought they knew is wrong.

Clara's example is reflective of the strong moral core that seems to run throughout the participants. Instead of judging other people's ignorance as a personal affront, Clara simply risks letting them think that she has no feelings by politely enlightening them. She believes that providing people with missing information is much preferable to protecting one's ego by retaliating against their ignorance. She explained that she grew up in a town where a greater degree of racial and cultural diversity existed in her home than in all the rest of the municipality. When one of Clara's younger sisters was in third or fourth grade and came home upset because the children at school were calling her Chinese, Clara advised her sister to tell the children, "I'm Korean, not Chinese." The children had nothing more to say on the subject. They knew little of China and far less of Korea. Their ignorance was kindly, if matter-of-factly, suggested to them, and, not getting the vulnerable or defensive response they may have expected, they settled on having a friend who simply looked different. Clara explained that she practices this form of activism daily in her classroom and in her life. She elaborated:

> Since I am in a position of power in the classroom, I have to use that power the very best way that I can. I always hated people who would use power to make other people feel like nothing. Since I did at one point feel like nothing, I know what it feels like, and it doesn't feel very good. So I do my very, very best to make people feel good about themselves, to give them confidence, because I don't want anyone to feel the way I felt.
>
> When I was growing up, since my mom liked to keep us well fed and to take the very best care of us that she could, I grew up as a very, very heavy child. So I was the butt of a lot of jokes and a lot of really harsh treatment.

There were many days when I would come home from school crying. I was always wondering why someone should be treated like that because it was horrible. Now, I don't want to give the impression that I'm Superwoman, but every time I see something unjust, someone being treated unfairly, I'll take the risk of speaking up and saying that that's not right, that there's no reason that we should be mean to somebody else. . . . A whole lot of times I think it really was class structure and the socioeconomic thing working against me. I found that a lot of people who are treated unfairly just get angry and make a lot of noise. I think that doesn't help at all. You need to educate people, to show them, "This isn't the way to do things." You have to risk your ego and just help people to learn.

Throughout the stories of the participants, there is evidence, both explicit and implied, that the participants became activists because they wanted to enhance the quality of life for others. Most lived by principles formed in the early years of their lives. John's aim was "to do something where I could make a difference in people's lives." Jerry's guiding principle was, "If morality is any good, it applies everywhere: in me, in my family, in my work, in my community, in my country." When Annie was twelve years old, she determined that she would "treat others like I want to be treated." All of the interviewees connected aspects of their activism to their actual life experiences. And a willingness to take risks for themselves and for others seemed to connect the entire life experience of each participant from their earliest days as children to the activism of their current lives. Their consistent willingness to take informed risks to effect positive change is testament to their optimism and to the personal responsibility that they have accepted for the *condition of things* in the world.

6 | Eyes Ahead of Us and Eyes Behind

Chapter 6
In Pursuit of Happiness

Let us briefly consider the costs and benefits to society of the education received by the seventeen men and women in this study. The interviews illustrate that society contributed far less to the participants' academic successes than to the education of students whom schools have traditionally valued. By contrast, as activists the participants give back to society at a rate well above that of contributions from average citizens. For society, the participants and others like them are gold mines discovered on undervalued ground. Not to develop these natural resources is wasteful, often mean-spirited, and even traitorous because it undermines the social and economic health of the nation.

In our brief consideration of the participants' educational costs and benefits to society, it is important to note the positive reverberations of their college degrees on their families. For example, Alex, whose father could not read or write, has a sister who has completed most of the coursework toward a bachelor's degree; a nephew who holds bachelor's and master's degrees and is a respected politician in a large city; a niece who is a lawyer; a niece who holds a bachelor's degree; several nieces who have completed some college coursework, including two with vocational or technical program certification; a grand nephew entering his junior year of college; and a niece entering her sophomore year. Alex's own child completed a bachelor's degree in six semesters and has just graduated from medical school. As an instrument of change, Alex has built a bridge from illiteracy to the highest levels of academic accomplishment. When he graduated from college and changed his standard of living, Alex's family's mindset shifted, and a college degree became a coveted goal. By his example, Alex switched the tracks for many members of his family from the lower- to the middle-class way of life.

Other participants similarly affected their siblings' and children's aspirations. Sadie, for instance, has four older siblings who went to college, following her lead. One became an aeronautical engineer, two others completed several college courses, and one earned an associate's degree. Sadie related how she urged her sister to enroll in the local community college and accompanied her to the campus to get a catalog, an application form, and other materials necessary to the admissions process. Her sister had lived in the same place for fifteen years, but once she earned her college degree, she acquired a better job and "moved on up to a better, different place." She has since received additional education and has landed even better jobs. Two of Sadie's nephews and two nieces have attended college.

Both of Steve's older siblings earned bachelor's and advanced degrees after he went to college. His younger brother also holds a degree, and all of his siblings are financially very successful. Fred, Ken, Jerry, Arlene, and Barbara all have children who have earned degrees. In fact, only two of the participants have a child old enough to earn a degree who has not done so at this time. The world needs more role models like those in this study, and finding their way to academic success, both as children and as college students, should be made easier. Consideration of how this can best occur deserves attention. Thus, in this chapter I examine the conjuncture between extant related research and the study's primary concepts on college choice, college persistence, and the effects of college and life experiences on activism. I then draw some conclusions based on these primary concepts, advance several recommendations for policy and practice, and end with recommendations for further research.

Support from the Literature

The Study's Primary Concepts and the Literature on College Choice

Since this study concerns the participants' entire educational and activist lives, it is important to connect their early family and life experiences with both their college success and their activism. Primary concepts from the study such as special status, positive naming, parental attitudes toward knowledge, and ascending cross-class identification seemed pivotal during the participants' early years and suggest a strong relationship to their academic and socioeconomic achievements and contributions to society as adults. Scant research exists, however, that acknowledges these concepts. Consequently, substantive support for them as foundations for the future academic and socioeconomic success of low SES, first-generation college students proved difficult to find.

As early as the 1960s, social psychologists were formulating a backdrop, relevant to some of these concepts, for the successful education of children through institutional or teacher acceptance and support. In *On Becoming a Person: A Therapist's View of Psychotherapy*, Rogers (1961) described teacher qualities geared toward promoting students' personal growth; openness to new experiences and to risk-taking; self-confidence and self-awareness; and willingness to learn—all of which were benefits of special status, positive naming, pre-mentoring, and teacher support. Related to this study's concept of parental attitudes toward knowledge, Rogers, as well as other social psychologists writing at the time, believed in the ability of families to positively influence their children's academic aspirations and achievement (Wolf 1963 and Davé 1964, cited in Gandara 1995). But these psychologists provide, at best, only indirect connections to this study's primary concepts.

Similarly, the literature on first-generation college students is basically silent on the concepts of special status and positive naming with a few isolated exceptions. One exception is found in LePage-Lees's (1997) study of women from low SES backgrounds who had been positively named in their youth as smart, special, or good. Another exception is Gandara's (1995) mention of the impact on a low SES Mexican American student who went on to become a physician after one of his teachers stated that he was "college material." Gandara supports the concept of special status in her example of college graduates who felt that being sickly and small as teenagers had influenced their spending most of their time and energy on schoolwork rather than on more socially integrative pursuits. Kinsella (1995) concluded that the special status of being the firstborn in a family was an effective predictor of academic achievement and persistence among sixty-seven first-generation college students, and Harrington and Boardman (1997), whose study was not exclusive to first-generation college students, found that being the oldest child in a small family or the youngest in a large family predicted a greater opportunity for upward mobility. While other literature on firstborns may support their achievement advantages as a result of birth order (Parker 1998; Nichols 1966 and Zajonc 1991, cited in Kinsella 1995), I found no studies that focused upon the role of special status in the academic success of first-generation college students.

The literature on first-generation college students, corroborated by the more generally directed research on college choice, presents a body of evidence that parental encouragement, educational levels, and socioeconomic standing are of crucial importance in a student's decision to attend college (Anderson 1985; Gandara 1995; Hossler, Braxton, and Coopersmith 1989; Hossler, Schmidt, and Vesper 1999; LaPaglia 1994; Levine and Nidiffer 1996; London 1978, 1986, 1989; McDonough 1997; Rendon 1994; Terenzini et al. 1996). While these studies and others support my finding that pre-mentors' positive attitudes toward knowledge affected the participants' decisions to go to college, I discovered no studies that emphasize the pivotal role of positive attitudes toward knowledge of functionally illiterate, low SES adults in predisposing children toward academic success. One loosely related exception is a study that examined twelve Mexican American high school students, who, limited in their English proficiency, were identified as learning disabled and relegated to special education classes. The children of immigrants seeking better living conditions for their families, these academically unsuccessful students persevered in school because they shared their parents' strong belief that education is the means to social and economic empowerment (Hayes 1992).

The literature on first-generation college students supports my finding that the homes, schools, and communities of the study's participants had significant impact, both positive and negative, on the participants' academic achievement, often working in near concert against them (Baca 1994; LaPaglia 1994; Lara 1992; LePage-Lees 1997; London 1986; Rendon 1994; Rodriguez 1982). A vivid example is provided in Cuadraz's (1993) study of Mexican Americans who earned doctorates from the University of California at Berkeley but believed that in their pre-college years, their teachers had assumed that they were not very intelligent and had not expected academic excellence from them. They reported that high marks on essays and tests were met with suspicion from their teachers, who wondered whether the students had done the work themselves. The teachers' evidence? The students' Mexican American ethnicity.

The participants in Cuadraz's (1993) study entered doctoral programs between 1967 and 1979, so their experiences as schoolchildren represent a chronological range of over two decades. However, more recent studies of pre-college students suggest the continuation of such obstructions to the success of first-generation students. For instance, Barahona's (1990) longitudinal study of the effects of first-generation status on the college aspirations of high school sophomores and seniors showed first-generation students to be at a marked disadvantage. Their aspirations to attend college, their actual college attendance, and their persistence in college were all negatively affected. Barahona concluded that the effects of first-generation status are well entrenched by tenth grade and that intervention programs should be implemented as early as the beginning of junior high school.

Related studies not limited to first-generation college students also lend support to my finding that members of the homes, schools, and communities played crucial roles in supporting or negating the academic well-being of the participants. Examples include a report by Galbo and Demetrulias (1996) that examined the impact of significant nonparental adults on the childhoods of

285 university students, and the work of Werner and Smith (1982, 1992), which examined the effects of community members on the lives of vulnerable but resilient children. Delgado-Gaitan and Trueba (1991) examined day-to-day experiences in immigrant children's lives, extending our understanding of the issues and meanings of children's worlds both inside and outside the school. Of major concern to the researchers was the necessity to empower immigrant parents and communities to interact with schools for the betterment of their children. Similarly, Lareau (1987, 1989) found that low SES parents tend to possess neither the knowledge about how schools work nor the degree of comfort within them to successfully intervene in the schools' operations on behalf of their children.

As this study shows, however, the depiction of family and community as friend and school as foe may be overly simplified; and the literature on first-generation college students presents, in fact, a more complex picture. While most college students must distance themselves from their pasts to some degree (Tinto 1987), the work of Anderson (1985), Gandara (1995), Hossler, Schmidt, and Vesper (1999), LaPaglia (1994), London (1986), McDonough (1997), Richardson and Skinner (1992), Zwerling and London (1992) and others has shown that families and communities, as well as schools, often erect substantial barriers to college enrollment for first-generation college students. Terenzini et al. (1994) reported that some families of first-generation college students, especially black, Hispanic, or Native American families, fear both their children's figurative and literal home-leaving and, as a result, may exacerbate their transition processes. Others such as Cross (1998), Vars and Bowen (1998), Wilson (1998), Kronley and Handley (1998), and Nisbett (1998), who focused upon African Americans' lack of social and economic opportunity, have asserted that long-standing environmental factors, including low life expectations and racial, ethnic, and economic discrimination, present considerable obstacles to students wishing to attend college. Not surprisingly, Harrington and Boardman (1997) found that all blacks in their study, even those from well-educated, middle-class families, reported more obstacles to their educational attainment and less redundancy of resources than whites, even those from low SES, undereducated families.

This study's primary concept that institutional and peer support appeared to be significant in the academic success of the participants is corroborated by the literature on first-generation college students. Terenzini et al. (1996) found that, compared with other students, first-generation college students exhibited lower educational aspirations and critical thinking skills, at least initially, and had spent less time interacting with their high school instructors and peers. Terenzini et al. (1994) reported that many of the first-generation college students they studied had been given the impression by their high schools, families, and peers that if they went to college, they would fail. Other writers assert the disadvantages suffered by first-generation college students who were relegated to lower academic tracks in high school (Oakes 1985), subjected to poor academic advice by counselors (Gandara 1995), and denied the academic preparation for college provided by rigorous high school courses (Darling-Hammond 1997).

York-Anderson and Bowman (1991) reported that first-generation college students received less familial support for going to college than did second-generation college students. Werner (1995) identified inadequate finances as the most crucial barrier to education for first-generation college students and a lack of familial encouragement and support as the second most important factor. He also found that Hispanic students' concern about educational barriers was inversely proportional to their identification with the Anglo culture. Studies by Brooks (1988) and Billson and Brooks-Terry (1982) looked at the difference in factors such as social and academic integration, academic rewards, commitment to the institution, and family influence between first-generation college students and their second-generation counterparts. Their findings suggested the advantages of being among the second as opposed to the first generation in one's family to go to college. By building ostensibly on the works of Hicks (1981), London (1989), McCarthy (1990), Stierlin (1974), and Weis (1985), in 1992 Weis found that there are significant tensions between same race and same gender college students from different social or economic classes. Thus, the negative impact of first-generation status can override even the supposed cohesiveness of race, ethnicity, and gender.

How the Study's Primary Concepts
Contribute to College-Choice Theory

Examined against a background of theoretical perspectives that help to define our understanding of the college-choice process, several of this study's primary concepts may suggest the need to adjust specific components of selected theoretical frameworks and findings regarding college choice. These theoretical perspectives include Anderson's (1985) identification of external and internal factors that influence a student's decision to go to college; the stages of the college-choice process as defined by Hossler, Braxton, and Coopersmith (1989); the definition of parental encouragement as a factor in the college-choice process (Anderson 1985; Hossler, Braxton, and Coopersmith 1989; Hossler, Schmidt, and Vesper 1999; LaPaglia 1994; Levine and

Nidiffer 1996; London 1978, 1986, 1989; McDonough 1997; Rendon 1994; Terenzini et al. 1996); the concept of "habitus" as defined by Bourdieu (1977, cited in McDonough 1997) and redefined by McDonough (1997); and the concept of "entitlement" as defined by McDonough (1997), extending the work of Bourdieu (1977, cited in McDonough 1997). While we must keep in mind that this study's sample population is too small for its findings to be generalizable, the study's primary concepts, nevertheless, may suggest the need for considerable adaptations of our views on which, how, where, and why low SES students from undereducated backgrounds decide to attend college.

The question before us is whether the aforementioned theoretical perspectives can more fully inform our understanding of the college-choice process if they are extended or enhanced by this study's primary concepts. To provide an answer, I briefly summarize pertinent aspects of these theories and findings and provide succinct descriptions of how their functions or meanings may be extended to consider the very real, continuing, and, I hope, increasing number of college students who are first-generation attendees from low SES families..

I begin with this study's primary concept that regardless of whether the participants' parents (or grandparents) were literate, their positive attitudes toward knowledge, education, or reading played an important role in the participants' earning college degrees. This primary concept is resonant of findings from the literature on college choice. For instance, and of particular interest here, Hossler, Braxton, and Coopersmith's (1989) description of the predisposition stage in the college-choice process asserts that the socioeconomic status and educational level of parents wield significant influence over whether their children will go to college. Though not contrary to Hossler, Braxton, and Coopersmith's assertion, this study suggests that their description may not be adequately practicable when applied to students or parents from poor, undereducated backgrounds.

This study shows that in spite of the low educational levels and socioeconomic status of the participants' parents, the influence of the parents was pivotal in the participants' decisions to attend college. Sixteen of the seventeen participants repeatedly stressed the fact that the degree of respect for or interest in knowledge, education, or reading held by their parents—despite their illiteracy in some cases—played a crucial role in whether the participants would earn a college degree. Current theoretical perspectives on college choice tend not to reflect the positive influence of such parents. Since fifteen of the participants had no degree of confidence that they would go to college, and since the parents of the participants generally had low levels of education, the participants' stories may demonstrate a strong connection between low SES parents' educational accomplishments and their children's confidence that they will attend college. It is possible that this connection could provide a point of inquiry about the predisposition stage of the college-choice process for low SES students. What seems certain is that scholars must pose questions and seek answers about the positive influence of undereducated parents from low SES backgrounds on their children's decisions to go to college.

In a similar vein, in his description of internal and external factors affecting college attendance, Anderson (1985), corroborated by a host of researchers (Hossler, Braxton, and Coopersmith 1989; Hossler, Schmidt, and Vesper 1999; LaPaglia 1994; Levine and Nidiffer 1996; London 1978, 1986, 1989; McDonough 1997; Rendon 1994; Terenzini et al. 1996), found that an external factor that influences a student's decision to go to college is parents who communicate to their children the value of a college education. My study, on the other hand, shows that while its participants found parental influence to be pivotal in their decisions to go to college, the positive impact of their parents was delivered in decidedly different ways. The difference lay in the fact that only two of the participants had parents who communicated to any consistent degree the value of a college education. Most of the participants' parents may not have understood the value of a college degree, and neither they nor their children generally envisioned a college education as a viable component of the children's futures. Similarly, many of the participants' parents were functionally illiterate and generally not supportive of their children's pursuing a college degree. Yet, with only one exception, the participants emphasized that they were influenced early, impressionistically, and deeply by the parents or grandparents whom they most admired and who held knowledge, education, or reading in high esteem. The participants described their parents in roles as pre-mentors who first influenced them to value learning and whose appreciation of education, reading, or knowledge played vastly important roles in the participants' journeys toward earning college degrees.

The point here is that Anderson's (1985), Hossler, Braxton, and Coopersmith's (1989), and many other researchers' (Hossler, Schmidt, and Vesper 1999; LaPaglia 1994; Levine and Nidiffer 1996; London 1978, 1986, 1989; McDonough 1997; Rendon 1994; Terenzini et al. 1996) findings on the influence of parental encouragement on students' decisions to attend college stop short of including in any important way the contributions made by low SES parents to their children's decisions to pursue a college degree. One reason for this lack may be suggested by the large time gap that existed between this study's participants' "pre-mentoring" experiences during childhood and their actual dates of college entrance. Because most of the parents did not exhibit the behaviors associated with positively influencing their children's college attendance during the years more immediately preceding college entrance, scholars might tend to ignore the effect that the early positive experiences might have had. Yet early educational experiences often comprise the foundation of one's educational attainment, and as Berger (2000a) has pointed out, by affecting a student's cultural capital, such experiences seem to influence whether the student will choose to go to college. This study suggests that the early positive influence of low SES, undereducated—even illiterate—parents is crucial and should be factored into theoretical perspectives on parental encouragement.

Also according to Anderson (1985), another external factor that encourages students to earn a college degree is the influence of peers from the same SES group who plan to go to college. Not surprisingly, this study shows that the participants were rarely influenced by these peers. Since the participants tended to be anomalies within their SES peer environments *because* they aspired to go to college, peer influence in electing to enter college was arrived at most often through ascending cross-class identification. This means that for the study's participants, peer influence came more often from students who knew they were going to college and who were from a higher SES group. A strategy widely used among the participants, ascending cross-class identification lent encouragement to pursue academic excellence and post-secondary education by providing the information required (1) to recognize and understand important benefits of a college education and (2) to determine and acquire the means to achieve a college degree.

The effect of ascending cross-class identification for peer support (when such support could be found) was no less than transformational for some of this study's participants. As a vehicle for acquiring cultural capital, ascending cross-class identification provided the participants with peers from higher SES groups who served as surrogate teachers, counselors, and other school personnel whose prescribed roles include aiding students in the college-choice process. A wide-reaching external factor, ascending cross-class identification seemed to enable the study's participants to achieve in varying degrees the internal factors that were found by Anderson (1985) to encourage the pursuit of a college degree: the academic skills required for college admission and graduation; academic motivation; personal and academic reasons for pursuing a college degree; career choices that require a college education; the self-assurance required for success in college; pleasure in reading; regard for a college education; and identification with college-educated role models. Ascending cross-class identification fostered academic survival and promoted academic persistence and achievement. To the degree that a participant's habitus did not provide the opportunity to develop her potential, ascending cross-class identification was necessary. As a tool employed by incredibly courageous and inventive children and students in their pursuit of an education, ascending cross-class identification extends the notion of cultural capital by indicating how it may be acquired by those who are lacking the valued variety. Along with those it might serve as a social-mobility vehicle, ascending cross-class identification deserves consideration in the theoretical frameworks that seek to illuminate the college-choice process.

In addition to its contribution to findings by Anderson (1985) and others on external and internal factors that influence college attendance, ascending cross-class identification may extend the meaning of Bourdieu's (1977, cited in McDonough 1997, 9) definition of "habitus" as expanded by McDonough (1997). According to Bourdieu, habitus is a "common set of subjective perceptions, experiences, and beliefs held by members of the same group or class that shapes an individual's expectations, attitudes, and aspirations." McDonough explained that members of the same group or class can be expected to aspire at similar levels since they have been influenced by the class-bound structures such as the families, schools, and communities that comprise their environments. Thus, students from middle- to upper-class environments receive academic encouragement, preparation, and enrichment privileges and services to prime them early in their schooling for college entrance and success. Conversely, students from low SES backgrounds and educational milieux most often receive academic preparation that is far inferior to that of their more affluent counterparts (McDonough 1997).

This study shows its participants—all from low SES backgrounds—appearing to counter some of the negative effects of their habitus through ascending cross-class identification. Briefly stated, while living within the class-bound contexts of their homes, schools, and communities, this study's participants acquired microscopic but substantive experience of more privileged environments. Through ascending cross-class identification, the participants seem to have experienced the narrow end of a funnel of privileged habitus, which gave them the mental wherewithal to view or imagine the increasing richness of life as the funnel spiraled outward to its widest expanse. Stated differently, even as the participants were experiencing the disadvantages of their neighborhoods, schools, and communities, through ascending cross-class identification they were gaining vital knowledge of how to acquire the education required to attain a life of greater options than their current habitus allowed. This study, then, may corroborate Bourdieu's definition of habitus, may support McDonough's conclusions about the effects of the low SES habitus on its children's academic aspirations, preparation, and achievement, and, most importantly, may describe the means by which this study's participants countered the debilitating effects of their low SES environments through ascending cross-class identification. As a means of reducing the del-eterious effects of the low SES habitus, the concept of ascending cross-class identification could make an important contribution to the theories and find-ings on college choice.

Finally, since a step in the ascending cross-class identification process is believing that one's imagined life of enhanced options is deserved and proper, this study may extend McDonough's (1997) extension of Bourdieu's (1977, cited in McDonough 1997) idea of entitlement. According to McDonough, entitlement refers to parents and their children's conviction that they deserve and are entitled to educational privilege that is commensurate with their habi-tus and socioeconomic status. The interviews in this study repeatedly demon-strate the participants' belief that their humanness entitled them to educa-tional excellence and social parity as the means to the pursuit of happiness and a fulfilling life. Where did they get this belief?

The sense of entitlement expressed by the participants seemed to derive not only from ascending cross-class identification, but also from two other primary concepts in the study, special status and positive naming. With regard to special status, the participants' stories suggest that because they knew at an early age that they were highly valued by someone, their levels of confidence were higher, enabling them to overcome obstacles to their goals. Likewise, positive naming—which aligned their obvious strengths with a profession, position, or condition without the assumption of anyone involved that the alignment would or should be heeded—seemingly affirmed the participants' aptitudes just as they were and guided them toward developing their potential. Generators of a kind of cultural capital, (Berger 2000a; Fowler 1997; McDonough 1997), special status and positive naming appear to have endowed this study's participants with academic advantages grounded in their enhanced senses of self. As Berger (102) stated:

> Bourdieu emphasizes that the accumulation of capital resources is cumula-tive in nature. The earlier one begins to accumulate capital in various forms, and the earlier one is able to begin optimizing those same resources, the greater advantage one will have later in the educational process.

The participants credit both special status and positive naming with en-couraging them to seek academic excellence and with influencing their deci-sions to attend college and strive for success once there. As appears true of parental attitudes toward knowledge, education, and reading and of ascending cross-class identification, special status and positive naming may extend Anderson's (1985), Hossler, Braxton, and Coopersmith's (1989), and other researchers' findings that parental as well as teacher and counselor encouragement is an important factor leading to a student's college matriculation. All of this study's primary concepts may suggest the need to develop theories on college choice that are more relevant to low SES students. The tendency of Anderson's theoretical perspectives on college choice as well as the model used by Hossler, Braxton, and Coopersmith is to treat college choice at a grand-theory level. The development of theory that focuses more directly on low SES students' predisposition and choice to attend college would heighten our understanding of the college-choice process while providing direction for policymakers and practitioners to advance academic achievement and college success among students from low SES, undereducated families.

The Study's Primary Concepts
and the Literature on College Persistence

The literature on the first-generation college student's transition to college provides support for my premise that belongingness and comfort zone were significant considerations for this study's participants. Many writers have pointed out that most first-generation college students enroll in two-year colleges, seeing them as more accessible and less intimidating than their four-year counterparts. LaPaglia (1994), the first in her family to go to college, recounts spending her freshman year at the local junior college not only for financial reasons but because she had to find the "audacity" (p. xiv) to go to the university. Rendon (1992), Rodriguez (1975, 1982), Lara (1992), and others have recounted their personal experiences as alienated first-generation college students. Research by Terenzini et al. (1994, 1996); Levine and Nidiffer (1996); Orozco (1995); Rendon (1995); McDonough (1997); Gandara (1995); LePage-Lees (1997); and Pounds (1998) have corroborated their stories. Still other researchers have addressed the feelings of discrimination experienced by first-generation and minority college students and the attendant negative effects on social adjustment, scholarship, and persistence (Harrington and Boardman 1997; Nora and Cabrera 1996; Steele 1999, 1993). Similarly, the effects of inadequate academic preparation for college (Anderson 1985), unrealistic positive assessments of black students regarding their academic readiness (Rowser 1997), and feelings of alienation as a precursor to dropping out (Mohr, Eiche, and Sedlacek 1998), while not limited to potential or actual first-generation college students, highlight some avenues of discomfort experienced by many who are the first in their families to go to college.

While this study's primary concept of ascending cross-class identification is not represented in the literature on first-generation college students, the literature does provide evidence of its necessity as an adaptive mechanism, along with the concept of belongingness, for those who must straddle two cultures without adequate knowledge of the way of life they are trying to enter. Lara (1992), Kiang (1992), Rendon (1992), and Orozco (1995) underscored some of the transitioning difficulties of first-generation college students. An immigrant student from the Dominican Republic, Lara recounted the confusion and trauma of trying to fit in as a first-generation, culturally different, minority student on an American college campus. Similarly, Rendon chronicled the difficulty of transition and the aids to persistence in her journey from the Mexican American barrio to having earned a doctoral degree and appointment as a university professor. Kiang's study showed how first-generation Asian immigrant and refugee students faced issues of cultural dislocation, identity, and mislabeling as model students. Orozco sampled 144 Mexican American students in order to examine levels of cultural adjustment among first-, second-, and third-generation college students. He found that first-generation students experienced greater degrees of cultural adjustment difficulties, as well as greater degrees of resultant stress, than did second- and third-generation college students.

Rendon's (1992) observations regarding the self-doubts of first-generation students supports their need for ascending cross-class identification as a way of knowing about the new world of college. In a related vein, Whitehall (1991) showed how issues of entitlement, especially as they relate to self-perceptions of academic ability, affect the success with which first-generation re-entry women dealt with the college-going process. McGregor et al. (1991) found that of three groups of college students, students whose parents had both attended college exhibited the highest levels of self-esteem while first-generation college students experienced the lowest levels. The ability to identify with the college-going experience and to feel that one belongs contributes favorably to the academic achievement and persistence of students (Attinasi 1989; Pounds 1998; Mohr, Eiche, Sedlacek 1998; Rendon 1995; Terenzini et al. 1994). While Rodriguez (1982) attributed his academic success, at least in part, to his disidentification with his Mexican American culture, others have asserted that students may neither need nor desire total assimilation in order to succeed academically (Gurin and Epps 1975; Rendon 1992; Portes and Zhou 1993). This study suggests that ascending cross-class identification might obviate some first-generation college students' belief that disidentification with their cultures is required for college success.

Support for my argument that belongingness was vastly important to the study's participants and that many of them began college as highly uncomfortable tourists who hoped to establish themselves as residents can be found in the literature on identity achievement. For example, the negative resolutions of Erikson's (1980) stages of psychosocial development, though spread across an entire life span, reflect many of the compressed complexities of this study's first-generation college students in their experiences as tourists. Feelings of guilt, inferiority, isolation, and even despair—all identified by Erikson—were central to the myriad aspects of many of the participants' identity fluctuations as college students. Similarly, Josselson's (1987, 1996) pathways to identity formation—by virtue of their intent to clarify the intersection of an identity in flux with the surrounding world—reflect my discussion of identity transmutation as experienced by some of this study's participants. Marcia's (1966, 1980, 1989) identity statuses likewise reflect the participants' campus lives at times as tourists and at other times as residents. In contrast to this study's findings, Harrington and Boardman (1997) reported that blacks in their study who were from low SES backgrounds tended to lose contact with their families and to hold negative feelings about their former environments. Though other discussions of racial identity, self-efficacy, and self-esteem (Helms 1990) make relevant connections to this study, the participants' accounts of identity-building, especially as it relates to ascending cross-class identification during their early years, seem to set them apart. I believe that their roles of agency during childhood—in constructing positive senses of self that may have influenced their college success—fall outside the contexts of much recent research on personality traits and identity acquisition (Siebert 1996; Scarr 1993; Scarr and McCartney 1983; and others).

The literature on first-generation college students offers support for my findings that the informal curriculum and interaction with the faculty were of great importance to the persistence and success of this study's participants. According to Astin (1993), the first and second most important influences on the growth and development of college students are peer groups and faculty, respectively. Tinto's (1987) student retention model connects students' academic success to their social integration, including their interactions with peers and with faculty. Terenzini et al. (1994) found that residential students reported encouraging each other, discussing classwork together, collaborating on group assignments, and generally helping each other to navigate the academic and social straits to college success. Rendon (1994, 1995, 1996) studied the effect of the informal curriculum on the academic progress of college students and identified a lack of faculty involvement with students as a barrier to education of first-generation college students. Hurtado (1990) addressed the difficulty that some colleges face in attracting and retaining minority students, many of whom are first-generation, because of the lack of connections between these students and their professors.

Other studies have shown that minority students in particular see faculty friendliness, fairness, and expressed belief in the students' academic ability as premium qualities among professors (Eimers and Pike 1996; Ferguson 1998; Nora and Cabrera 1996; Ogbu 1974, 1981; Poock 1999; Steele 1993, 1999), with student leadership roles greatly enhancing student persistence and graduation from college (Astin 1975; Fuertes and Sedlacek 1993). Building upon the work of McKeachie (1969), Lowman (1984), Pascarella (1980), Pascarella and Terenzini (1991), Kuh (1993), Kuh, Schuh and Whitt (1991), and Boyer (1987), Mayo, Murguia, and Padilla (1995) found that most students reaped greater academic benefits from formal than from informal social integration through their involvement with faculty and with student organizations. But support for my concept of the professor as change agent may be most vividly expressed in personal accounts such as Albom's (1997) *Tuesdays with Morrie* or Carson's (1996) report of 222 college graduates' stories of their transformations as a result of their professors' influence. Additionally, the writings of Freire (1970) and Palmer (1983, 1998), the empirical research of Macrorie (1984), Brookfield (1987), Conrad, Haworth, and Millar (1993), Harrington and Boardman (1997), and Haworth and Conrad (1997), and the personal accounts of many previously cited authors whose works speak specifically to the first-generation college student experience, all strongly support the need for critical awareness and dialogue between student and professor in fostering student achievement and persistence in college.

How the Study's Primary Concepts
Contribute to College-Persistence Theory

In addition to heightening our understanding of college choice, this study's primary concepts may contribute to current theoretical perspectives on the college-persistence process. Specifically, several of the culture-based propositions about premature student departure advanced by Kuh and Love (2000) as extensions of Tinto's (1993) theory of student departure, may, in turn, be extended by primary concepts in this study. In "A Cultural Perspective on Student Departure," Kuh and Love enumerate and explain eight propositions that focus upon students for whom the likelihood of persisting is particularly low, including students from historically underrepresented groups. In a discussion of how this study's primary concepts correlate with Kuh and Love's cultural perspective on student departure, I examine Propositions 1, 2, 3, 5, and 6.

The authors' first proposition states that "[t]he college experience, including a decision to leave college, is mediated through a student's cultural mean-ing-making system" (Kuh and Love 2000, 201). Kuh and Love posit that pre-mature student departure is not caused by the organizational or structural qualities of an institution but by the student's perception of those organiza-tional or structural qualities. The student's perception grows out of his "mean-ing-making system," which is "comprised of values, assumptions, and beliefs about what to expect from college, the role of being a college student, and the value of a college degree." The authors further state that students from low SES Alaskan Native, Native American, and African American groups "may appear to be committed to the institution but this 'commitment' is based on inaccurate information" and is, therefore, illusory, contributing to the students' premature departure.

In concurrence with Kuh and Love (2000) and along with many other schol-ars (Anderson 1985; Darling-Hammond 1997; Gandara 1995; Kiang 1992; LaPaglia 1994; Lara 1992; Orozco 1995; Rendon 1992), this study's partici-pants indicated that their college-going experiences—and in most cases their pre-college experiences as well—were fraught with problems stemming from a lack of pertinent information about educational processes, a complaint that is common among low SES, first-generation college students. However, the participants' interviews provide a wealth of details asserting that "the struc-tural and organizational properties per se" (Kuh and Love, 201) of their pre-college and baccalaureate institutions presented some of the greatest barri-ers—as well as inducements—to their persistence. Because pre-college education builds the foundation upon which college access and success gener-ally rests, this study's participants were made especially vulnerable by academic-success-deterring organizational and structural properties of their pre-college institutions, and many of these properties were replicated in the collegiate setting. If Berger and Braxton (1998) are correct, and this study suggests that they are, the presidential and administrative styles at higher education institu-tions are examples of organizational characteristics and processes that may promote student persistence as well as student departure (Also see Astin and Scherrei 1980, cited in Braxton 2000). According to Berger (2000b), the organizational functioning of the bureaucratic, collegial, political, and anar-chical models of colleges and universities (Birnbaum 1991) may contribute to both college departure and college persistence. As Braxton (2000, 261) states, ". . . research shows that such organizational attributes as institutional com-munication, fairness in the administration of rules and policies, and participa-tion of students in decision-making also exert influences on social integration and departure (Braxton and Brier 1989; Berger and Braxton 1998)." Considerable support exists for the premise that while aspects of the college experience, including a decision to persist or to leave college, may be mediated through a student's cultural meaning-making system, the organizational or structural qualities of the institution may also promote or deter student persistence.

Also suggesting the need to amend Kuh and Love's (2000) explanation of Proposition 1 is the commitment to college demonstrated by all of this study's participants. Appearing to have benefited greatly from information gleaned through ascending cross-class identification, the participants described deep and abiding commitments to college, based in part on a growing body of information, which influenced their academic success and culminated in their college graduation. Their information gathering may have provided an outlet for some of the participants' activist tendencies. For instance, when Clara discovered that informational meetings were held on each floor of her college dormitory, she would attend meetings on the same subject on two different floors. "I had a double chance to learn," she said. "I became an expert on financial aid so I could help other people who were like I had been." In cases where participants left college before degree completion as a result of their institutions' organizational or structural functioning, their commitment to education per se led them to different colleges and, ultimately, to graduation. In these instances, the participants' incomplete information about college appeared far less influential in their decisions to depart than were the institutions' organizational or structural properties. This study suggests that the assumptions underlying Kuh and Love's discussion of Proposition 1 may preclude the positive effects, in particular, of ascending cross-class identification, but also of concepts such as special status, positive naming, and parental attitudes toward knowledge, education, or reading on low SES, first-generation college students' commitment to college.

Kuh and Love's (2000) second proposition, that "[o]ne's cultures of origin mediate the importance attached to attending college and earning a college degree," may also exclude the probable positive effects on low SES students of special status, positive naming, parental attitudes toward knowledge, education, or reading, or ascending cross-class identification. For this study's participants, cultures of origin appeared to inform their belief that they could not go to college but, contrary to Proposition 2, not the importance that the participants attached to college attendance or to earning a college degree. In light of their struggles to earn a degree, the importance that they attached to doing so seems unquestionable. Not only did attending college and earning a degree become a significant goal for each of the participants, several were supported—at least emotionally—by members of their families. If Annie's parents, for instance, had not attached importance to Annie's college education, they likely would not have endured being run off the land with their crops still in the fields to live in a corn crib where they huddled in terror as gun shots—fired by whites angry that black sharecroppers would send their daughter to college—hit the tin roof of their shelter. Instead, at the beginning of their trouble with the landlord over Annie's college education, they would have avoided these and other sacrifices by assuring their proprietor that Annie was not going to college and by withdrawing their support for her attendance. Annie's special status as the seventh child was a culturally significant fact observed by others in her family and may have influenced their acceptance of her educational aspirations from childhood onward. As the stories of Annie, Sadie, Maria, and Jorge illustrate, some low SES, undereducated parents harbor dreams for their children that are similar to those of their middle- and upper-class counterparts (Comer 1985, 1988, 1989, 1997; Fliegel 1993; Gandara 1995; Levine and Nidiffer 1996; Wilson 1987). These low SES parents may lack the belief that their dreams for their children can be realized because they have no knowledge of how to make them happen. As a result, their apparent inertia regarding higher education for their children—stemming at least in part from ignorance and economic powerlessness—may seem akin to a value system which places no importance on earning a college degree. This study's participants show that value system to be uncharacteristic of some low SES parents and their children as well.

Proposition 3 states: "Knowledge of a student's cultures of origin and the cultures of immersion is needed to understand a student's ability to successfully negotiate the institution's cultural milieu" (Kuh and Love 2000, 203). Yet this study's participants seemed to gain a degree of understanding about their cultures of immersion through ascending cross-class identification that was basically independent of their cultures of origin, prompting their success in earning at least baccalaureate degrees. This means that knowledge of the participants' cultures of origin might not include any or most of the academic-success-promoting distinctions that benefited them as children and as students. Consequently, such knowledge might provide inaccurate information as support for judgments about their "ability to successfully negotiate the institution's cultural milieu" (203). This study shows that in various instances some knowledge of the participants' cultures of origin was used not only in the lowering of expectations for them in their cultures of immersion but also in diminishing their opportunities for academic excellence. A more practicable proposition, according to this study, would align knowledge of a student's culture of origin and the culture of immersion with the knower's ability to anticipate or recognize barriers or inducements to the student's successful negotiation of the institution's cultural milieu.

According to Proposition 5, "[s]tudents who traverse a long cultural distance must become acclimated to dominant cultures of immersion or join one or more enclaves" (Kuh and Love 2000, 204). Similarly, Proposition 6 states that "[t]he amount of time a student spends in one's culture of origin after matriculating is positively related to cultural stress and reduces the chances they will persist" (205). In their discussion of Proposition 5, Kuh and Love offer the examples of first-generation college students (1) renouncing some aspects of their cultures of origin and (2) joining subcultures that espouse norms reflective of their cultures of origin as a way of spanning the cultural divide between home and college. In their discussion of Proposition 6, the authors state that shifting between two distinct cultures adds to the stress of students who do not deny or renounce parts of their cultures of origin—and this contributes to their departure.

Interestingly enough, most of this study's participants evinced no consideration of denying or renouncing their cultures of origin, and most maintained strong connections with home and family even when familial support for attending college was weak or nonexistent. In this respect, this study corroborates Rendon, Jalomo, and Nora's (2000) contention that students from minority groups tend not to deny or renounce their cultures of origin in order to gain membership in a culture of immersion. (Also see Gurin and Epps 1975; Portes and Zhou 1993; Rendon 1992.) Most of this study's participants seemed to succeed in reconciling their identities as college students with their identities of origin by recognizing and accepting the differences in customs, conditions, experiences, and badges between the two cultures. Prior to college, through ascending cross-class identification, most participants had gained some positive knowledge and experience of a different culture or standard of living and, once at college, were able to attain the level of biculturalism needed to move from tourist to resident within the college milieu. As aspiring dual residents, on occasions when their family members entered the world of college, the participants endeavored to make them comfortable by making their visits as culturally familiar as possible.

By developing strong senses of self and enhancing their cultural capital through the study's primary concepts such as special status, positive naming, and ascending cross-class identification, most of this study's participants seem to have enhanced their abilities to cope with the cold comfort zone of college. Perhaps their respect for who they were plus a sense of economy—a belief that subtracting one's identity would be both unreasonable and too costly a prerequisite to adding a college education—augmented their understanding that they could, in time, become comfortable with both feet planted in whichever culture they happened to find themselves.

This was fortunate for the participants, especially those who had a great deal of trouble breaking into the culture of college once they had arrived and who had neither the time nor the opportunity to join an enclave. As Rendon, Jalomo, and Nora (2000) have stated, the option of joining an enclave may not be open to some students whose cultures of origin are distant from the culture of immersion. For several of this study's participants, affirmation, validation, and positive naming by faculty were among the realities of the informal college curriculum that influenced persistence, while joining enclaves—with the exception of work—or renouncing their cultures of origin were not. (See related discussions by Comer 1997; Eimers and Pike 1996; Ferguson 1998; Harrington and Boardman 1997; Ogbu 1974, 1981; Steele 1999; Nora and Cabrera 1996; Rogers 1961; Terenzini et al. 1994.)

It should be noted that the recommendations given here for broadening the assumptions underlying Kuh and Love's (2000) propositions, especially Propositions 5 and 6, are mediated by ascending cross-class identification. These suggested modifications would refocus the lens of Kuh and Love's cultural perspective to include low SES students from undereducated backgrounds whose academic capabilities may not be fairly predicted by the prevailing wisdom on their cultures of origin.

The Study's Primary Concepts and the Literature on Activism

Some degree of support for my findings regarding the interviewees' lives as activists can be found in the life stories of nationally and globally acclaimed contemporary Americans who were the first in their families to go to college and who lead activist lives. Examples include Benjamin Carson, the renowned surgeon who rose from humble beginnings in Detroit to become director of pediatric neurosurgery at Johns Hopkins University Hospital (Carson and Murphy 1990); Dick Gregory, the political activist and comedian; Jocelyn Elders, former Surgeon General of the United States; Jesse Jackson, the political activist and preacher; and Ruth Simmons, president of Brown University, whose high school drama teacher donated some of her own apparel so Ruth would have more than the clothes on her back when she arrived at college (Picker 1996). Also included are Willie Gary, a personal injury lawyer who grew up in abject poverty but gave ten million dollars to his alma mater, Shaw

University, a historically black college that was near bankruptcy in 1991, and helped to raise an additional seventeen million dollars for the school (Harr 1999; Haygood 1992); Maya Angelou, college professor, author, actor, director, and producer for stage, film and television; and Oprah Winfrey, television talk show host and movie star. Another example is Michael Eric Dyson, the one-time high school dropout turned welder who was labeled by the *Village Voice* as an "intellectual for our times." Of his experience at an elite boarding school to which he won a scholarship when he was sixteen, Dyson writes:

> That short distance [thirty miles] had divided me from a world I had never known as a poor black inner-city youth: white wealth, power, and privilege. I had never gone to school with white kids before, much less wealthy white kids, many the sons and daughters of famous parents, a banking magnate here, a film giant there. I immediately experienced a Hitchcockian vertigo about the place, its seductive grandeur, warming grace, and old-world elegance not enough to conceal the absurdity of racism that lurked beneath its breathtaking exterior. I left Cranbrook near the end of my second year, returning to Detroit and obtaining my diploma in night school, and taking a succession of jobs in the fast-food industry in maintenance work, and in construction. I finally became an employee at my father's alma mater, the Kelsey-Hayes Wheelbrake and Drum company, becoming an arc-welder and later unloading trains brimming with brake drums. (1993, xxvii)

Though drawn from a pre-college experience, Dyson's words are illustrative of the first-generation college student's disorientation within the collegiate world. As professor, minister, author, and social activist, he epitomizes what a poor child can become.

Beyond such accounts of individuals' lives, the literature draws scant connections between first-generation college graduates and their lives as activists. A study based on the stories of one hundred interviewees, *Common Fire: Lives of Commitment in a Complex World* (Parks Daloz et al. 1996) identified conditions that seem to foster the commitment to purposeful lives of helping others. But the study did not include first-generation college student status, college graduation, or low SES familial background as criteria to inform its selection of subjects. Similarly, Astin's (1985) theory of student involvement and Rhoads' (1998) research on student activism are primarily concerned with involvement and activism among the general student population prior to college graduation. Harrington and Boardman's (1997) study, whose "Path-makers" or subjects from low SES backgrounds were neither necessarily college graduates nor activists, showed that when altruism was present in their subjects, it was stronger, but not more frequent, in those from low SES backgrounds. Neither the Harrington and Boardman study nor any of the others I examined provided substantive support for my premise that a willingness to take risks and to live relatively simple lives advanced the participants' commitment to activism.

How the Study's Primary Concepts Contribute to College-Effect Theory

This study's primary concept that the participants decided to lead lives of activism based upon their past experiences and augmented by their willingness to take risks and to live relatively simple lives may extend Astin's (1993) theoretical perspective on the impact of college on students as well as his (1985) theory of student involvement. Involvement theory holds that the quality and degree of growth that a student experiences in college is determined by the quality and degree of the student's involvement with college resources (Astin 1985; Pascarella and Terenzini 1991, cited in Rendon, Jalomo, and Nora 2000). Astin (1984, 1985) determined that students who spend large amounts of time on their academic studies, are active members of student organizations, spend considerable time on the campus, and connect with faculty on a frequent basis are more satisfied with their college experience, more successful academically, and more prone to persist. Student involvement, Astin (1985) found, is promoted, among other factors, by student services, assessment and feedback, and instruction—areas that colleges and universities should aggressively support as important ways to enhance the college student experience. In his research on the effects of college on students, Astin (1993) determined that the college experience influences students' involvement in social activism. He identified college students who are most prone to social activism as those who participated in discussions with peers on race- or ethnicity-related subjects, spent time socializing with students from diverse racial and cultural backgrounds, took courses in ethnic studies, and attended workshops designed to raise cultural and racial awareness. The uninvolved student's goal for attending college, Astin (1985, 1993) reported, was to acquire a job that would produce wealth. Not only did he find that students' involvement in service-oriented learning experiences during undergraduate school improves their college experiences, Astin also determined that such social involvement has lasting effects on students. He discovered that a positive relationship exists between the amount of time students commit to volunteering in college and their commitment to social service after graduation, including their greater propensity to help those in need and to perform civic services.

This study suggests that college may have a profound impact on activism, an impact that seems to be more directly related to the social, economic, and political enfranchisement derived from the conferral of a baccalaureate degree than to the properties of involvement theory as described by Astin (1985). Each of the participants in this study seems to have been transformed by college graduation into one who is actively committed to educational or social activism. Selection of the seventeen first-generation college graduates from low SES backgrounds as the participants in this study required potential subjects to have been involved as activists for at least five years after college graduation—five years, I reasoned, being enough time for them to have established a history of verifiable activist programs and behaviors. While a few of the participants had been involved in activist events during college or had begun to manifest evidence of their future activism, most of the participants seem to have immersed themselves in service to others almost immediately upon college graduation. In fact, one of the most pivotal factors in their having earned a college degree appears to have been the degree's power to increase the opportunity and the means by which the participants could discover or design and implement ways of serving others. In this respect, college graduation was a portal to activism made possible by the participants' heightened social, economic, and political power.

The point of the preceding paragraph is that the effect of college on the activism of this study's participants may mark a departure from the impacts of college described by Astin (1984, 1985, 1993). A number of the participants fit various aspects of Astin's definition of student involvement while they were in high school as well as in college, but for some of the participants, Astin's theory was actualized primarily in the area of faculty validation (See Rendon 1994; Rendon, Jalomo, and Nora 2000.), emphasizing the significance of faculty to the academic and social well-being of some first-generation college students (Astin 1985, 1993; Eimers and Pike 1996; Ferguson 1998; Hurtado 1990; Nora and Cabrera 1996; Ogbu 1974, 1981; Poock 1999; Steele 1993, 1999; Terenzini et al. 1994; Tinto 1987). Indeed, the transformative pedagogy and power of their professors is reflected in the ways some of the participants have elected to live, work, and carry out their programs of activism. Arriving at college with cultural capital that was different from the collegiate currency; dividing most of their out-of-class time between working and studying; being preoccupied with fear of academic failure; and lacking the confidence to discover which avenues of involvement would be welcoming, of interest, and affordable in terms of time and money were only a few of the reasons that some of this study's participants, as appears true of other low SES first-generation college students (Bowen and Bok 1998; Comer 1997; Ferguson 1998; Harrington and Boardman 1997; Rendon, Jalomo, and Nora 2000; Steele 1999, 1993; Steele and Aronson 1998; Wilson 1998), may not readily have become more generally involved . While Astin (1975, 1977, 1993) discovered that full-time as well as outside employment were among the detrimental forms of student involvement, all of this study's participants held part-time or full-time jobs during college either in off-campus or on-campus settings or both, emphasizing the financial necessity of work for many low SES students. As Astin (1993), Tinto (1993), and Rendon, Jalomo, and Nora (2000) have indicated, institutional accountability for student involvement may reach beyond offering opportunities for heightened participation to more active and responsible encouragement of at-risk students to become involved. Corroborating Astin's (1985, 1993) findings on faculty influence (See Eimers and Pike 1996; Ferguson 1998; Hurtado 1990; Nora and Cabrera 1996; Ogbu 1974, 1981; Poock 1999; Steele 1993, 1999; Terenzini et al. 1994; Tinto 1987.) and involvement, some of this study's participants indicated that they took a more substantial part in college life after a professor, using positive naming, reached out to them with a suggestion for greater involvement.

Though the activism of this study's participants is primarily post-college, the participants share goals that are reflective of Astin's (1985) theory of student involvement. Astin found that the altruistic goals of involved students differ from the goals of the uninvolved, who see a college degree as an avenue to acquiring a great deal of money. However, this study's participants also expressed and have demonstrated in their daily living a preference for relatively simple lifestyles that enable them to allocate more of their time and financial resources to activist endeavors. In addition, this study suggests that the participants' willingness to take risks on behalf of others, seemingly derived from the study's primary concepts such as special status, positive naming, and ascending cross-class identification, may be another trait of the first-generation college graduate who leads a life of activism. As such, this study may move beyond Astin's (1984, 1985, 1993) description of the involved college student—including the social activist during college—by identifying what may be specific characteristics of social or educational activists from undereducated, low SES backgrounds who have earned a college degree.

With the exception of their possible effects on the participants' decisions to persist to graduation, most aspects of Astin's (1993) theoretical perspective on college impact seem not to bear direct connections to this study's participants' decisions to become social or educational activists. Far more pronounced in the participants' histories regarding their activism are the connections between their personal experiences and identity issues up until college graduation and the activist behaviors and programs that they launched after earning their college diplomas. This study shows that the participants selected programs of activism that would (1) counteract the types of difficulties that they and others in their environments had experienced and (2) replicate or enhance in the lives of others remedies for those experiences.

This study's primary concept on activism suggests that if society would wholeheartedly promote the opportunity for low SES children and students to receive excellent educations and to earn college degrees, the benefit to the nation and to the world might be exponentially increasing, lifelong contributions by new members of the middle and upper classes. Switching the economic, social, and political tracks for themselves out of the lower class through attainment of a college education might enable these first-generation college graduates to become key sources for ascending cross-class identification in the lives of children and students who lack the cultural capital required to improve their own circumstances. By examining the activist lives of first-generation college graduates from low SES, undereducated backgrounds; by describing the social mobility vehicles that may have influenced their academic achievement; by identifying and describing personal characteristics that seem to foster their activism; and by connecting their activism to the improvement of underprivileged lives, this study may extend Astin's (1993) theoretical perspective on the effect of college on students as well as his (1985) theory of student involvement.

How the Study Extends Current Writings on First-Generation College Graduates

While some of the primary concepts of this study are grounded in existing research and scholarly writings, the concepts, overall, contribute to our understanding of the still-emerging field of first-generation college students. I discuss four such contributions here: first-generation college graduates' lives of activism; undereducated, low SES parents' and community members' academic-success-promoting behaviors on behalf of their children; the role of ascending cross-class identification in academic success; and the roles of risk-taking and simple living in first-generation college graduates' decisions to lead activist lives.

First, this study is novel in that it examines the activist lives of first-generation college graduates. Its participants confirm the conventional wisdom that first-generation college graduates from low SES backgrounds tend to give back, not only through their increased public contributions to the civic and economic good of society, but also through a more personalized commitment to others. Though not concerned with first-generation status, *The Shape of the River* (Bowen and Bok 1998), a definitive study of black and white graduates from highly selective colleges, reported that blacks, especially males, were more active in community and civic endeavors than were their white counterparts and, by extension, provided greater returns to society by more successfully using their academic achievements for the societal good. Conversely, Harrington and Boardman (1997) reported that the white males and black females in their study were more service-oriented than were the black males and white females. I hold that autobiographical as well as biographical accounts provide intriguing support for first-generation college graduates' value as activists, yet I found no existing research that substantively examines activism as a quality of these graduates. By examining the participants' choices to lead activist lives in light of their childhood, pre-college, and college-going experiences, this study begins to illuminate the processes by which the participants became the activists that they are today. From the purely practical standpoint of looking out for the nation's welfare, findings from this study invite our reappraisal of the enormous advantages inherent in (1) successfully educating children who might become first-generation college graduates and (2) continuing to promote their academic success as they traverse the collegiate pipeline.

Second, this research identifies and examines new concepts which invite our reevaluation of the roles played by family and community members, no matter how uneducated they may be, in their children's education. While the role of parental involvement in their children's schooling has long been represented in the literature, this study identifies and recognizes special status, positive naming, and pre-mentoring as academic-success-promoting behaviors of family members and others whose children are among the least likely to go to college. In its exploration of these behaviors, which are generally absent from the literature, this study suggests that more democratic approaches to academic excellence among the poor are in order. More specifically, the study points to the participants' poor, undereducated families and community members as primary resources for the identification of practices that might help more low SES children to become first-generation college graduates and activist members of the middle class.

Third, the study identifies the phenomenon, ascending cross-class identification, as key to the genesis, development, and achievement of college-going aspirations among the participants and to their means for achieving them. Absent from the literature, ascending cross-class identification invites us to reconsider our understanding of identity formation and how it is influenced by environment. According to Jerome Groopman (2000), professor of medicine at Harvard University, psychologist Jane Holmes Bernstein believes that neither an individual's personality nor his behavior can be considered separately from his environment. Groopman's discussion suggests to me that an environment that promotes academic ineptness also promotes adaptive mechanisms. Most of this study's participants lived in environments designed to guarantee their academic ineptness by forcing their adaptation to debilitating environmental stimuli. Through ascending cross-class identification, the participants were able to escape society's trap. "An adaptive mechanism can always become nonadaptive," Bernstein states (Groopman, p. 55). Even though the participants in my study successfully resisted society's prescribed adaptive behaviors as well as their devastating results, they were compelled to fight those behaviors throughout childhood, high school, and college, and, to some degree, may have to fight them throughout their lives. While the study's sample is too small for its primary concepts to be generalizable, the significance of ascending cross-class identification in the participants' lives is arresting. Additional study should examine further the salience of ascending cross-class identification in the lives of first-generation college students and should investigate its impact on goals formation and achievement, especially among children from low SES backgrounds.

Fourth, though writers such as Palmer (1983, 1998), Lowman (1984), Macrorie (1984), Belenky et al. (1986), Shrewsbury (1987), and Haworth and Conrad (1997) have emphasized the value of risk-taking environments for effective teaching and learning, I found no existing studies that examined the role of risk-taking on the social, educational, and activist lives of first-generation college graduates. Moreover, I found no research that identified a preference for relatively simple living as an important variable in the study of these lives. As is discussed in the previous chapter, a willingness to take informed risks may be an important component in the academic success and activist endeavors of this study's participants. Their willingness to live modestly may bolster their feelings of efficacy as well as their reserves of time and money that can then be used for the well-being of others. This study advances the possibility of a connection between risk-taking, activism, and relatively simple lifestyles among first-generation college graduates and highlights that connection as an area for future inquiry.

Conclusions

> In my life, I try to learn, and I try to share with others what I know. I know that peace, love, and understanding start right here, with me. . . . What kind of experience do I want today? What I project is the kind of experience that I can have.
>
> *— Arlene*

Throughout most of these chapters, my primary concern has been the identification of factors that may have contributed to the academic successes of the first-generation college graduates in this study and to their decisions to become educational or social activists. In these final pages, my focus turns to translating what I have learned from the participants' life stories into effective practices for creating academic success for first-generation college students. Since the study suggests a number of measures that are easily accessible by individuals, groups, and organizations, my paramount objective is to share ideas that can readily shorten the pipeline from researcher and findings to practitioners and students. In this spirit, I offer the following conclusions drawn from the study.

1. The processes by which the participants in this study may have succeeded in becoming the first in their families to attend college and to earn a college degree were not part of a comprehensive plan.

The literature on pre-college and college education presents a wealth of support for the need for comprehensive programs designed to improve the learning experience at all levels of education The results of this study indicate that family and life experiences that may have increased the participants' chances of earning college degrees arose from diverse, largely piecemeal sources that were unconnected by a comprehensive plan or vision for the students' educational well-being. These experiences, nevertheless, may have helped the participants to become academically successful almost in spite of the institutions whose rightful job it was to ensure their academic achievement.

Some of these aids came from sources totally outside the educational arena. One example is pre-mentors who, despite their own illiteracy in some cases, predisposed the interviewees to value education. At largely the same time, significant adults gave them special status, and others positively named them. Teachers and community members were among those who exposed the participants to worlds far different from the environments that they had known.

And the participants took advantage of the opportunities afforded them, turning bleak outlooks into exceptional lives.

The participants' exceptionality is evident in their examples of ascending cross-class identification; they demonstrated the ability to envision their circumstances as different from others in their communities and showed the wherewithal to persist in turning their visions into reality. In numerous instances, through ascending cross-class identification, the participants appear to have resisted many of the familial, societal, and cultural adaptive mechanisms common to their places and times. How difficult was it for these individuals, in most cases as young children, to rebel against the dictates governing their lives in order to create future circumstances for themselves far superior to the mold for which they had been cast? Fred related with awe and anger that in a speech delivered on the banks of the James River in 1712, William Lynch, a white slaveholder, spoke the terrifying truth when he predicted that if his methods of slave-breaking were followed, blacks would comport themselves in a manner befitting slaves for hundreds of years to come with little or no remediation. "But if you can make a slave, you can unmake one," Fred stated. Indeed, the interviewees are involved in the unmaking of slavery in its many guises of poverty, illiteracy, second-class citizenship, poor self-concepts, and other social ills, and most seem to have begun with the unmaking of slavery in themselves through ascending cross-class identification. By striving to be different, most of the participants countervailed the conditioning of countless generations. Remembering that their climbs toward success were the results of disparate, often disconnected forces helps us to understand the tenuous nature of their ascensions. Without a comprehensive plan to chart their courses, their successes appear to have depended largely upon happenstance.

2. Conditions seen by the participants as leading to their successes in academics and as activists are identifiable and replicable.

One of the most important conclusions of the study is that the success experienced by the participants is not solely the result of their extraordinary powers. To the contrary, the study begins to demystify the participants' differences from others in their environments. By showing how they appeared to be—and why they could be—so different from their siblings and others, the study clarifies the processes by which the interviewees' metamorphoses may have taken place. By isolating these practical processes, this research begins to make them readily replicable.

The processes by which Jerry and many others in the study appear to have become academic successes, for example, seem clearly identifiable and include the benefits of pre-mentoring. As the youngest of five children, Jerry was taught the alphabet and the rudiments of reading by an older sister before he was of school age. "I've been a quick study all my life," Jerry stated, and the coaching and modeling in reading provided by his sister proved of great benefit. However, when he left the public school system for third grade at St. Jerome Catholic School, he was demoted to second grade because his skills were lacking.

While many of Jerry's years as a public school student were downright uninspiring, he was saved by his increasing ability to read and his love of books:

> I'd read ahead in texts and get other things to read. I did an awful lot of reading. There were books in our house the other kids had in school. . . . My mother would say, "You're going to ruin your eyes," and I'd be under the covers at night reading with a flashlight. If you can't read, you really close the door on knowledge.

As a result of pre-mentoring by his sister, Jerry developed a lifelong practice of reading every day. In his case—as well as in the cases of most of the participants in the study—other concepts such as special status, positive naming, ascending cross-class identification, positive connections with professors, and the ability to forge a positive sense of self were identifiable and appear crucial in his success in academics and activism. Through means such as "fresh air" camps, Head-Start-type programs, mentoring programs in various academic disciplines—including the humanities where few such programs exist (Gandara 1999)—and community-based tutoring and mentoring programs, those concepts can be fostered for other potential and actual first-generation college students. And educating the public about them is a good way to start.

3. The participants perceived that developing a positive sense of identity and belonging within the college setting greatly influenced their college success.

In keeping with the related literature, the interviewees indicated that their college success was greatly influenced by their ability to find their places within the collegiate setting (Anderson 1985; Astin 1993; Gandara,1995; Hossler, Schmidt, and Vesper 1999; LaPaglia 1994; London 1986; McDonough 1997; Rendon 1992, 1994; Richardson and Skinner 1992; Zwerling and London

1992). For many, this was a difficult task since they were prone to enter college "by hook or by crook"—without adequate advisement, academic preparation, financial aid, or encouragement. Such backdoor access tended to cast the participants—in their own views as well as in the minds of others—as imposters or interlopers, which exacerbated their feelings of not belonging.

In many cases participants' self-doubts were compounded by the need to reconcile their identities of home with their emerging identities as college students. (Related discussions can be found in Gandara 1995; Harrington and Boardman 1997; LaPaglia 1994; Lara 1992; Levine and Nidiffer 1996; Rendon 1992; Rodriguez 1975, 1982). In *This Fine Place So Far from Home*, Law (1995) describes the price of not reconciling the two:

> My mother, I know, was proud of me and glad that I was doing well in a world she had never known. What she could not have guessed, though, was that in the course of my teacher training, I learned, through myriad covert (and some not so covert) pressures and practices, to feel increasingly ashamed of my home, of my family. Again and again, I heard that children who do not read, whose parents work too hard and who have little time or skills to read to them, whose homes are not "literate" but oral and often pretty nonverbal as well, children who have never been taken to an art museum or who do not have library cards, these are the ones at risk, the ones most likely to fail (be failed by?) the traditional academic setting . . . the ones who make a teacher's job so frustrating. Never once did any of my professors entertain the thought that I or any of my classmates could possibly have been one of those children. . . .
>
> It becomes the university's job to help children of the working class, when by some fluke or flash of good fortune they become undergraduates, to overcome their backgrounds. As Laurel Johnson Black writes . . . "It's about every child's nightmare of losing her family and the ways in which the academy tries to make that nightmare come true, to make it not a nightmare but a dream, a goal." I eventually made that dream my own and day by day betrayed myself in order to gain acceptance in the academic community; my strategy was silence and lies. I never confessed that I recognized my own home in the patronizing, contemptuous examples of my well-intentioned professors, which every day increased my resolve to erase my past and elude the humiliation of being found an imposter. (p. 2–3)

My research shows some ways by which the participants came to understand their own senses of vulnerability and how this awareness led them to reconcile their identities of home with their identities of college. Reconciliation, in turn, seems to have enabled the participants to work toward a wholeness of personality that could comfortably span two worlds. My research underscores the participants' becoming, rather than their losing, themselves. It shows them adding to, rather than subtracting from, their senses of self. It shows many of them expressing objective truths about their parents, rather than being embarrassed by them. By developing positive senses of identity, the participants seemed able to create for themselves comfort zones in both the culture of home and the culture of college, thereby reducing fear, fragmentation, and other similar detractions from the ability to learn. (See related discussions by Eimers and Pike 1996; Ferguson 1998; Nora and Crabera 1996; Ogbu 1974, 1981; Poock 1999; Steele 1993, 1999.)

This study also stresses the significance of personal connections that these first-generation college students made with professors, peers, and others through in-class and out-of-class experiences, including work. Most of the participants attributed to such connections a great deal of responsibility for their ability to establish positive identities and a sense of belonging on the campus. Professors were important to the participants' academic successes far beyond their duties as instructors and often enhanced the participants' lives by simply communicating that they cared (Comer 1997; Eimers and Pike 1996; Ferguson 1998; Harrington and Boardman 1997; Ogbu 1974, 1981; Steele 1999; Nora and Cabrera 1996; Rogers 1961; Terenzini et al. 1994). The interviews indicate that the current debate over the dual professorial roles of researchers versus teachers should contain a third component that includes more directly the nurturing and mentoring of students (Cienkus, Haworth, and Kavanagh 1996; Comer 1997; Harrington and Boardman 1997; Haworth and Conrad 1997; hooks 1994; Levine and Nidiffer 1996; Mayer 1997). Through abundant examples, my research demonstrates that the ability to make affirming connections with others was often the adhesive that helped a participant stick with the pursuit of a college degree. As a case in counterpoint, when Dorothy could not connect with anyone or forge an identity on campus, she dropped out:

> They didn't do a very good job of supporting students. That is the problem with many huge universities. Nobody gets to know you. You don't talk to your professors. You talk to your T.A.'s if they happen to care. Right before dropping out, I went in to the student center and I said, "Well, gee, I need to talk to someone; I'm depressed." And that was sort of like being in a mill somewhere. You go in there, and they time you. "Okay, you have five min-

utes. What's your problem?" I was depressed because I didn't understand my purpose anymore for being there. I didn't feel sure anymore. I didn't have anyone to talk to, and I needed some help. His solution to me . . . was to go to a health clinic and get some Lithium. That's when I went home.

4. A willingness to take informed risks presented itself as a probable factor in the educational success of the participants and in their decisions to become activists. Their satisfaction with living relatively simple lives seems to have accompanied their success as activists.

A final primary conclusion of this study concerns the tendency of the participants to take significant risks in an effort to prevail over seemingly insurmountable obstacles, to achieve success in those efforts, and then to take additional risks to overturn similar obstacles on behalf of other people. Harrington and Boardman (1997) posited that the low SES achievers in their study were reward-oriented rather than cost-oriented, and therefore more willing to take a risk with the objective of achieving a distant goal. In a study of abuse survivors, Higgins (1994) contended that positively channeling one's fury over past injustices can provide the impetus for "convictional mettle" (228). My research, I believe, provides strong evidence that a sense of security or self-worth may have enhanced the participants' propensity to take informed risks for their own and for others' benefits. Perhaps the participants' willingness to live unostentatiously manifests their senses of self-worth. I was struck by the interviewees' apparent lack of compulsion to build their egos by accruing great personal riches. Moreover, evidence from the study points to affirmations gained through special status, positive naming, and ascending cross-class identification as foundations for the confidence and self-esteem sufficient to promote risk-taking. The interviews suggest that when the participants were secure enough to believe that they could recover from making a mistake, they were more willing to take an informed but high risk with the possibility of commensurate, though long-range, payoffs. Having been "special" in some way during their early lives, they seemed to know their right to pursue their dreams. Perhaps as a result of having been positively named, they believed that for them better circumstances were in store. And ascending cross-class identification may have enlightened the participants as to what those circumstances might be. However destitute or uncertain they attest to having felt, the participants may have evinced the royalty that is latent, according to Emerson, in everyone. Their empowerment, one might argue, stemmed from their deep and abiding understanding that they counted:

The world has been instructed by its kings, who have so magnetized the eyes of nations. It has been taught by this colossal symbol the mutual reverence that is due from man to man. The joyful loyalty with which men have everywhere suffered the king, the noble, or the great proprietor to walk among them by a law of his own, make his own scale of men and things and reverse theirs, pay for benefits not with money but with honor, and represent the law in his person, was the hieroglyphic by which they obscurely signified their consciousness of their own right and comeliness, the right of every man. (Emerson 1841, 514)

Recommendations for Policy and Practice

If I clap my hands, I want the sound that goes out to be a positive rather than a negative sound because I believe that it travels forever through the universe. That's where the love is, then. It's in our actions and in our intentions.

— John

With regard to their social, economic, and educational backgrounds, many of this study's participants came from families reminiscent of those sought by Lady Liberty. Indeed, the inscription at the statue's base is a noble, if paternalistic, invitation. "Give me your tired, your poor, / Your huddled masses yearning to breathe free, / The wretched refuse of your teeming shore," (Lazarus 1883, 510) it intones without intimation of its long-range plans for such a dubious gift. Nor does it concede in its magnanimity the value of the huddled masses or teeming refuse beyond its recognition of their humanness in wanting to be free. This study presents a somewhat broader view that may be implicit in the Statue of Liberty's offer. First, even though the study's focus is on people from low SES backgrounds, it suggests the indisputable value of its participants as well as the relative pittance of debt that they owe to society when compared to the immense contributions that they make. Second, it indicates the level of care that may be required by such individuals on their way to becoming first-generation college graduates who are educational or social activists. And third, it prescribes specific ways in which society may be able to aid in the development of ultimate citizens simply by paying its debt to children and students. Accordingly, in this section, I offer five broad recommendations for policy and practice affecting the education of first-generation college students.

1. Adopt comprehensive plans as effective road maps to educational outcomes.

In *Race, Class, and Education: The Politics of Second-Generation Discrimination,* Meier, Stewart, and England (1989) argue that ability-grouping in elementary schools and tracking in junior high and high schools comprise the core of a wildly successful comprehensive plan in U.S. schools to perpetuate post–*Brown v. Topeka* educational discrimination *within the law.* Bowen and Bok (1998) provide clear evidence that comprehensive college admissions plans under affirmative action worked much more effectively to ensure equality of educational opportunity for underrepresented groups than many of us had known. Similarly, a wide range of comprehensive education programs, from preschool through graduate school, that have been described in the literature and replicated in schools, communities, and colleges have helped students, including those from poor, minority, and undereducated backgrounds, to become academic successes. Examples include Head Start, the Algebra Project (Jetter 1993), and the MURALS program (Gandara 1999). My purpose is not to discuss those programs here, but rather to recommend strongly that policymakers influence the adoption of comprehensive plans that meet the teaching and learning needs of children and students at every level of the educational pipeline.

Caution, however, is in order. Comprehensive plans cannot be effectively designed or applied on a one-size-fits-all basis (Fliegel 1993; Green 1997; LePage-Lees 1997; Mayer 1997; Shor 1996; Werner 1997). As Wilson (1998) has warned and my research has shown, what students from the black underclass need may be quite different from what is required for those from the black middle class. At pre-college levels, decisions regarding comprehensive plans should reflect dialogue among major stakeholders such as administrators, teachers, parents, researchers, community members, and policymakers (Comer 1985, 1988, 1989, 1997; Darling-Hammond 1997; Fliegel 1993; Kozol 1991; Levine and Nidiffer 1996; Werner, 1997). Unfortunately, in their zeal to promote student assessment, policymakers have often imposed upon schools their deeply entrenched assumptions about what curriculum and skills are appropriate at a certain grade level, which pedagogical practices should be employed, and how, once defined, outcomes should be measured (Comer 1985).

Students would be better served, I think, if policymakers were to begin with a clear perception of the question: If these children are to have a chance at acquiring the good life and at becoming productive citizens, what behaviors and skills must we teach them (Comer 1997)? When the question is currently posed, the very real students whom policymakers would serve are often replaced in their educational visions by cut-outs from the middle class. Like a physician who treats a syphilis sufferer for another patient's bad cold, such policymakers may not literally kill their charges, but they do little to improve their conditions, with spiraling lifelong negative repercussions. Comprehensive plans must be fine-tuned to meet the actual needs of the students they serve and must include provisions for equitable access to knowledge; qualified and committed teachers, counselors and administrators; the application of appropriate strategies for teaching and learning; and a genuine respect for the students and their cultures. Whether or not one agrees with Mayer's (1997) contention that parental beliefs and practices are more predictive of how children will achieve academically than anything money can buy, the importance of parental contributions to their children's academic success is common knowledge and should inform the design of a school's comprehensive educational plan.

This study suggests that early influences in the participants' lives that may have aided in their becoming college graduates were disparate events that were neither connected to any comprehensive plan nor necessarily extended to the participants' siblings. Educators' and policymakers' can ensure the timely occurrence of these events in the lives of entire families by systematically encouraging low SES parents, relatives, and community members—whether literate or not—to serve as pre-mentors and positive namers of children, to provide them with opportunities for ascending cross-class identification, and to award them special status. None of this suggests that children should be encouraged to compete with each other for affection or attention from adults. To the contrary, it is the adults who must be challenged to gain the attention of the children, and even as few as one or two adults may be able to provide these services for dozens of youth (Rodkin 1999). Maria, one of this study's participants, was the older of two children, both of whom were positively named, pre-mentored, awarded special status, and provided with opportunities for ascending cross-class identification by their undereducated parents. The parents expected that Maria and her sister would go to college, and they went. A key element in Maria's and her sister's success was that their parents realized their worth, role, and responsibility in preparing their children to better their lives. They planned their daughters' pathway to a future that they themselves had not experienced. Many other low SES adults have done so for their children, and others can learn to do the same.

Networks of parents, schools, and communities should be established to empower low SES parents, grandparents, and others to prepare their children for the academic arena (Levine and Nidiffer 1996). Ventures such as the

"America Reads" campaign are excellent templates for establishing such networks and promoting their message on national television and in public venues such as grocery stores, laundromats, public libraries, and public schools. The problem of illiteracy that "America Reads" highlights, however, is most often found in the very parents, grandparents, and community members whose help is needed in the promotion of literacy. Instead of being inadvertently cast as the problem, undereducated parents and other relatives should be recognized as potentially significant contributors to the solution.

As an adjunct to its brilliant strategy of featuring celebrity promoters of reading, "America Reads" and similar organizations could be urged to highlight undereducated, low SES adults as reading advocates in their national promotions. At the same time, since society has given its schools—particularly in the minds of the undereducated—authority in educational matters, the overture to form new coalitions for learning should be initiated by schools, especially those where low SES children are part of the student population. By joining forces with publishers of books, magazines, and newspapers, as well as with local libraries, governmental bodies, and service organizations, schools and their constituents could enrich low SES homes by providing families with free literature. In conjunction with their local cable television companies, schools could widen the scope of marketing "Family Reads" programs. Asking simply that families set aside and observe time for reading each week, "Family Reads" programs whose advertisements honestly and sensitively increased the public stature of all groups within their intended audience, would elicit and affirm the contributions that low SES adults can make in helping to educate their children in their own homes and on their own time.

2. Provide students with high-quality educational opportunities as a time-honored way of ensuring their academic success.

Unfortunately, as was true for many of this study's participants, children of the poor and of minorities disproportionately attend inadequately funded schools (Kozol 1991) that are staffed by the least prepared teachers (Miller 2000) and commonly offer substandard curricula, including fewer advanced classes in English, science, foreign languages, and mathematics—skill areas closely associated with college success (Darling-Hammond 1997). Despite these disadvantages, low SES, minority, and first-generation students are expected to win admission to college based on their standardized test scores as valid measures of their academic ability (Comer 1997). Their plight is further exacerbated by the recent derailment of affirmative action policies, arguably aimed at slamming the doors of baccalaureate institutions in the faces of minority and low SES students, whether they would be first-generation college students or not.

The preceding observations are important points for policymakers who may be as susceptible as the general population to the mythology surrounding low SES, first-generation, and minority students. Bowen and Bok (1998) have pointed out that contrary to common beliefs, basing affirmative action policy on low SES alone (thereby excluding race and ethnicity) would do little to maintain diversity in colleges and universities since minority children represent fewer than half of all the nation's poor children and comprise only 16 percent of low SES students who finish high school in the top ten percent of their classes. Clearly, affirmative-action-based education programs are desperately needed by low SES children, but the substandard schooling provided many of these students does little to prepare them to take advantage of affirmative-action-based opportunities (Wilson 1987). That middle-class minorities are more prepared than their low SES counterparts to gain college admission through affirmative action should not be regarded by policymakers as a mitigating factor in the repeal of affirmative action policy. Middle-class and minority first-generation college students face many of the same educational obstacles (see Policy Recommendations 3, 4, and 5) as low SES students, with the demise of affirmative action programs drastically reducing the number of blacks, Hispanics, and Native Americans in four-year colleges and universities regardless of their socioeconomic status (Gandara 1999). Policymakers need to work toward the re-enactment of affirmative-action-type policies while designing new policy that incorporates and extends the benefits of affirmative action's principles.

As a partial solution to the problems of unequal educational opportunity facing minority, low SES, and first-generation college students, policymakers might consider, for example, Fishkin's principle of equalizing life chances (cited in Wilson 1987). Fishkin reasonably concludes that the poor have less political influence and fewer benefits from health care, legal, and other social systems; that their environments thwart the normal development of their children's abilities and dreams; and that society should redress these inequities by carrying out race- and ethnicity-blind programs aimed at helping the truly disadvantaged.

From my perspective, ideas such as Fishkin's are exemplary as a corollary to—not as a replacement for—affirmative action policy. Equalizing life chances would prepare poor children to succeed in college *at some future time*, while affirmative action policies help minority students, some of whom are neither first-generation college attendees nor low SES (Wilson 1987), gain admission to college and succeed academically *today*. Moreover, although recent research presents compelling arguments that money or economic class is an important variable in the promotion of educational excellence (Mayer 1997; Steele 1993, 1999; Steele and Aronson 1998), as Gandara (1999) has pointed out, many of the middle-income students who would have profited from affirmative action have barely arrived at middle-income status and require most of the support (e.g., mentoring, in-depth advisement, academic tutoring, and peer-relationship building opportunities) needed by the continuing poor. Additionally, the confluence of realities and perceptions about race, culture, identity, and inferiority appears to take its academic toll on minority students, especially African Americans, regardless of their economic backgrounds (Bowen and Bok 1998; Comer 1997; Ferguson 1998; Harrington and Boardman 1997; Steele 1993, 1999; Steele and Aronson 1998; Wilson, 1998).

Policymakers must be reminded that according to current research (Bowen and Bok 1998; Gandara 1999), minority college graduates, many of whom may have benefited from affirmative action policies, make larger contributions (including tutoring and mentoring low SES children) to the underclass and others than do their majority counterparts, indirectly connecting affirmative action in college admissions to low SES students not yet ready to take firsthand advantage of it for themselves. If policymakers work successfully to establish equality of life chances and affirmative-action-type policies as complementary efforts (Hodgkinson 1991, 1996, 1998), the former will begin to address issues of education and life quality affecting low SES children and their families, while lessening the gulf separating them from the more advantaged. The latter will broaden the pool of activists willing to help the underclass and will guarantee the continued momentum of low SES, first-generation, and minority students in attaining college degrees.

3. Faculty, counselors, administrators, and staff must be encouraged to positively affect students' lives.

This study suggests that educators often play a transforming role in the academic success of low SES, minority, and first-generation students from the earliest years of schooling through graduate school. However, many of the participants pointed to teachers, professors, and counselors whose discriminatory treatment of them detracted from their educational opportunity. Low SES and minority students who feel devalued by school authority figures often are at risk of abandoning their academic goals (Comer 1997; Fliegel 1993; hooks 1994; Steele 1993, 1999; Steele and Aronson 1998). As early as third grade, some children respond to a negative reception at school by ceasing to aspire and by marking time until they are old enough to drop out (Fliegel 1993). Others may continue through high school graduation in educational tracks that prepare them neither for vocations nor for college (Keller 1992). Still others may go to college for a short while before dropping out, discouraged and unprepared for the rigors of academic life. Such students often become lost souls whose special purgatory is minimum-wage employment, illegal employment, or no employment at all. Students' fear of current and historical discrimination may be complicit in the fact that the most academically prepared first-generation and minority students who succeed at college do so at levels far below those of commensurately prepared white students (Ferguson 1998; Steele 1993, 1999; Steele and Aronson 1998).

In their efforts to address problems of educational inequality, policymakers must remember that sources of educator discrimination against students are not confined to teaching faculty. As many of this study's participants indicated, counselors intentionally withheld advice from them when they were undergoing the college admissions process. Equally important as college counseling was the advisement in academic course-planning that students need prior to high school. Because low SES parents may know little or nothing about academic preparation for college, without advice from school counselors or teachers, their children may be clueless about which courses they need to take during junior high or middle school if they are to qualify for college preparatory courses in secondary school. High school students may not know which academic areas they must master—and at what levels of proficiency— if they are to earn competitive scores on college entrance examinations. Students and their parents need access to this information early. Finding out at the last minute, as Clara, one of this study's participants, did that the ACT exists and is required for admission to many colleges could derail a students' college-going plans.

Policymakers must seek ways to solve such problems for low SES, first-generation, and minority students. One way would be to hire faculty, counselors, and staff who are committed to excellent educational practices for all students and to adopt meaningful employee evaluation plans that address issues of equity and excellence (Archer 1998; Burke 1997; Danielson 1996; Danielson and McGreal 2000; Duke and Stiggins 1990; Haefele 1993; Hawley and Valli 1999; Scriven 1994; Wolf, Lichtenstein, and Stevenson 1997). Policies affecting teacher and counselor evaluation should require review proceedings in which individual counselors and teachers are observed by supervisors and peer committees while performing their jobs—just as teachers in many institutions are commonly observed. Students should systematically be encouraged to evaluate their advisement as well as their classroom experiences.

The implementation of such reviews could raise the morale of excellent faculty and counselors and would serve as notice to others that the dereliction of duty to their students will not go unnoticed and will not be tolerated.

A second way to improve the learning environment for low SES, first-generation, and minority students is to provide educators—from preschool through graduate school—with workshops, courses, teacher preparation programs, and other training (Archer 1998; Burke 1997; Danielson 1996; Egger and Kauchak 1996; Hawley and Valli 1999; Scriven 1994; Werner 1997) on how best to meet the academic needs of these students. Not only might such training produce better teachers pedagogically, but it also might curtail blind bias in the classroom. An educator may be unaware of reflecting bias toward a student, thereby impeding the student's sense of belonging and, consequently, his academic achievement.

A third method of eroding the effects of bias while improving academic success is to implement a mentoring plan in which school employees, community members, and others would advocate within the schools for low SES, minority, and first-generation students even as they mentored the students within the community. Such a mentoring plan would extend services already provided in most schools, reducing the probability that students who are among the most vulnerable would not be served. This study's participants provided many examples of effective community-based mentorships, both on their own behalf as students and as part of their activist agendas. Maria spoke of her role as a mentor:

> When I was in high school, I would have insulted my mom to ask her for help with algebra because I knew she had no clue. I have a godson who's in high school and a cousin who's a junior getting ready to take the ACT. I'm constantly helping them because I know their parents aren't able to help them. I've spent Saturday nights working on algebra problems with my godson. We figure out word problems, and he has caught on. I've helped my cousin to develop good writing skills. We have a part-time clerk here who was going to a technical institute and failed math that was just fractions and decimals. Now that I am aware of her struggles, I constantly offer my help. I don't want them to go through what I had to, and I think they will automatically do better just knowing that they're not in it alone, that they can go for help, and that it doesn't mean that they're dumb.

Students are a ready source of social and academic aid to their peers, and high schools and colleges would do well to include peer advisors in their comprehensive advisement plans. Several of this study's participants indicated that in high school their college-bound peers were their most important sources of information about the college-going process. Similarly, Astin (1993) found that students' peers have the single most significant impact on their growth and development in college. At many colleges, junior counselors aid first-year students in making the transition to college, a practice that could be replicated in pre-college settings. Junior counselors at the high school level might prove beneficial to incoming students, who are certainly no more likely to approach upperclassmen for advisement or other help than are college freshmen. A caution for policymakers is that neither untrained peers nor junior counselors are professionals in the field, and just as peer tutors would not be regarded as replacements for classroom teachers, junior counselors must not be considered replacements for their professionally trained counterparts.

4. Seek ways to promote belongingness among low SES children and first-generation college students in their respective educational environments.

Most of this study's participants indicated that a lack of belongingness in school and college settings presented a significant obstacle to their academic success. Some participants related that at the hands of pre-college teachers and counselors as well as college professors, they were denied advisement, told that they would never succeed academically, placed in lower tracked classes, referred to by ethnic slur rather than by name, graded unfairly, and generally treated with contempt. Without exception the participants have made inclusion and fair play an important part of their programs of activism. Their stories demonstrate that the message that discrimination is not condoned and will not be tolerated should be clearly articulated and supported at the highest levels of a school's administration and should be reiterated and supported at every other level within the institution. Such messages begin to allay the fears of first-generation and minority students that they are going to have to contend—far above and beyond the efforts of those who "belong"—with alienation and hardship at every turn.

Alex, one of this study's participants, talked about the stance taken by the administration when he took his daughter to undergraduate school at Harvard. In his address to the hundreds of incoming freshmen and their parents, the dean referred to the racial incidents occurring on many college campuses. He indicated that such behavior would not be tolerated by the university. "If you do not believe that the atmosphere here is right for you, go home now," he admonished. In spite of having earned a bachelor's degree, two master's degrees, and a doctorate, Alex, a minority, needed to hear those words from the institution where he would leave his daughter. He needed an indication that his daughter would belong. Believing that institutions have collective consciousnesses and that their leaders are the most powerful forces in raising or lowering them, Alex was reassured by the Dean's words.

While a school's leaders may set the tone for inclusion at their institution, the role of faculty in promoting students' achievement by reducing their fears of not belonging should not be underestimated. Continuing his work on achievement levels of women, African Americans, and other minorities attending predominantly white colleges, Steele (1999) found that students, regardless of race or ethnicity, who thought they were or would be negatively stereotyped at college did less well academically than when they did not feel threatened by others' stereotypic thinking. Steele concluded that the degree of success achieved by the academically strong black students he studied was less related to motivation and expectations, as was commonly reported in the literature, than to trust that others' stereotypic thinking would not negatively affect the evaluation of their schoolwork. When considered against his earlier finding that black students earning a C+ average had an ACT score in the 98th percentile, while white students earning the same grade at the same college had ACT scores in the 34th percentile (Steele 1993), Steele's contention regarding stereotype threat assumes added significance.

The good news is that Steele (1999) found that when white faculty told their black students that they believed the students could attain the professors' high standards for their classes, the students were able to take the professors' criticisms of their work at face value and to respond with motivation and success equaling that of white students at their ability levels. Without their explicitly stated belief in the students' ability, white professors were suspected of bias by their black students, eroding the students' trust that they would be accepted or treated fairly and undermining their ability to achieve their best in class—whether they actually had been discriminated against or not. As Faludi (1991) contended in her study of women, the disenfranchised have been conditioned to enforce discrimination upon themselves.

Another pertinent conclusion from Steele's (1993, 1999) research is that weekly informal rap sessions among minority and white students allay fears of stereotype threat, promote belongingness, and enhance vulnerable students' academic achievement—perhaps by demonstrating that regardless of race, most students deal with many similar concerns. The challenge for policymakers is clear: If administrators are trained to set the tone for fair treatment of all students, if faculty are trained to follow suit by reducing stereotype threat for vulnerable students, and if communication is systematically fostered among diverse student groups, belongingness and academic success may be more readily achieved by female students in traditionally male dominated disciplines, minority students (especially those who are high achieving), and actual or potential first-generation college students who may fit all three categories.

5. Seek ways to promote informed risk-taking and activism among low SES, minority, and first-generation students.

This study seems to show that the participants developed the self-confidence to take calculated risks as a result of having felt affirmed or special in some way. Unlike most others in their environments, they seemed capable of envisioning a new way of life and striving successfully to achieve it. And their desire to help others seems as strong as their desire to help themselves. Policymakers and educators can do much to foster these conditions in all students, but intervention is especially needed for those from low SES backgrounds.

As I argued a few pages ago in my discussion of comprehensive educational plans, policymakers can ensure that low SES parents, as well as community members, are solicited as contributors to the design and implementation of educational programs affecting their children (Comer 1985, 1988; Fliegel 1993; Hooks 1994). Not only may such power-sharing endeavors be affirming for all stakeholder groups, but they may also prove practical and beneficial in other ways. Even though children generally live in close proximity to their schools, the cultures of low SES children's homes and communities are often quite different from those of their teachers and administrators. Instead of waiting expectantly for students and their families to discover the culture and traditions of the school, through stakeholder sharing sessions educators could learn more about their students' and their families' cultures, traditions, aspirations, realities, and ways of living. Gaining a more intimate understanding of who students are may create opportunities for teachers, administrators, counselors, and staff to award them with special status, to positively name them, to provide them with opportunities for ascending cross-class identification, to enhance their sense of belonging, and to pre-mentor them in life-affirming qualities such as compassion, intellectual curiosity, integrity, and activism. These qualities, in turn, and the educators and staff who foster them could become catalysts for transformation in the lives of children who otherwise might have little chance of becoming well-educated, excellent citizens and members of the middle class. Once empowered, the students will emulate the teachers, counselors, administrators, and others who are positive role models, thereby bestowing immortality, of sorts, upon them. This study's participants have demonstrated that the positive influence of their benefactors lives on through them and spirals outward with every person that they influence. The possibilities for good from one benefactor's acts are endless. How could a benefactor lose?

The study's primary concepts should serve as a basis for policymakers and educators to develop administrator, faculty, staff, parent, and community training directed at improving learning experiences and opportunities at low SES and minority schools and at colleges and universities whose student populations include first-generation, low SES, and minority students. Selectively applied to students at different stages in the education pipeline, the primary concepts outlined in this book can be replicated for preschool, elementary, junior high, and high school students, parents, and educators, and for first-generation college and graduate students and their professors and administrators as well. Based on well-orchestrated planning, the results in realized human potential of such efforts would be even more striking than this study's participants, producing—as comprehensive plans would—comparable giants in vastly incomparable numbers.

Recommendations for Further Research

> One of the great influences in my life was Florence Rome, an older, black professor at Bethune-Cookman College. She knew Mrs. Bethune— had been her personal secretary—and was just the most inspiring, the most helpful person I ever met. When they assigned me to teach the honors course, I was just petrified. We shared a double section. Once she came in and said, "I've just lost them this week." Shocked to hear this from an excellent, experienced teacher, I asked, "What will you do?" She said, "Just keep on trying."
>
> — *Ken*

One problem with replicating the progress made by outstanding individuals is overcoming the perception that they *are* outstanding. Too often we see human exceptionality as beyond the pale of possibility for others. Thus, we discount examples of, as well as processes and opportunities for, societal progress because we do not believe that they are realizable. While this study shows the myopic nature of such beliefs regarding educational attainment for potential and actual first-generation college graduates and activists, it leaves salient questions unanswered.

First, the study does not address the degree, if any, to which the participants' successes in school, in college, and as activists are attributable to the *je ne sais quoi*, the unknown factor that may simply lie within them as particular and unique individuals. A second and corollary question is "How much of their success is due to other extrinsic causes undetected or unexamined in this study?" The question is pertinent for all seventeen of the cases. As I indicated at the beginning of this book, the study does not address structural or physiological attributes of the participants.

John provided an intriguing example of the question's relevance. Upon analysis of the interviews, I found John's independent actions as a child, as an adolescent, and as an adult to be especially interesting among the cases—not so much because of their difference from the actions of the other participants as because of the unique foundation of support on which he acted. While the school, the home, and the community were not supportive of John in terms of caring human awareness and interaction, the community appears priceless when considered simply as physical environment. John described his situation:

> I grew up by my own devices, pretty much on my own. My mom and dad sort of let me go. Whatever I did was okay. It was as if they forgot about me . . . and I was able to roam the hillsides with my bow and arrow when I was a kid . . . I loved it because you could see the ocean, which was five miles away. I could just be a boy. I don't think kids in a town . . . can be that way today.

John stated that he knew, after the birth of his son, that because of his early life of detachment from his parents, the disconnected way of bringing up a child "couldn't possibly work." However, in spite of the debilitating effects of aloneness and isolation on children, John's lack of connection to his parents netted him an early discovery of freedom that appears to have influenced everything he has done in life. Other participants' stories depict humans as their primary aids on their paths toward success. John's foundation appears to have come mainly from nature and the freedom that it afforded. Further study of John's childhood circumstances and of similar cases might reveal helpful insights into the role of nature in human resilience and productivity.

Third, it would be worthwhile to study in depth the effects on familial relationships—especially on parents, spouses, siblings, and children—when first-generation college students work toward and earn college degrees. While a large number of first-generation college students are recent high school graduates, many others are of nontraditional age and have established families of their own before entering college. What are the costs and benefits of college attendance to their family members? The stories of traditional- and nontraditional-aged first-generation college students could tell us much that might illuminate how to abate the dissonance between the cultures of home and college for these students.

Fourth, further exploration of some of the links between this study's primary concepts and their implications for college choice, college retention, and the effects of college on students is needed. Especially important to such an inquiry would be specific implications for theory, practice, and policy affecting children from low SES, undereducated backgrounds and first-generation college students. As this chapter has suggested, the needs and realities of these students may not be adequately reflected in the theoretical underpinnings that influence how students are aided in the college-choice and college-persistence processes. Likewise, current theories on the effects of college may prove impracticable when applied to students from low SES, undereducated backgrounds. Additional research examining connections between this study's primary concepts and extant theories and research on college choice, college persistence, and the effects of college on students could enhance our understanding of how to make college success more attainable for all students, especially those who are poor and among the first in their families to go to college.

Finally, while a few studies have begun to venture down this path, additional research is needed that further isolates and identifies family, life, and college-going experiences that have had a positive effect on the academic successes of first-generation college graduates (Cuadraz 1993; Gandara 1995; Levine and Nidiffer 1996) and on their decisions to become educational or social activists. The benefits of this group to the nation—in purely practical terms—is certainly great, and the efforts that may have aided in their successful educational development deserve replication. But the first and best reason for aiding those who would become first-generation college graduates is that it is the right thing to do. For them, also, the pursuit of happiness is an inalienable right.

References

Albom, M. 1997. *Tuesdays with Morrie: An old man, a young man, and life's greatest lesson.* New York: Doubleday.

Anderson, E. 1985. Forces influencing student persistence and achievement. In *Increasing student retention.* Edited by L. Noel, R. Levitz, D. Saluri, & Associates. San Francisco: Jossey-Bass.

Archer, J. 1998. Students' fortune rests with assigned teacher. *Education Week*, 9.

Astin, A. W. 1975. *Preventing students from dropping out.* San Francisco: Jossey-Bass.

———. 1977. *Four critical years.* San Francisco: Jossey-Bass.

———. 1984. Student involvement: A developmental theory for higher education. *Journal of College Student Personnel* 25: 297–308.

———. 1985. *Achieving educational excellence: A critical assessment of priorities and practices in higher education.* San Francisco: Jossey-Bass.

———. 1993. *What matters in college? Four critical years revisited.* San Francisco: Jossey-Bass.

Attinasi, L. 1989. Getting in: Mexican Americans' perceptions of university attendance and the implications for freshman year persistence. *Journal of Higher Education* 60: 247–277.

Baca, R. 1994. Persistence and secession: Toward an understanding of first-generation Mexican binational migrant students in high school. *Dissertation Abstracts International* 56/05-A, 1689.

Barahona, D. 1990. The first-generation college student: a longitudinal study of educational outcomes. *Dissertation Abstracts International* 51/02-A, 423.

Barr, R., and J. Tagg. 1995. From teaching to learning: A new paradigm for undergraduate education. *Change* 27, no. 6: 12–25.

Becker, H. S. 1978. The relevance of life histories. In *Sociological methods.* Edited by N. K. Denzin. New York: McGraw-Hill.

Becker, H. S., B. Geer, and A. L. Strauss. 1961. *Boys in white: Student culture in medical school.* Chicago: University of Chicago Press.

Belenky, M., B. Clinchy, N. Goldberger, and J. Tarule. 1986. *Women's ways of knowing: The development of self, voice, and mind.* New York: Basic Books.

Berger, J. 2000a. Optimizing capital, social reproduction, and undergraduate persistence. In *Reworking the student departure puzzle*. Edited by J.M. Braxton. Nashville: Vanderbilt University Press.

————. 2000b. Organizational behavior at colleges and student outcomes: A new perspective on college impact. *Review of Higher Education* 23: 177–198.

Berger, J., and J. M. Braxton. 1998. Revising Tinto's interactionalist theory of student departure through theory elaboration: Examining the role of organizational attributes in the persistence process. *Research in Higher Education* 39: 103–119.

Billson, J., and M. Brooks-Terry. 1982. In search of the silken purse: Factors in attrition among first-generation students. *College and University* 58: 57–75.

Birenbaum, W. 1986. From mass to class in higher education. In *The community college and its critics*. Edited by L. S. Zwerling. San Francisco: Jossey-Bass.

Birnbaum, R. 1991. *How colleges work: The cybernetics of academic organization and leadership.* San Francisco: Jossey-Bass.

Bogdan, R., and S. Biklen. 1992. *Qualitative research for education: An introduction to theory and methods,* 2nd ed. Boston: Allyn & Bacon.

Bonsangue, M. 1992. The effects of calculus workshop groups on minority achievement and persistence in mathematics, science, and engineering. Ann Arbor: UMI Dissertation Service

Bowen, W., and D. Bok. 1998. *The shape of the river: Long-term consequences of considering race in college and university admissions.* Princeton: Princeton University Press.

Boyer, E. 1987. *College: The undergraduate experience in America.* New York: Harper & Row.

Braxton, J. M. 2000. Reinvigorating theory and research on the departure puzzle. In *Reworking the student departure puzzle*. Edited by J.M. Braxton. Nashville: Vanderbilt University Press.

Braxton, J. M., and E. M. Brier. 1989. Melding organizational and interactional theories of student attrition. *Review of Higher Education* 13, no. 1:47-61.

Brookfield, S. 1987. *Developing critical thinkers: Challenging adults to explore alternative ways of thinking and acting.* San Francisco: Jossey-Bass.

Brooks, T. 1988. Tracing the disadvantages of first-generation college students: An application of Sussman's option sequence model. In *Family and support systems across the life span.* Edited by S. K. Steinmetz. New York: Plenum Press.

Budhos, M. 1996. Ruth Sidel: Crusading for change. *The Monthly Forum on Women in Higher Education* 1, no. 4: 27–31.

Burger, J. P. 2000. Optimizing capital, social reproduction, and undergraduate persistence: A sociological perspective. In *Reworking the student departure puzzle*. Edited by J. M. Braxton. Nashville: Vanderbilt University Press.

Burke, K. 1997. *Designing professional portfolios for change.* Arlington Heights, Ill.: IRI Skylight Publishing.

Cagampang, F. 1992. What parents know about preparing for college and how it affects their children's academic performance: Parents' information in the college choice decision. *Dissertation Abstracts International* 54/06-A, 2003.

Caine, R. N., and G. Caine. 1997. *Education on the edge of possibility.* Alexandria: Association for Supervision oand Curriculum Development.

Carson, B. 1996. Thirty years of stories: The professor's place in student memories. *Change* (November/December): 11–17.

Carson, B, and C. Murphy. 1990. *Gifted hands.* Grand Rapids: Zondervan Publishing House.

Chaffee, J. 1992. Transforming educational dreams into educational reality. In *First-generation students: Confronting the cultural issues.* Edited by L. S. Zwerling and H. B. London. San Francisco: Jossey-Bass.

Chase, S. 1996. Taking narrative seriously: Consequences for method and theory in interview studies. In *Interpreting experience: The narrative study of lives.* Edited by R. Josselson and A. Lieblich. Thousand Oaks, Calif.: Sage Publications.

Chatman, K. 1994. A study of the University of Tennessee Ronald McNair post-baccalaureate achievement program: Factors related to graduate school enrollment for first-generation, low-income and under-represented college students. *Dissertation Abstracts International,*56/02-A, 491.

Cienkus, R., J. Haworth, and J. Kavanagh, eds. 1996. *Mentors and Mentoring/Peabody Journal of Education* 71, no. 1. Mahwah, N. J.: Lawrence Erlbaum Associates.

Clemens, S. L. 1977. *The adventures of Huckleberry Finn.* New York: W.W. Norton.

Comer, J. 1985. Demand for excellence and the need for equity. In *Education in school and nonschool settings: Eighty-fourth yearbook of the National Society for the Study of Education,* part I. Edited by M. D. Fantini and R. L. Sinclair. Chicago: University of Chicago Press.

———. 1988. Is "parenting" essential to good teaching? *NEA Today,* 6, no. 6: 34–40.

———. 1989. Child development and education. *Journal of Negro Education* 58, no. 2: 125–139.

———. 1997. *Waiting for a miracle: Why schools can't solve our problems—and how we can.* New York: Penguin.

Connelly, F. M., and Clandinin, D. J. 1990. Stories of experience and narrative inquiry. *Educational Researcher* 19, no. 5: 2–14.

Conrad, C., J. Haworth, and S. Millar. 1993. *A silent success: Master's education in the United States.* Baltimore: Johns Hopkins University Press.

Cross, T. 1998. Explaining the gap in black-white scores on IQ and college admission tests. *Journal of Blacks in Higher Education* 18 (winter): 94–97.

Crowson, R. L. 1987. Qualitative research methods in higher education. In *Higher education: Handbook of theory and research,* vol. 3. Edited by J. C. Smart. New York: Agathon Press.

Cuadraz, G. 1993. Meritocracy (un)challenged: The making of a chicano and chicana professoriate and professional class. Ann Arbor: UMI Dissertation Services.

Danielson, C. 1996. *Enhancing professional practice: A framework for teaching.* Alexandria: Association for Supervision and Curriculum Development.

Danielson, C., and T. McGreal. 2000. *Teacher evaluation to enhance professional practice.* Princeton: Educational Testing Service.

Darling-Hammond, L. 1997. *The right to learn: A blueprint for creating schools that work.* San Francisco: Jossey-Bass.

Delgado-Gaitan, C., and H. Trueba. 1991. *Crossing cultural borders: Education for immigrant families in America.* Bristol, Pa.: Falmer Press.

Duke, D., and R. Stiggins. 1990. Beyond minimum competence: Evaluation for professional development. In *The new handbook of teacher evaluation.* Edited by J. Millman and L. Darling-Hammond. Newbury Park, Calif.: Sage Publications.

Dyson, M. 1993. *Reflecting black: African-American cultural criticism.* Minneapolis: University of Minnesota Press.

Egger, P., and D. Kauchak. 1996. *Strategies for teachers: Teaching content and thinking skills.* Needham Heights, Mass.: Allyn & Bacon.

Eimers, M., and G. Pike. 1996. Minority and non-minority adjustment to college: Differences or similarities? Paper presented at the annual forum of the Association for Institutional Research, Albuquerque, N. Mex.

Eliot, T. S. 1952. *T. S. Eliot: The complete poems and plays.* New York: Harcourt, Brace & World.

Ely, M., M. Anzul, T. Friedman, D. Garner, and A. McCormack-Steinmetz. 1991. *Doing qualitative research: Circles within circles.* New York: Falmer Press.

Emerson, R. W. 1841. Self-Reliance. In *Major writers of America.* Edited by Perry Miller. New York: Harcourt, Brace & World.

Erikson, E. 1968. *Identity: Youth and crisis.* New York: W. W. Norton.

————. 1980. *Identity and the life cycle.* New York: W. W. Norton.

Faludi, S. 1991. *Backlash: The undeclared war against American women.* New York: Crown.

Ferguson, R. 1998. Can schools narrow the black-white test score gap? In *The black-white test score gap.* Edited by C. Jencks and M. Phillips. Washington, D.C.: The Brookings Institution.

Fliegel, S. 1993. *Miracle in east Harlem: The fight for choice in public education.* New York: Times Books.

Fowler, B. 1997. *Pierre Bourdieu and cultural theory: Critical investigations.* London: Sage Publications.

Freire, P. 1970. *Pedagogy of the oppressed.* New York: Seaview.

Fuertes, J., and W. Sedlacek. 1993. Barriers to the leadership development of Hispanics in higher education. *NASPA Journal* 30, no. 4: 277–283.

Galbo, J., and D. Demetrulias. 1996. Recollections of nonparental significant adults during childhood and adolescence. *Youth and Society* 27, no. 4: 403–420.

Gandara, P. 1995. *Over the ivy walls: The educational mobility of low-income Chicanos.* Albany: State University of New York Press.

————. 1999. *Priming the pump: Strategies for increasing the achievement of underrepresented minority undergraduates.* A report to the College Board. University of California, Davis.

Gardner, J. N. 1996. Helping America's first-generation college students. *About Campus* (November/December): 31–32.

Garland, M. 1993. The mathematics workshop model: An interview with Uri Treisman. *Journal of Developmental Education* 16 (spring): 14–22.

Geertz, C. 1973. *The interpretation of cultures.* New York: Basic Books.

———. 1983. *Local knowledge: Further essays in interpretive anthropology.* New York: Basic Books.

Glaser, B., and A. Strauss. 1967. *The discovery of grounded theory: Strategies for qualitative research.* Chicago: Aldine Press.

Green, M. 1997. *Transforming higher education: Views from leaders around the world.* Phoenix: The Oryx Press.

———, ed. 1989. *Minorities on campus: A handbook for enhancing diversity.* Washington, D.C.: American Council on Education.

Groopman, J. 2000. The doubting disease: What's wrong with obsession? *The New Yorker,* April 10, 52–57.

Gubrium, J., and J. Holstein. 1996. Biographical work and new ethnography. *In Interpreting experience: The narrative study of lives,* vol. 3. Edited by R. Josselson & A. Lieblich. Thousand Oaks, Calif.: Sage Publications.

Gurin, P., and E. Epps. 1975. *Black consciousness, identity, and achievement.* New York: Wiley.

Haefele, D. L. 1993. Evaluating teachers: A call for change. *Journal of Personnel Evaluation in Education* 7: 21–31.

Harr, J. 1999. The burial. *The New Yorker,* November 1, 70–95.

Harrington, C., and S. Boardman. 1997. *Paths to success: Beating the odds in American society.* Cambridge: Harvard University Press.

Hawley, W., and L. Valli. 1999. The essentials of effective professional development: A new consensus. In *Teaching as the learning profession: Handbook of policy and practice.* Edited by L. Darling-Hammond & G. Sykes. San Francisco: Jossey-Bass.

Haworth, J., and C. Conrad. 1997. *Emblems of quality in higher education: Developing and sustaining high-quality programs.* Boston: Allyn & Bacon.

Hayes, K. 1992. Attitudes toward education: Voluntary and involuntary immigrants from the same families. *Anthropology and Education Quarterly* 23, no. 3: 250–267.

Haygood, W. 1992. The remarkable journey of Willie Edward Gary. *Boston Globe Magazine,* May 24, pp. 12–15, 21–24.

Helms, J. 1990. *Black and white racial identity.* New York: Greenwood Press.

Hewlett, J. 1981. First-generation college students who are college graduates. *Dissertation Abstracts International* 42/10-A, 4344.

Hicks, E. 1981. Cultural marxism: Nonsynchrony and feminist practice. In *Women and revolution.* Edited by L. Sargent. Boston: South End Press.

Higgins, G. 1994. *Resilient adults: Overcoming a cruel past.* San Francisco: Jossey-Bass.

Hill, D. 1994. Stand and deliver, act II. *Education Week* (March 30): 20–23.

Hodgkinson, H. 1991. Reform versus reality. *Phi Delta Kappan* (September): 9–16.

———. 1996. Who will our students be? Demographic implications for urban and metropolitan universities. *Metropolitan Universities: An International Forum* 7, no. 3: 25–39.

————. 1998. The demographics of diversity. *Principal* 78, no. 1: 26, 28, 30–32.

Holt, J. 1972. *Freedom and Beyond.* New York: E. P. Dutton.

hooks, bell. 1994. *Teaching to transgress: Education as the practice of freedom.* New York: Routledge.

Hossler, D., J. Braxton, and G. Coopersmith. 1989. Understanding student college choice. In *Higher Education: A handbook of theory and research,* vol. 5. Edited by J. C. Smart. New York: Agathon Press.

Hossler, D., J. Schmidt, and N. Vesper. 1999. Going to college: *How social, economic, and educational factors influence the decisions students make.* Baltimore: Johns Hopkins University Press.

Hummel, M., dir. 1991. The 21st century program brochure. University of Michigan. Ann Arbor.

Hurtado, S. 1990. Campus racial climates and educational outcomes. University of California, Los Angeles. Ann Arbor: University Microfilms International, no. 9111328.

Jetter, A. 1993. Mississippi learning. *New York Times Magazine,* February 21, pp. 30–35, 50, 64, 72.

Josselson, R. 1987. *Finding herself: Pathways to identity development.* San Francisco: Jossy-Bass.

————. 1996. Imagining the real: Empathy, narrative, and the dialogic self. In *Interpreting experience: The narrative study of lives,* vol. 3. Edited by R. Josselson and A. Lieblich. Thousand Oaks, Calif.: Sage Publications.

Josselson, R., and A. Lieblich. 1996. Introduction. In *Interpreting experience: The narrative study of lives,* vol. 3. Edited by R. Josselson and A. Lieblich. Thousand Oaks, Calif.: Sage Publications.

Joyce, B. 1987. "First-generation" college students: A study of college choice. *Dissertation Abstracts International* 49/11-A, 3278.

Karabel, J. 1986. Community colleges and social stratification in the 1980s. In *The community college and its critics.* Edited by L. S. Zwerling. San Francisco: Jossey-Bass.

Keller, G. 1992. Revolutions in American society since 1900. Paper presented at the Community College Consortium's Strengthening Leadership Institute, Ann Arbor.

Kiang, P. 1992. Issues of curriculum and community for first-generation Asian Americans in college. In *First-generation students: Confronting the cultural issues.* Edited by L. S. Zwerling & H. B. London. San Francisco: Jossey-Bass.

Kinsella, M. 1995. Predictors of performance of graduates of pre-college enrichment programs. *Dissertation Abstracts International* 56/05-A, 1688.

Kozol, J. 1991. *Savage inequalities: Children in America's schools.* New York: Crown.

Kronley, R., and C. Handley. 1998. *Miles to go: A report on black students and post secondary education in the south.* Atlanta: Southern Education Foundation.

Kuh, G. 1993. In their own words: What students learn outside the classroom. *American Educational Research Journal* 30: 277–304.

Kuh, G., and P. Love. 2000. A cultural perspective on student departure. In *Reworking the student departure puzzle*. Edited by J.M. Braxton. Nashville: Vanderbilt University Press.

Kuh, G., J. Schuh, and J. Whitt. 1991. *Involving colleges: Successful approaches to fostering student learning and development outside the classroom*. San Francisco: Jossey-Bass.

Lareau, A. 1987. Social class differences in family-school relationships: The importance of cultural capital. *Sociology of Education* 60: 73–85.

———. 1989. *Home advantage: Social class and parental intervention in elementary education*. New York: Falmer Press.

LaPaglia, N. 1994. *Storytellers: The image of the two-year college in American fiction and in women's journals*. DeKalb, Ill.: LEPS Press.

———. 1995. The interplay of gender and social class in the community college. In *Gender and power in the community college*. Edited by B. Townsend. San Francisco: Jossey-Bass.

Lara, J. 1992. Reflections: Bridging cultures. In *First-generation students: Confronting the cultural issues*. Edited by L. S. Zwerling and H. B. London. San Francisco: Jossey-Bass.

Law, C. L. 1995. Introduction. In *This fine place so far from home*. Edited by C. L. B. Dews and C. L. Law. Philadelphia: Temple University Press.

Lazarus, E. 1883. The New Colossus. In *The American pageant: A history of the republic*. Edited by T. A. Bailey & D. M. Kennedy. Lexington, Mass.: D.C. Heath.

Leichter, H. 1985. Families as educators. In *Education in school and nonschool settings: Eighty-fourth yearbook of the national society for the study of education, part I*. Edited by M. Fantini and R. Sinclair. Chicago: University of Chicago Press.

LePage-Lees, P. 1997. *From disadvantaged girls to successful women: Education and women's resiliency*. Westport: Praeger Publishers.

Levine, A., and J. Nidiffer. 1996. *Beating the odds: How the poor get to college*. San Francisco: Jossey-Bass.

Lincoln, Y., and E. Guba. 1985. *Naturalistic inquiry*. Beverly Hills: Sage Publications.

London, H. B. 1978. *The culture of a community college*. New York: Praeger Publishers.

———. 1986. Strangers to our shores. In *First-generation students: Confronting the cultural issues*. Edited by L. S. Zwerling and H. B. London. San Francisco: Jossey-Bass.

———. 1989. Breaking away: A study of first-generation college students and their families. *American Journal of Education*, 97, no. 2: 144–170.

———. 1996. How college affects first-generation students. *About Campus* (November/December): 9–13.

Lowman, J. 1984. *Mastering the techniques of teaching*. San Francisco: Jossey-Bass.

MacDermott, K. 1987. The influence of parental education level on college choice. *Journal of College Admissions* 115: 3–10.

Macrorie, K. 1984. *Twenty teachers*. New York: Oxford.

Marcia, J. 1966. Development and validation of ego identity status. *Journal of Personality and Social Psychology* 3: 551–558.

————. 1980. Identity and adolescence. In *Handbook of adolescent psychology*. Edited by J. E. Adelson. New York: Wiley.

————. 1989. Identity and intervention. *Journal of Adolescence* 12, no. 4: 401–410.

Matthew, J. 1998. *Class struggle: What's wrong (and right) with America's best public high schools*. New York: Times Books.

Mayer, S.E. 1997. *What money can't buy: Family income and children's life chances*. Cambridge: Harvard University Press.

Mayo, J., E. Murguia, and R. Padilla. 1995. Social Integration and Academic Performance Among Minority University Students. *Journal of College Student Development* 36, no. 6: 542-552.

McCarthy, C. 1990. *Race and curriculum: Social inequality and the theories and politics of difference in contemporary research on schooling*. Philadelphia: Falmer Press. McDonough, P. 1997. *Choosing colleges: How social class and schools structure opportunity*. New York: State University of New York Press.

McDonough, P. 1997. *Choosing colleges: How social class and schools structure opportunity*. New York: State University of New York Press.

McGregor, L., M. Mayleben, V. Buzzanga, and S. Davis. 1991. Selected personality characteristics of first-generation college students. *College Student Journal* 25, no. 2: 231–234.

McKeachie, W. 1969. *Teaching tips: A guidebook for the beginning college teacher*. Lexington, Mass.: D. C. Heath.

Meier, K., J. Stewart, Jr., and R. England. 1989. *Race, class, and education: The politics of second-generation discrimination*. Madison: University of Wisconsin Press.

Miller, Z. 2000. Ten crucial things the next president should do for colleges. *Chronicle of Higher Education* (July 14): B4–B6.

Mohr, V., K. Eiche, and W. Sedlacek. 1998. So close, yet so far: Predictors of attrition in college seniors. *Journal of College Student Development* 39, no. 4: 343–354.

Neumann, A., and E. M. Bensimon. 1990. Constructing the presidency: College presidents' images of their leadership roles: A comparative study. *Journal of Higher Education* 61: 678–701.

New Cassell's German dictionary. 1971. New York: Funk & Wagnalls.

Nisbett, R. 1998. Race, genetics, and IQ. In *The black-white test score gap*. Edited by C. Jencks and M. Phillips. Washington, D.C.: The Brookings Institution.

Nora, A., and A. Cabrera. 1996. The role of perception in prejudice and discrimination and the adjustment of minority students to college. *Journal of Higher Education* 67, no. 2: 119–148.

Oakes, J. 1985. *Keeping track: How schools structure inequality*. New Haven: Yale University Press.

Ogbu, J. 1974. *The next generation: An ethnography of education in an urban neighborhood*. New York: Academic Press.

————. 1981. Origins of human competence: A cultural-ecological perspective. *Child Development* 52, no. 2: 2–21.

Orozco, C. 1995. Factors contributing to the psychological adjustment of Mexican American college students. *Dissertation Abstracts International* 56/05-A, 1714.

Padron, E. 1992. The challenge of first-generation college students: A Miami-Dade perspective. In *First-generation students: Confronting the cultural issues.* Edited by L. S. Zwerling and H. B. London. San Francisco: Jossey-Bass.

Palmer, P. 1983. *To know as we are known: A spirituality of education.* San Francisco: Harper Collins.

———. 1998. *The courage to teach.* San Francisco: Jossey Bass.

Parker, W. 1998. Birth-order effects in the academically talented. *Gifted Child Quarterly* 42, no. 1: 29–38.

Parks Daloz, L. Keen, J. Keen, and S. Daloz Parks. 1996. *Common fire: Lives of commitment in a complex world.* Boston: Beacon.

Parks Daloz, L., C. Keen, J. Keen, and S. Daloz Parks. 1996. Lives of commitment: Higher education in the life of the new commons. *Change* (May/June): 11–15.

Pascarella, E. 1980. Student-faculty informal contact and college outcomes. *Review of Educational Research* 50: 545–590.

Pascarella, E., and P. Terenzini. 1991. *How college affects students: Findings and insights from twenty years of research.* San Francisco: Jossey-Bass.

Patterson, W. 1999. Certificate programs raise important issues. *Communicator* 32, no. 3: 1–3.

Picker, L. 1996. Lessons from some of America's most successful women. *Parade Magazine*, April 21, 4–5.

Piorkowski, G. 1983. Survivor guilt in the university setting. *Personnel and Guidance Journal* 61, no. 10: 620–622.

Poock, M. 1999. Students of color and doctoral programs: Factors influencing the application decision in higher education administration. *College and University* 74, no. 3: 2–7.

Portes, A., and M. Zhou. 1993. The new second generation: Segmented assimilation and its variants. *Annals, AAPSS* 530: 75–96.

Pounds, A. 1998. Black students' needs on predominantly white campuses. In *Responding to the needs of today's minority students: New directions for student services.* Edited by D. J. White. San Francisco: Jossey-Bass.

Ravitch, D. 1983. *The troubled crusade: American education 1945–1980.* New York: Basic Books.

Rendon, L. 1992. From the barrio to the academy: Revelations of a Mexican American "scholarship girl." In *First-generation students: Confronting the cultural issues.* Edited by L. S. Zwerling & H. B. London. San Francisco: Jossey-Bass.

———. 1994. A systemic view of minority students in educational institutions. National Center on Postsecondary Teaching, Learning, and Assessment. Washington, D. C.: Office of Educational Research and Improvement.

———. 1995. Facilitating Retention and Transfer for First-Generation Students in Community Colleges. Paper presented at the New Mexico Institute, Rural Community College Initiative, Espanola, N. Mex.

————. 1996. Life on the border. *About Campus* (November/December): 14–20.

Rendon, L., R. Jalomo, and M. Nora. 2000. Theoretical considerations in the study of minority student retention in higher education. In *Reworking the student departure puzzle*. Edited by J.M. Braxton. Nashville: Vanderbilt University Press.

Rendon, L., P. Terenzini, and M. Upcraft. 1994. Voices of transition: First-year students and the transition to college. National Center on Postsecondary Teaching, Learning, and Assessment. University Park, Penn.: National Center on Teaching, Learning, and Assessment.

Rhoads, R. A. 1998. *Freedom's web: Student activism in an age of cultural diversity*. Baltimore: Johns Hopkins University Press

Richardson, R., and E. Skinner. 1992. Helping first-generation minority students achieve degrees. In *First-generation students: Confronting the cultural issues*. Edited by L. S. Zwerling & H. B. London. San Francisco: Jossey-Bass.

Rodkin, D. 1999. Quality Time. *Chicago Tribune*, August 1, sec. 10, p. 10.

Rodriguez, R. 1975. Going home again: The new American scholarship boy. *The American Scholar* 44: 15–28.

————. 1982. *Hunger of memory: The education of Richard Rodriguez*. Boston: Godine.

Rogers, C. 1961. *On becoming a person: A therapist's view of psychotherapy*. Boston: Houghton Mifflin.

Rowser, J. 1997. Do African American students' perceptions of their needs have implications for retention? *Journal of Black Studies* 27, no. 5: 718–726.

Scarr, S. 1993. Biological and cultural diversity: The legacy of Darwin for development. *Child Development* 64, no. 5: 1333–1353

Scarr, S., and K. McCartney. 1983. How people make their own environments: A theory of genotype. *Child Development* 54, no. 2: 424–435.

Scriven, M. 1994. The duties of the teacher. *Journal of Personnel Evaluation in Education* 8: 151–184.

Shor, I. 1996. *When students have power: Negotiating authority in a critical pedagogy*. Chicago: University of Chicago Press.

Shrewsbury, C. 1987. What is feminist pedagogy? *Women's Studies Quarterly*, 15: 6–13.

Siebert, A. 1996. *The survivor personality*. New York: Berkley Publishing.

Simelton, V. 1994. An evaluation of the educational talent search program at the University of Arkansas at Little Rock, Arkansas. *Dissertation Abstracts International* 55/08-A, 2284.

Staff. 1995. College enrollment by racial and ethnic group, selected years. *The Chronicle of Higher Education Almanac* 42, no. 1: 14.

Steele, C. 1993. Race and the schooling of black Americans. *Atlantic Monthly*, March, 22–38.

————. 1999. Thin ice: "Stereotype threat" and black college students. *Atlantic Monthly*, August, 44-54.

Steele, C., and J. Aronson. 1998. Stereotype threat and the test performance of academically successful African Americans. In *The black-white test score gap*. Edited by C. Jencks and M. Phillips. Washington, D.C.: The Brookings Institution.

Stein, W. 1992. Tribal colleges: A success story. In *First-generation students: Confronting the cultural issues.* Edited by L. S. Zwerling and H. B. London. San Francisco: Jossey-Bass.

Stierlin, H. 1974. *Separating parents and adolescents: A perspective on running away, schizophrenia, and waywardness.* New York: Quadrangle/New York Times.

Terenzini, P., L. Rendon, L. Upcraft, S. Millar, K. Allison, P. Gregg, and R. Jalomo. 1994. The transition to college: Diverse students, diverse stories. *Research in Higher Education* 1: 57–73.

Terenzini, P., L. Springer, P. Yaeger, E. Pascarella, and A. Nora. 1996. First-generation college students: Characteristics, experiences, and cognitive development. *Research in Higher Education* 37, no. 1: 1–22.

Thoreau, H. D. 1854. Walden. In *The individual American.* Edited by E J. Gordon and C. Feidelson, Jr. Boston: Ginn.

Tinto, V. 1987. *Leaving college: Rethinking the causes and cures of student attrition.* Chicago: University of Chicago Press.

————. 1993. *Leaving college: Rethinking the causes and cures of student attrition.* Chicago: University of Chicago Press.

U.S. Department of Education, Office of Educational Research and Improvement. 1998. *Toward resiliency: At risk students who make it in college.* Washington, D.C.: Author.

Van Maanen, J. 1988. *Tales of the field: On writing ethnography.* Chicago: University of Chicago Press.

Vars, F., and W. Bowen. 1998. Scholastic aptitude, test scores, race, and academic performance in selective colleges and universities. In *The black-white test score gap.* Edited by C. Jencks and M. Phillips. Washington, D.C.: The Brookings Institution.

Warner, N. 1992. From their perspective: Issues of schooling and family culture of four African American first-generation college students. *Dissertation Abstracts International* 53/08-A, 2674.

Weber, M. 1968. *Economy and society: An outline of interpretive sociology.* Translated by E. Fischoff et al. New York: Bedminster Press. Original work published 1946.

Webster's ninth new collegiate dictionary. 1986. Springfield, Mass.: Merriam-Webster Inc.

Weiland, S. 1996. Life history and academic work: The career of Professor G. In *Interpreting experience: The narrative study of lives,* vol. 3. Edited by R. Josselson and A. Lieblich Thousand Oaks, Calif.: Sage Publications.

Weis, L. 1985. *Between two worlds: Black students in an urban community college.* Boston: Routledge & Kegan Paul.

————. 1992. Discordant voices in the urban community college. In *First-generation students: Confronting the cultural issues.* Edited by L. S. Zwerling and H. B. London. San Francisco: Jossey-Bass.

Weis, L., and M. Fine, eds. 1993. *Beyond silenced voices: Class, race, and gender in United States schools.* Albany: State University of New York Press.

Werner, E. 1997. Conceptual and methodological issues in studying minority children: An international perspective. Paper presented at the Biennial meeting of the Society for Research in Child Development, Washington, D.C.

Werner, E., and R. Smith. 1982. *Vulnerable but invincible: A longitudinal study of resilient children and youth.* New York: McGraw-Hill.

———. 1992. *Overcoming the odds: High risk children from birth to adulthood.* Ithaca: Cornell University Press.

Werner, L. 1995. An investigation of the relationship between biculturalism and barriers perceived by Hispanic students in higher education. *Dissertation Abstracts International* 56/05-A, 1692.

Whitehall, C. 1991. Issues of entitlement: Self-perceptions of intellectual competence in late-entry women who are the first in their families to attend college. *Dissertation Abstracts International* 52/10-B, 5078.

Willett, L. 1989. Are two-year college students first-generation college students? *Community College Review* 17, no. 2: 48–52.

Wilson, W. 1987. *The truly disadvantaged: The inner city, the underclass, and public policy.* Chicago: University of Chicago Press.

Wilson, W. 1998. The role of the environment in the black-white test score gap. In *The black-white test score gap.* Edited by C. Jencks and M. Phillips. Washington, D.C.: The Brookings Institution.

Wolf, K., G. Lichtenstein, and C. Stevenson. 1997. Using teaching portfolios in teacher evaluation. In *Teacher assessment and evaluation: A guide for research and practice.* Edited by J. Stronge. Thousand Oaks, Calif.: Corwin Press.

Wolfe, T. C. 1942. *You can't go home again.* Garden City: Sun Dial Press.

York-Anderson, D., and S. Bowman. 1991. Assessing the college knowledge of first-generation and second-generation college students. *Journal of College Student Development* 32: 116–122.

Zwerling, L. S. 1976. *Second best: The crisis of the community college.* New York: McGraw-Hill.

———. 1986. Lifelong learning: a new form of tracking. In *The community college and its critics.* Edited by L. S. Zwerling. San Francisco: Jossey-Bass.

Zwerling, L. S., and H. B. London, eds. 1992. *First-generation students: Confronting the cultural issues.* San Francisco: Jossey-Bass.

Index